The Catholic
as Historian

The Catholic as Historian

Edited by Donald J. D'Elia & Patrick Foley

Sapientia Press
of Ave Maria University

Table of Contents

 Preface

AS IS TAUGHT regularly at the academic level, the discipline of history centers on recovering civilizations' pasts through the study of written records. One who engages in this scholarly pursuit is referred to as a historian. It must be understood, however, that this form of researching involves more than seeking factual knowledge. The historian must be learned in various areas of study, inasmuch as he or she has to intellectually, spiritually, and in other ways interpret the substances of people's lives individually and communally within historical settings. Such is especially true when the deepest, most substantive natures of various societies' heritages are being investigated and written about—those of their religious bases. Historians, often using different languages, research into literature, try to comprehend philosophies and situate them in the particular circumstances of historical periods, analyze political developments, and much more, while attempting to unearth the essences of cultures' foundations. Nowhere is such more obvious than in the centuries-old tradition of the Catholic as historian.

Eusebius, consecrated bishop of Caesarea in A.D. 314, is seen as the first Catholic historian. It was he who initiated the tradition of writing Catholic history. He saw the story of the Church as all-encompassing regarding the early Christians: who they were, what they came to believe and teach about Jesus of Nazareth, how they worshipped, where they lived, how they were organized, and more. The best-known of his numerous works, being published in ten books slightly more than a decade after he became bishop, about A.D. 325, was translated as *The History of the Church*. Much of what is known about the first three centuries of Christianity, essentially up to the Council of Nicaea, comes from Eusebius's writings. The second personage to mature as an influential Catholic historian was the English monk of Jarrow on the Tyne, the venerable Bede (673–735). His most profound tome was *Ecclesiastical History of the English Nation*. For Bede the narrative of the Church was the story of the nation, the term "nation" being used precisely to mean "people."

With the passage of time, from the decline of the Roman Empire to the Renaissance, divisions grew within Christendom between the Greek, Syrian, and Coptic East and the Latin West, centered on Rome. For a lengthy period of several centuries in the West the Holy Roman Empire, which had come into being with the crowning of Charlemagne as the first emperor on Christmas Day in the year 800, mirrored a union of the ecclesiastical and the civil authorities. Yet, eventually the unity of Christendom—of which the Holy Roman Empire developed as a major aspect— was weakened, due to both the rise of nation-states and the schisms within Christianity that the Protestant Reformation effected.

As nations, and in some cases empires, evolved and the Catholic unity of the West became splintered through the Reformation, nations retained a Christian identity—several assuming a Protestant character of one kind or another, but many remaining Roman Catholic. Thus, the efforts of the Catholic historian took on a more demanding challenge: to study Catholic historical legacies within a broad panorama of increasingly varied Christian national and cultural environments. Within this context came, first, colonialism—Catholic and Protestant—Enlightenment thinking, revolution, predictable materialism, secular humanism, and in one form or another modernism and neo-modernism. Throughout all of this to current times, the Catholic as historian has had to research and write with fidelity to his or her Faith as well as scholarly calling.

Within this milieu almost countless names of Catholics who were, and are, outstanding historians come to mind. To highlight a mere handful of these scholars, Andrés Pérez de Ribas published in Spain in the year 1645 his classic work *Historia de los triumphos de nuestra santa fe entre gentes las mas bárbaras y fieras del Nuevo Orbe (History of the Triumphs of Our Holy*

Faith amongst the Most Barbarous and Fierce Peoples of the New World). In 1880, the Spanish historian Marcelino Menéndez Pelayo produced his classic two-volume defense of Catholic Spain against the assault of the Spanish liberals, *Historia de los heterodoxos Españoles*. A half-century later, in 1933, the French Catholic historian Robert Ricard brought out his excellent tome on the efforts of Catholic missionaries in sixteenth-century Mexico, *Conquete Spirituelle du Mexique (The Spiritual Conquest of Mexico)*.

Virtually anyone even slightly familiar with the Catholic presence in Texas has heard of the still predominant seven-volume series that Carlos Eduardo Castañeda authored under the auspices of the Knights of Columbus of Texas between the latter 1930s and his death in 1958, *Our Catholic Heritage in Texas*. At the same time, no student of the Catholic history of the American South can ignore Roger Baudier's 1939 *The Catholic Church in Louisiana*. And few question the validity of Jesuit historian Fr. Martin P. Harney's valuable book, *The Catholic Church through the Ages* (1973). In even more recent days, Warren H. Carroll's multi-volume study, *A History of Christendom*, is drawing rave reviews. And many college and university professors use as a textbook in their upper division history of Christianity courses English scholar Owen Chadwick's quite recent (mid-1990s) pictorial history, *A History of Christianity*.

Savoring this hope for fealty to the Faith, as well as realizing the obligations of scholarship, the authors of this series of essays titled *The Catholic as Historian* have divided their eleven essays into three major headings: "History, Philosophy, and Culture: Inseparable to the Catholic Historian"; "God at the Center of History: A Purview of Permanence"; and "The Catholic Historical Complexion: Two Specific Areas of Study."

In the first section Donald J. D'Elia, co-editor of the book, establishes the overall tone of this study in his "The Catholic as Historian: Witness in Every Age to Christ's Presence among Us," stressing the responsibility of the Catholic historian to show that in true history focus always is on Christ. It is His mission of salvation that exists as the center of history—what some thinkers might refer to as an Augustinian view. The other contributors to this section—Michael Ewbank, Rocco Buttiglione (with John F. Crosby as translator), Robert A. Herrera, and Glenn W. Olsen—develop their studies around such themes as the enduring role of the Catholic historian; nature, culture, and history; Christianity and the philosophy of history; and finally the parallelism of Christian philosophy and Christian history.

The second section, faithful to the general prospectus of the tome, hones in on the teaching of Catholic history and why it is so important. The scholars of this group of essays include Warren H. Carroll, Thomas Molnar, James Hitchcock, and Edward King. Topics discussed are why it is fundamental that scholars not rule out the action of God in history; why it is necessary to teach history; things hidden since the beginning of the world; and secularized Christendom and the Age of Revolution.

The third and final section of the study applies much of what is argued about the role of the Catholic as historian to two specific areas of historical interpretation. Carl B. Schmitt, Jr., and Patrick Foley—the latter being the other co-editor of the book—wrote the pieces for this area of coverage. Discussed first is the issue of a Catholic student wrestling with the Enlightenment. How does history usually treat this arena of study? Then, how has history narrated the growth and influence on the American character of the Catholic Southwest and West? Puritan New England, for example, is virtually always discussed in any religious, cultural, or socio-economic study of the United States, but the Catholic Southwest and West are given attention only occasionally.

Collectively these essays develop variations of the thesis that God has always been at the center of human life. His Church remains eternally the dispenser of the sacraments, holder of the Magisterium, teacher of doctrine, upholder of morals, and molder of culture within the Catholic tradition. Moreover, in spite of many attitudes constantly exhibited around the world that are in and of themselves anti-Catholic, the Catholic as historian must always remind society of the true heritage of a Christ-centeredness legacy in history. ◆

—Patrick Foley
Donald J. D'Elia

Contributors

Rocco Buttiglione is an internationally known scholar, journalist, and editorialist who has for decades focused on the study of politics, philosophy, social ethics, and economics, especially as such have matured within the Roman Catholic range of vision. Buttiglione, who is Full Professor of Political Science at Rome's Saint Pius V University, is an expert on the thought of Pope John Paul II. He has been Professor and Acting Chancellor of the International Academy of Philosophy at Liechenstein and as well has taught at the Catholic University of Lublin. The latter institution awarded him an honorary degree in philosophy in 1994. At present he serves as European Union Policy Minister of Italy. Professor Buttiglione has compiled an impressive list of publications in several different languages, many of them treating the thought of Pope John Paul II.

Warren H. Carroll is a leader in the restoration of orthodox Catholic liberal arts education in America. His wife, Anne, is a noted Catholic scholar and educator. A convert to the Roman Catholic Faith in 1968, Dr. Carroll founded Christendom College in Front Royal, Virginia, and served as that institution's first president (1977–1985). He was, in addition, a member of the college's board of directors and chair of its History Department until his retirement in 2002. Dr. Carroll is perhaps best-known for his prodigious list of intellectually demanding and spiritually profound books and articles, all written from a Catholic perspective. He is currently working on his projected six-volume history of Christendom from the Incarnation through the twentieth century. Several volumes already have been published. Dr. Carroll earned his B.A. cum laude from Bates College and his M.A. and Ph.D. degrees in history from Columbia University.

John F. Crosby received his B.A. from Georgetown University in 1966 and his Ph.D. in philosophy from the University of Salzburg, Austria, in 1970. At Salzburg he studied under Dietrich von Hildebrand and Josef Seifert. Dr. Crosby served on the faculties of the University of Dallas 1970–1987, and the International Academy of Philosophy, Liechenstein, 1987–1990. He has been professor and chair of the Philosophy Department at Franciscan University of Steubenville since 1990. From 1983 to 1993, he taught at the John Paul II Institute for Marriage. Dr. Crosby has published extensively on the thought of John Henry Cardinal Newman as well as that of Pope John Paul II.

Donald J. D'Elia is Professor Emeritus of History at the State University of New York (SUNY), New Paltz, where he taught from 1965 to 2005. Dr. D'Elia has also served on the faculties of Bloomsburg State College, Bloomsburg, Pennsylvania; Marist College, Poughkeepsie, New York; New York University; and Regnum Christi Center, Wakefield, Rhode Island. He has been a visiting lecturer at Dickinson College, Carlisle, Pennsylvania; Manhattanville College, Purchase, New York; Christendom College, Front Royal, Virginia; Washington College, Chestertown, Maryland; the Opus Dei Center, New York City; Columbia University, New York City; and Thomas More College, Merrimack, New Hampshire. Dr. D'Elia has published extensively on colonial America. He earned both his B.A. and M.A. degrees in history and philosophy from Rutgers University and his Ph.D. in history and philosophy from the Pennsylvania State University. Dr. D'Elia has done postdoctoral work at the Angelicum in Rome.

Michael B. Ewbank is Professor of Philosophy at the Seminarium Fraternitatus Sacerdotalis S. Petri in Denton, Nebraska. From 1988 to 1997 he taught philosophy at Loras College, Dubuque, Iowa. Dr. Ewbank taught philosophy at Stonehill College in North Easton, Massachusetts, 1982–1985; and in 1977–1978 taught courses in English to university professors at Spain's Universidad de Salamanca. Dr. Ewbank earned his B.A. in philosophy at the University of Dallas and his Ph.D. in philosophy at the Universidad de Salamanca. From the latter institution he also received a licentiate in philosophy. Beyond these, he has engaged in graduate studies in philosophy at St. Louis University. He was awarded a Fulbright Post-doctoral Research Grant to carry out research in Spain, 1985–1986. Dr. Ewbank has to his credit more than forty publications, many of them published in Spain, France, Germany, or French Canada.

Patrick Foley is Editor Emeritus of *Catholic Southwest: A Journal of History and Culture* and Consulting Editor for *The Catholic Social Science Review.* A specialist on Catholic Texas, Catholic Spain, and the American Vincentians, Dr. Foley has numerous publications. In 1987, he wrote the official history essay of the Church in Texas that was sent to Pope John Paul II for the pontiff's study in preparation for his pastoral visit to Texas that year. For that effort Dr. Foley was awarded a papal medallion. During the summer of 1974 he studied in Madrid, Spain, and in 1995, he presented several lectures on Spain's Catholic heritage at Salamanca. Dr. Foley is Professor Emeritus, Tarrant County College, Fort Worth, Texas, and serves on the faculty of Columbia College of Missouri's Fort Worth campus. He has taught at the University of San Francisco; the College of Notre Dame, Belmont, California; Chaminade University of Hawaii; the College of Santa Fe; the College of Saint Thomas More in Fort Worth; and the University of Texas at Dallas. Dr. Foley earned his B.A. in history from Chico State College in California; his M.A. in history from Santa Clara University; and his Ph.D. in history from the University of New Mexico.

Robert A. Herrera is Professor Emeritus of Philosophy, Seton Hall University, having retired from that institution in 1998. He has also been on the faculties of Baruch College, Rutgers University, and the New School for Social Research. He specializes in the philosophy of history and the history of ideas. The several books that Professor Herrera has published show clearly that he penetrates deeply and with scholarly fineness the intellectual and spiritual essence of many of the profound thinkers of the past in regard to the history of ideas. Perhaps the better known of his subjects of study are Juan Donoso Cortés and Orestes Brownson. Professor Herrera studied in the United States, Spain, and Cuba, and earned his Ph.D. from the New School for Social Research, studying under Hans Jonas.

James Hitchcock is Professor of History at St. Louis University. Before this he served on the faculties of St. John's University in New York, the New School for Social Research, and Long Island University. Dr. Hitchcock was a Woodrow Wilson Fellow, is a former Editor-in-Chief of Communio, is a member of the advisory board for *The Catholic Social Science Review*, and is a former president of the Fellowship of Catholic Scholars. The latter group named him as a recipient of its prestigious John Cardinal Wright Award. This Catholic scholar also is on the Board of Advisors of the Marian Institute for Advanced Studies. Professor Hitchcock has numerous publications—books, contributions to books, scholarly journal articles, and reviews among them. His wife, Helen Hitchcock, is a noted Catholic apologist. Dr. Hitchcock received his A.B. in history from St. Louis University and earned his M.A. and Ph.D. in history from Princeton University. In addition, he has received honorary degrees from Benedictine College and Franciscan University of Steubenville.

Edward King, in 1997, founded the Christopher Dawson Centre of Christian Culture in Kanata, Canada. He is the director of the Centre and editor of its *Newsletter*. For many years he worked closely with the late John J. Mulloy, writing articles for Mulloy's *The Dawson Newsletter*. Edward King was born in Ottawa, Ontario, Canada, in 1940. Educated in Montreal by Sisters of Saint Joseph at the elementary school level and Jesuits in secondary school, in 1961 he earned his B.A. in history at Loyola College in Montreal. King undertook graduate studies in history at the University of Toronto, Assumption College, and the University of Windsor. From 1967 to 1995, he taught mostly religion at the Montreal Catholic School Commission. In 1968, King married Christina Murphy. In 1976, they adopted two boys. Over the years Edward King has become an internationally known scholar on the life and works of Christopher Dawson. King and his wife have visited numerous sites—especially several in England—containing Dawson's works.

Thomas Molnar has been Professor of Religious Philosophy at the University of Budapest since 1991. He has also taught philosophy and has been a visiting professor at the University of Dijon, Yale University, Potchefstroom University in South Africa, Hillsdale College, and other colleges and universities in the United States and Europe. He holds an honorary degree from the University of Mendoza in Argentina. In addition, he received the Medal of Achievement in French Political Thought from the City of Nice and has been awarded the Moi, Symmaque prize (Paris, 1999), the Szecheny prize (Hungary, 2000), and the Stephanus prize (Hungary, 2002). Among his many highly influential books are *Bernanos: His Political Thought and Prophecy* (1960); *The Decline of the Intellectual* (1962); *Utopia: The Perennial Heresy* (1967); *The Counter-Reformation* (1969); *God and the Knowledge of Reality* (1974); *The Pagan Temptation* (1987); *Twin Powers, Politics and the Sacred* (1988); *The Church Pilgrim of Centuries* (1990); *Az idealis allam kritikaja* (1991); *The Emergence of Atlantic Culture* (1994); and *L'hegemonie liberale, Age d'homme* (1992).

Glenn W. Olsen is Professor of History at the University of Utah, specializing in Christianity and medieval history. His particular interest is Western civilization to 1300, Medieval Spain, Christianity in the ancient and medieval world, and early and late medieval social and cultural history. Professor Olsen has a long list of distinguished publications centering on such areas of study as Christianity and the making of Europe; history as seen by Hans Urs von Balthasar; John of Salisbury and humanism; the Catholic ideas of history as interpreted by Christopher Dawson; America, Catholicism, and the Enlightenment; and more. Dr. Olsen is active in several scholarly associations and is in demand as a speaker and panelist at scholarly gatherings, especially where contributions from the Catholic world are needed. Dr. Olsen earned his Ph.D. in history from the University of Wisconsin in 1965.

Carl B. Schmitt, Jr. is a Catholic intellectual devoted to a scholarly and spiritual quest to show how Christ lives through history—history is centered on Christ. Dr. Schmitt was born in Wilton, Connecticut, in 1929, the eighth son of well-known artist Carl Schmitt and his wife. While attending public schools, he resided in Rome from age ten to twelve, there receiving his First Confession and First Communion. Dr. Schmitt graduated from Harvard College in 1951 magna cum laude, with a senior thesis on St. Augustine's philosophy of history. Subsequently, he studied at the University of Paris Institut Catholique and received a Fulbright Fellowship to the University of Florence. He completed his Ph.D. in history at Harvard and commenced a career of teaching, writing, and developing educational programs that reflected his view of Christ and history. Dr. Schmitt taught at Harvard and the City University of New York, and later was an educational consultant in New York City. He played a role in setting up the Stillman Chair of Catholic Studies at Harvard. Dr. Schmitt has developed as foundation to support the memory of his father's works in the original Schmitt home in Wilton, Connecticut. ◆

History, Philosophy, and Culture: Inseparable to the Catholic Historian

The Catholic as Historian: Witness in Every Age to Christ's Presence among Us

Donald J. D'Elia

Progress in Christianity is not linear and horizontal, it is vertical. It aims at eternity, not the spinning out of time. The reason for the existence of time is that we should move out of it, soul by soul. When the number of souls foreseen by the Lord has been reached, time will come to an end, whatever the condition of humanity may be at that moment. . . .

—Antonin Gilbert Sertillanges

The Mystical Body unites all ages into one company, and I can talk to Augustine, not as to a memory, as to a man. . . .

—Frederick D. Wilhelmsen

History, the greatest work of God. . . .

—Christopher Dawson

"ANYBODY can make history," Oscar Wilde once remarked, turning the familiar adage on its head, "only a great man can write it." In a sense beyond anything that Wilde probably had in mind at the time he made this observation, there is much truth in it. For it indeed does take a great man or woman to write history with a fidelity to the past, great in the only true Christian sense of the word. It takes a great man, the kind of man who—before Christ's redemptive passion and death—was not possible in pagan antiquity. The only really great man, the Christian knows, is one who, in the words of St. Peter, is called to be a "partaker of divine nature" (2 Peter 1:4).

This man, now made worthy of God because of grace, is the only true historian, because the only true man, "God became man, so that man could become God." This is the ancient wisdom about man and history, about all things. Because the Word became flesh and died for us on a cross, man may even now begin to see with the eye of Christ, the God-Man, as he continues his pilgrimage to the fullness of Truth in the Beatific Vision. And the Truth about history, and about all things, is not mere propositions. "The believer's act [of Faith] does not terminate in the propositions, but in the realities [which they express]"[1] Truth Himself has told us (John 14:6).

But a discussion of this kind belongs properly to the realm of theology, and the kind reader should look elsewhere for one competent to provide a theology of history. My purpose in this essay is much less ambitious. It is simply to share reflections that I have garnered in a career of over thirty-eight years of teaching and writing American and European history in a number of colleges and universities.

Modernity and the Decapitation of God

There is a book close at hand as I write, which has become recognized as a little masterpiece, and to which we can resort for one of the most preliminary observations about Catholic and history. While it is true that the Dominican historian Bede Jarrett was writing about understanding the social theories of the Middle Ages in his book by that title, his insistence on the need to refer to the "idea of Christendom," of the Faith as the background of that study, applies not only to medieval thought, but to all Western thought as well. There is, in fact, no other way to make intelligible—to make sense of—our history since the end of the Middle Ages.

Fr. Jarrett, after emphasizing the primacy of faith in medieval thought, that is, that for medieval thinkers "perfect love was not possible without perfect faith," discusses the forces emerging from the Middle Ages that in the end would destroy Christendom and the "common unity of the Faith."[2] Together these forces shaped modern times and, even more significant to our purpose here, the new postmedieval understanding of history.

Fairly recent secular assumptions, that is, unconscious metaphysics of history, gradually came to be accepted in the study of the past, and this emerged as the greatest "revolution" of all, culminating in the triumph of a bogus value-free positivism, foisted on unsuspecting contemporary man as no metaphysics at all. "No science can be more secure than the unconscious metaphysics which it tacitly presupposes." The twentieth-century philosopher Alfred North Whitehead has warned us, "All reasoning apart from some metaphysical reference is vicious." And without "metaphysical presupposition there can be no civilization."[3] But Whitehead and Catholic realism notwithstanding, it is positivism, naturalism, and other metaphysical theories that continue to dominate man's historical consciousness. If he or she does nothing else, the Catholic as historian must strive to expose the philosophical assumptions that underlie these popular petit bourgeois attitudes toward the past.

The emerging forces were nationalism, secularism, and conciliarism. And these progressions have led, as another English historian, Christopher Dawson, has shown, to the decline of authentic Christianity and Christendom, and the rise of pseudo-religions such as materialism, Marxism, and nationalism itself. Secularism, which became even more popular as the result of religious diversity at the time of the Protestant Reformation, seemed to leave the state—for example, in the thought of Bodin and the early Alexander Hamilton—as the only acceptable "universal" community, with responsibilities hitherto assigned to the medieval Church. It was only a matter of time before religious diversity and the secular Renaissance conception of an increasingly absent God produced deism in all its forms and the contracted, decentralized "natural law" of the Enlightenment. What Eric Voegelin called the "decapitation of God" in our own time seemed to be inevitable.[4]

History, like those other ancient studies now named "economic" and "political science"—reflecting their separation from moral philosophy—became just one of the "social sciences" thought to be made possible by the Scientific Revolution. "We shall measure what is measurable," Galileo made his terrible boast in the name of the Modern Age that was dawning, "and we shall make measurable what is not." Forced to lie on the Procrustean bed of the new quantitative spirit, and excised of the life-giving mysticism that defies bourgeois calculation and that mankind from time immemorial has recognized as vital to man, the study of history was reduced more and more to that mere episodic, traditionless document-shuffling that Hilaire Belloc and other historians complained about.[5]

As Christianity, the dynamic element of metaphysics (Whitehead) of Western Civilization lost its influence among men, the "social sciences" over the centuries mirrored the new metaphysical theories by growing more secularistic, mathematical, and behavioristic. The Industrial Revolution radically accelerated the process of de-Christianization and of isolating Western man from his past. History, that living tradition in the Christian sense of the mystical transcendent, supra-individualist community (the Church) existing through the ages, had served hitherto to protect Western man's personhood and authentic existence. But now, modern man, traditionless, autonomous, and solitary, in both formation and free exercise of conscience, was his own authority and alone faced the terrible responsibility of choosing his relationship to society and "church" (social contract).[6]

Christopher Dawson has described this "artificial" situation in *The Crisis of Western Education*:

> On the one hand, man is sheltered from the direct impact of reality, while on the other he is subjected to a growing pressure which makes for social conformity. He seldom has to think for himself or make vital decisions. His whole life is spent inside highly organized artificial units— factory, trade union, office, civil service, party—and his success or failure depends on his relations with this organization. If the Church were one of these compulsory organizations modern man would be religious, but since it is voluntary, and makes demands on his spare time, it is felt to be superfluous and unnecessary.[7]

The modern pseudo-religion of the autonomy of the individual, along with the autonomy or self-dependence of nature and culture, severs man's relationship to God and all things, including history, and blasphemously converts the individual into the final Absolute, a self-worshipping creature, the ultimate idol, a god.[8]

It is the living Faith, the true historical consciousness, right tradition that enables man to be what he is meant to be in Christ, "The way, the truth, and the life" (John 14:6). Maurice Blondel has described this tradition in all its fullness as conveying:

> much more than ideas susceptible of logical formulation. It embodies a life that involves, all in one, sentiments, thoughts, beliefs, aspirations

and deeds. It hands on in a kind of fruitful contact that which successive generations must become imbued with and in turn impart as a permanent condition to a vivification and participation in a reality that admits of being drawn on indefinitely by individual and successive effort without being thereby exhausted.

Implicit in this tradition, for Blondel, who urged modern man to take the fact of Revelation seriously, is "the spiritual communion of souls that feel, think, and will within the unity of a single patriotic or religious ideal." Tradition, he continues:

> remains a condition of progress insofar as it allows of certain portions of the truth, that as a whole can never be completely defined, to be made to pass from a state of being explicitly known. For as the principle of unity, continuity. and fecundity, tradition which is at one and the same time initial, anticipative, and final, precedes all attempts to effect a synthetic reconstruction and survives every endeavor to subject it to searching analysis.

Only in the Church, the "communion of saints," can man attain full stature in what Blondel calls "theandrical symbiosis," and this "indwelling of the Trinity" is possible only in mankind's authentic historical existence, protected by Christ's Church against Gnostic modernist discontinuities of time and space.[9]

Blondel's and Dawson's contemporary, the German Catholic philosopher Peter Wust, also warned against renouncing the "will to heroic action," which in his country and elsewhere seemed to be leading to the appearance of those "nihilistic personalities who in the absence of Christian 'constructive personalities'—always come forward to carry out their work of destruction."[10] Only one tradition, Christopher Dawson agreed, that of the Catholic Church, was "capable of satisfying the whole of human nature," forming the true personality of man, and bringing the "transcendent reality and spiritual Being into relation with human experience and the realities of social life."[11] Jacques Maritain called this "integral humanism . . . integral wholeness . . . the humanism of the Incarnation." It was man in "the integral wholeness of his natural and supernatural being and setting no apriori limits to the descent of the divine into man."[12]

"For Apart from Me You Can Do Nothing" (John 15:5)

Peter Wust's alarm about the "nihilistic personalities" of modern Germany and the West in general was not clarion enough to save his country from the Nazis, the "little gods" of the new anti-Christian world that Nietzsche had had his prophet Zarathustra sing about in the nineteenth century.

Man was not created in the image and likeness of his Creator, Nietzsche proclaimed to a modern world eager to listen; man was an "unfixed animal" and could be made into whatever he liked. There was no transcendent order, no supernatural values—as in Platonism and Christianity—to which man must submit. Nietzsche rejected Kierkegaard's plea for a true Christendom, free of the corruption and hypocrisies of their contemporaries. The temporal order was all that existed, the world of becoming in which man was a bridge to the superman of Zarathustra's teaching. God is dead, declared Nietzsche. In the next century, his disciple, Adolph Hitler, and the Third Reich's high priests Alfred Rosenberg and Joseph Goebbels created the new mass religion of Nazism with its new man, the "nihilistic personality," who numbered in the millions and who owed his absolute allegiance to the God-state.

"Once the 'autonomous state' has broken all bonds," Romano Guardini was among the first to see, "it will be able to deliver the last *coup de grace* to human nature itself."[13] Eric Voegelin aptly called this new religion the "mysticism of contracted existence," denying as it did revelation and supernatural values. The source of order, the Catholic student of history must agree with Voegelin, lies only in the transcendental, in the beyond. "Political" religions such as Nazism, Fascism, and Marxism seek divine order within the contents of the world, where it cannot be found. As a result, man is deformed by trying to live within this radically secular, radically artificial, contracted pseudo-existence, and his extreme alienation from his creator and himself soon leads to destruction.[14]

Why the Catholic Church should know this best is explained by a great historian of the twentieth century, Etienne Gilson: "Catholicism alone knows exactly what is nature and what is the world, and what is grace, but it knows it only because it keeps its eyes fixed on the concrete union of nature and grace in the Redeemer of nature, in the person of Jesus Christ."[15] Neither Calvinism nor Lutheranism, with their despair of nature, nor the "foolish hope" of naturalism should distract the Catholic from the truth that the grace of Jesus Christ heals and restores. The "world" is nature apart from God's direction. Nature was created by God, and subject to Him it will attain its end, but when perverted, self-governed, nature become the "world," and is deflected from the end for which God created it.

It was the world that triumphed in Nazi Germany: Nature, human and otherwise, turned against its Creator. "Nihilistic personalities" such as the Gestapo agents who tortured the student members of the anti-Hitler "White Rose" and the SS guards at Dachau and Buchenwald, were modern men in revolt against God, living the lie of a contracted existence that closed them off from the higher transcendental life that Jesus Christ offers to man through faith and the sacraments. The spiritual life of mankind is its true existence, as a contemporary of Nietzsche and a greater historian, John Henry Newman, taught.[16] And this spiritual life, which Newman knew from his study of history men and women are always seeking, attains its fullness and perfection only in Christ and His Church.

The Italian priest and founder of Christian Democracy, Luigi Sturzo, warned his contemporaries against the Fascist version of this new mass man and "nihilistic personality" whose rise to power in the West was nothing less than a diabolical attempt to reject the Incarnation in history. "The moment in time is 'the Word was made flesh,' the Word Who manifests 'the glory of the Only begotten of the Father,'" Don Sturzo explained the centrality of the Incarnation as the living, ever-present Divine reality in the Catholic meaning of history: "The repetition of that day is in every day; that moment is every moment. The moment in time has not and cannot have any other significance, any other value than that of mirroring the eternal moment when 'in the beginning was the Word, and the Word was God,' and 'was made flesh.'"[17] With the Incarnation, the Second Person of the Holy Trinity had engrafted Himself into history and become:

> a factor of human progress without diminishing man's freedom to choose between good and evil, between heaven and earth. Nor is this all. Although God respects our human liberty—for without that of course there could be no voluntary participation in the divine—in the spiritual and historical life of man, God cannot be other than unfolding truth, compelling, winning love.[18]

The mass, "nihilistic personality" was the fragmented disintegrated "man" that Christ had come to redeem, the storm trooper, the concentration camp "desk murderer," the monster-product of centuries of "revolt against God." "For the first time," Henri de Lubac wrote, "a mass persuasion has arisen, powerful as a tidal wave, that man's hour was struck at last. And in that hour the finite being, self-sufficient in his finitude and his imma-nence, takes to himself all the prerogatives of God. It is the folly of Kirilov in *The Possessed*, of Zarathustra, of Feuerbach, the folly alike of 'humanist' and 'superman.'"[19]

The modern, necessarily secular "technology of man," this manipula-tion of man, led the biologist Julian Huxley to declare in 1923 "that man had finally achieved the conscious control of evolution" and that mankind would no longer have to be subject to the "mechanism of chance."[20] It was the realization of a dream, going back at least to Condorcet, Comte, Marx, and Nietzsche—the dream of a "man-made being" that would be far superior to the "sorry creature of God's making."[21] "This is the task of our century," Alfred Rosenberg, the leading spokesman of Nazi ideology, wrote in his *Myth of the Twentieth Century* (1925), "to create a new human type from a new life-mythus. . . . The new man of the approaching first German Reich will have but one answer for all doubts and questions: Alone, I will."[22]

It was this "new" man of Hitler's and Rosenberg's, the product of Godless history and the "technology of man" that staffed the death camps. "For without Me you can do nothing," Jesus taught (John 15:5). The record of men following their own wills, apart from God, is not "history." It is evil. It is literally nothing, as we learn from the Lord of History and the Truth of Himself.[23]

Alfred Delp, unlike Hitler and Rosenberg, was German-born; as a convert to Catholicism and a Jesuit priest he understood—with St. Paul—that the only "new man" worthy of the name is a man transformed in Jesus Christ. Rejecting any Heideggerian doctrine of the "utter and total finiteness" of man, he saw modern man as a "tragic" figure compared with true man, who was called as the very "image of God" to see "every histor-ical moment" as "an opportunity for the kingdom of God."[24] "Everywhere today," Fr. Delp wrote about life in the 1930s, "existence is in some way endangered and pure, authentic life is threatened." But the Gestapo, powerful and ubiquitous as it was, their agents watching his every movement in his small parish in Munich-Bogenhausen, could not destroy in Fr. Delp's mind the great truth that man is God's noblest creature and that he is gifted with creative freedom.

Nor could the Nazi state, with all its techniques of human degradation, abolish true history. In his book *Der Mensch und die Geschichte*, dedicated to his parishioners at St. George, Fr. Delp angered the Gestapo by publicly defending that universalism which the Church has zealously guarded down the centuries. Hitler and the Nazi historians condemned such Jesuit-taught universalism as Jewish and Catholic internationalism designed, in reality, to enslave the German people to foreign leaders. But National Socialism itself was, Fr. Delp knew, a species of that "irrational particularism" or anti-intellectualism, holding as it did that truth was racial and national.[25]

Man, created in the image and likeness of God, is at the center of history, Fr. Delp wrote in his book. And then, faithful to his Augustinian-Thomistic understanding of that history taught by the Church, he alluded to the Nazi challenge of his own times. "If history or one of the moments within it is corrupted, then in that hour, men, though bound not to betray their relationship with history, are equally bound not to surrender their freedom or the immediacy of their relationship with God."[26] Man in his God-like creative freedom was not in this view the abstracted individual of classical liberalism, a mere part of the whole man, but the human person in all of his biblical fullness—man in the Mystical Body of Christ.

Man, Fr. Delp had written in an earlier work, *The Christian and the Present Day*, is "the meeting place between things of the world, the historical and the transcendent, the unhistorical." As the image of God, every human being, whatever his time or place, had the responsibility of witnessing to the "divine life" of "faith, hope, and charity" available to man by the historic Catholic fact of the pouring out of Christ in the continuing Incarnation.[27] "The Christian has to be redeemed of his age. Man must see that we are redeemed today." And this means that today, this very moment, we must seek and find in Christ and His Church—in Faith and Holy Sacraments—that "perfect life" that the Savior of the world won for us in His precious blood on Calvary.

This is the Christian meaning of history, and it is very different from Nazi, Marxist, and other Gnostic distortions of man's past and present that, as Eric Voegelin, notably, has argued, seek to "immanentize" human existence by replacing religious faith with philosophy. "The attempt at immanentizing the meaning of existence," he has written, "is fundamentally an attempt at bringing our knowledge of transcendence into a firmer grip than the *cognito fidei*, the cognition of faith, will afford, and the Gnostic experiences offer this firmer grip insofar as they are an expansion of the soul to the point where God is drawn into the existence of man."[28] But as the Lord of History Himself has said when asked whether the time had come for the restoration of the Kingdom of Israel: "It is not for you to know times or dates that the Father has established by His own authority" (Acts 1:6–7; Ecclesiastes 3:1–22).

In rejecting the Gnostic reduction of the mysteries of life, this "contracted existence," in his defense of Catholic universalism against the narrow, totalitarian particularism of Nazism, Fr. Delp urges contemporary man to claim the God-given "creative freedom" that is his birthright. This was the "homeland" not only of his German contemporaries, but of all men and women created as they are in the image and likeness of God. The highest vocation of man, in every generation, is to help others see this: to guide them in the recognition of "this inclination and this longing . . . so that men are once again free to view existence in its entirety with all its commitments and obligations and components."[29]

The "nihilistic" men Peter Wust had warned about came for Fr. Delp on July 28, 1944. The charge was membership in the Kreisau Circle, an important resistance group, and implication in the failed attempt on Hitler's life in the July Plot a week earlier. From his prison cell, where he remained until his condemnation and death by hanging on February 2, 1945, Fr. Delp continued to write to his parishioners and friends about God, man, and the mystery of man's relationship to divine reality, present and past.

"When the decision will come," he wrote at the beginning of December, anticipating the Nazi death sentence, "is once again up in the air. Yesterday it looked as if the matter would drag on until Christmas. Today the word is, it will come as early as next week. In any case, I now know what it means to live in His hand. That is what we should always have done. But often I have lived very much in reliance on my own powers and certainty—and by reason of this remain indebted for so much to so many people."[30]

"I am the vine, you are the branches," the Lord of History and all reality has said; "He who lives in Me and I in him, will produce abundantly, for apart from Me you can do nothing" (John 15:5).

Christ, Eucharistic Prisoner and Liberator

It was above all in receiving the Holy Eucharist, the Body and Blood of Christ, Priest and Victim, Fr. Delp tells us, and in his "hours of grace" in adoration before the Blessed Sacrament, that the martyr-priest discovered more intensely who he was as an image and likeness of God, and knew that the Nazi guards, for all the beatings they inflicted upon him, "would not succeed in annihilating me."[31] The Almighty God, the Lord of Hosts, Whom the universe could not contain, out of His infinite love for man made Himself a fellow "Prisoner" in the tabernacle of Fr. Delp's cell. "Even if the new paganism no longer wishes love," the Dutch Carmelite priest Titus Brandsma had prophesied before the war and his own martyrdom in Dachau, "we shall overcome paganism with this very love. Love will conquer the hearts of the pagans for us."[32]

"Adoration and love"—in Fr. Delp's words the "only two realities that make existence worthwhile"—reveal the meaning of man's life and history. "Only if we worship, love and live according to God's divine commandments are we human beings and really free."[33] Only if we do this—in our creative freedom grow more perfect in our love of God and neighbor—can we become whole and fully intelligible "personalities" in Christ rather than stunted individualities following our own creaturely wills.[34] It is these unfragmented, integrated men and women—the saints—who alone have a "history," and it is Christ's presence among them, His sacramental action, especially in the Eucharist, that creates "history." Jesus Christ, "Emmanuel," in His Incarnation in time and His permanent Incarnation, the Church, creates the only true history, "Sacred history," by radically altering human existence and setting down "a qualitative frontier between the Before and the After."[35] Jesus Christ and His sacramental actions give to time its "ontological integration and unified intelligibility."[36] The sacred actions of Christ while on earth continue in His Church in man's present and future, but the fullest realization of the sacraments, their "realized eschatology," will come only with the Parousia and when the last soul has been liberated from "spiritual captivity." This is "the mission," Jean Cardinal Danielou writes, that "constitutes the reality hidden under the appearances of secular history." By it is constituted progressively in charity the incorruptible body of Christ which will cross through the fire of judgment. This "mission" is the work of the Holy Spirit. It is the continuation of the great works of the *mirabila Dei* of the two Testaments. This is the same Spirit that, through its power, liberated the people from Egypt, liberated Christ from death, and liberated man by baptism. It is by the "preaching of the Word and by the Sacraments" that this "work of the Spirit" is accomplished.[37] It is this Augustinian understanding of history as Christian "sacred history," time integrated sacramentally in Christ's living presence among men, that inspired Fr. Delp's heroism in opposing the neo-paganism of the Nazis. The City of God must not be absorbed gnostically into the City of Man.[38] Even though he was so deeply influenced by the existentialist philosophy of his day, Fr. Delp understood that his decision not to submit to Nazi totalitarianism was not merely a declaration of his liberty as an individual, however nobly given, but a Christian affirmation of sacred history, where man "inserts himself into the web of an economy which goes beyond him and which constitutes an objective plan."[39] This is the divine "pedagogy," as St. Irenaeus called it, the Father's plan in Christ to bring man home.

In this plan, true history begins with Christ, is directed to Christ as its object and final cause, and is centered on Christ. There can be no history without Christ and the Church that He founded—"the translation of our world into the eternal fullness of God." Christ in His sacraments, especially the Eucharist, gathers all the days of men to Himself. All creatures, in the words of St. Bonaventure, are vestiges, traces, or images of God (man), and are truly known only when they are known in relation to God and the end to which they tend.[40] Christ is the Alpha and Omega of all reality, concentrating it in Himself, in His Eucharistic presence in the tabernacles of men. He is that clarification the Marxists, Nazis, and other Gnostics seek in their dialectics within history, in their immanentisms, not realizing that the ultimate ground and clarification of all things, the

Logos, the "Word made flesh," has made Himself a "Prisoner" of men in the Blessed Sacrament, reserved in the tabernacle of the humblest chapel.

The "nihilistic" men who came to take Fr. Delp to Plotzensee prison to be hanged on February 2, 1945, were victims and agents of the false historical consciousness of Nazism. But it could have been any form of totalitarianism that denies the transcendence of Christianity and Judaism, trying to replaced them with the contracted existence of a "civil theology." Wrote the German theologian Johannes Pinsk:

> Indeed, the incarnation of the Son of God opens up for the entire cosmos and for all mankind an entirely new dimension. The individual manifestations of life in its various categories do not lie now merely on the horizontal plane of cosmic and historical events, they are also drawn into the great perpendicular, which leads by way of Christ's humanity into the innermost life of God. In consequence of this perfect union of the Godhead with humanity in Christ, religion has found its absolute perfection.[41]

The Incarnation and the sacraments, Christ's presence among us today in history, the Divine-human mystery of the Church, these transcendent realities give the lie to the Gnosticism and caesaro-papism of the Nazis, as they did to the French Revolutionaries before them. That man in this world can partake of God's conscious life because God became man destroys every kind of Gnosticism and non-Christian civil religion that Hitler and his "nihilistic" monster-men tried to construct. "The light of lights cannot be quenched under the bushel of nationality."

The Eucharist, the "Sacrament of Sacraments," as taught by the Church, provides each man and woman in their daily lives with Christ—the Pascha (Heb. *Pesah*), the "break-through," the "Fullness of God's life"—the ultimate reference point in human history. Christ in the Eucharist rescues man from existential isolation in the narrow circumstances of his personal life, integrating past, present, and future and making a whole (i.e., holiness) of his life as well as the lives of all men and women in the Mystical Body of Christ.[42]

By His action in the Eucharist, His Real Presence, as notably St. Irenaeus argued in *Adversus Haereses*, the Gnostic (Nazi, etc.) heresy of absorbing transcendent divine revelation into religious philosophy (civil religion and theology) is prevented. Matter, held by the Gnostics to be co-eternal and opposed to God, is vindicated as a creature of God and therefore good. The very human body of Christ—like all human bodies—is proved to be real and good and the Eucharist the real flesh and blood of the Redeemer, which God Himself has commanded us to eat.[43] No wonder that the Nazis hated the Eucharist, the ultimate Pasch, symbol and break-through to Absolute Transcendence! "Happiness is achieved only in the fullness which personality gains in the community of a Church filled with the infinity of God" in the Sacraments, a Church that alone is the bearer of Christ's divine Life and that alone fulfills all personal being. "The man, therefore, who seeks life in its totality will of necessity discover the Church. For the individual Christian, no less than for Christ Himself, 'the Church is his *pleroma*,' his completion" (Ephesians 1:23).[44]

It is the teaching of the Church, in the famous words of St. Catherine of Siena, that "all the way to Heaven is Heaven." The spiritual doctrine of Blessed Elizabeth of the Trinity, in our own day, confirms this truth against Gnosticism, that is, that the work of sanctification, of the indwelling of the Holy Trinity in the souls of men and women, begins now on this earth and in history. History is not an essence that can be deified as in the Gnostic systems of Joachim of Fiore, Hegel, and Marx. Only human beings made in the image and likeness of God can be deified, can be completed by being incorporated in Christ. And the Eucharist is the Bread of the voyager, the *Viaticum* of the Christian, who is free—"creative freedom" in Fr. Delp's words—and in *statu viatoris* rather than created in Beatitude.[45]

As for St. Maximilian Kolbe in Auschwitz and Blessed Titus Brandsma in Dauchau, when Fr. Delp adored the Blessed Sacrament in his prison cell he was in the Real Presence of his creator, on his way to the beatific vision and yet in a true sense already there. Time breaks through to absolute transcendence because the Man-God is among us. Heraclitus weeps no more for men and women condemned to eternal recurrence.[46]

It was his belief in the Eucharistic Presence that led Jacques Maritain to request of Pope Paul VI the privilege of having the Blessed Sacrament in his monastic cell when, near the end his life, he went to live with the Little Brothers of Jesus in Toulouse. Like Fr. Delp, Blessed Titus Brandsma, and St. Maximilian Kolbe, in the crueler days of the Nazi occupation of Europe, the great Catholic philosopher and mystic knew where the Lord of History and of all reality could be found. It was in the Blessed Sacrament, in his monk's cell, that Jacques Maritain confirmed that transcendent "hope against hope," as he had during a long lifetime of assisting at the Holy Sacrifice of the Mass and Eucharistic visits in the grand cathedrals and plain country chapels of Europe and America.

History's Surrender to the "Word"

Just as it was that "hope against hope" that had turned him and his beloved Raissa back from suicide in their youth when as students at the Sorbonne they had been desperate about the meaning of life, so Jacques Maritain took up the great theme of Christian hope as a contemplative in his monk's cell. But even earlier, in his book *Christianity and Democracy,* the French Catholic thinker had surveyed the ruins of World War II and called upon his fellow men not to despair about the future.[47]

The war had shown, he wrote in 1944, that hope was a "spiritual weapon, as necessary a dynamic agent of effective transformation and victory as material weapons and munitions." During the war, not only under the swastika—the anti-Church, the idol of nationalism—but everywhere and at all times, the "obscure hope of millions of men" was "at work in the underground recesses of history." Hope is the "true enfranchisement of human life . . . a deliberate will to hope." It is our "historic duty, a duty to our brothers, and to future generations to keep hope firm." We must not be discouraged. "It is a work of courage and hope, of confidence and faith, which must begin with an effort of the mind determined to see clearly at all cost, and to rescue from the errors which disfigured them the great things in which we have believed and in which we believe, and which are the hope of the world."[48]

But this hope, Maritain cautions, can exist only when coupled with the Gospel law of brotherly love:

> If it fails to recognize its supra-human origins and exigencies, this hope risks becoming perverted and changing into violence to impose upon a "brotherhood or death." But woe to us if we scorn this hope itself, and deprive the human race of the promise of brotherhood. The human race has been exalted by it, it will renounce it only at the cost of becoming more fierce than before.[49]

This was clear from the horrors of World War II. "This hope is holy in itself, it corresponds to the deepest and most ineradicable desires of human nature. It places souls in a communion of pain and longing with all of the oppressed and the persecuted; it has a divine power for transforming human history.[50] "Again and again"—the words are Fr. Delp's, but they could be Maritain's—"history will surrender to the Word because history too knows its Master and cannot exist away from its true source."[51]

It is significant that Fr. Delp smuggled the consecrated Host—the Lord of History—into the Nazi courtroom where he was condemned to death for being a "Christian and a Jesuit." And Jacques Maritain spent his last days alone with the Incarnate Meaning of History.[52]

America and the Christian Life Force

Jacques Maritain, who lived and taught in the United States for many years, loved the American people. Like Christopher Dawson and the native-born theologian Fr. John Courtney Murray, Maritain believed that American Catholics had a "particularly important historic role, if they fully understood the mission, especially their intellectual mission, in cooperating in the forward movement of the national community as a whole. True, in its 'historic roots, and in the cast of mind of its Founding Fathers, as well as in the moral structure of its secular consciousness' the United States was more Protestant than Catholic. Still, Maritain believed, at least when he wrote in the mid-fifties, that in this country 'the notion of a Christian-inspired civilization is more part of the national heritage than in any other spot on earth.' "[53]

The federal Constitution, for example, Maritain pointed out, appeared in the history of ideas as a lay—even, to some extent, rationalist—fruit of the perennial Christian life force, which despite three centuries of tragic vicissitudes and spiritual division was able to produce this momentous temporal achievement at the dawn of the American nation. Certainly much more could have been achieved for mankind had the scandal of division between Protestant and Catholic not taken place and the "integrity and unity of faith" been preserved. But the "release at that given moment of humbler, temporal Christian energies must at any cost penetrate the historical existence of mankind."[54]

The American Constitution—and doubtless the French philosopher regarded the Declaration of Independence the same way—could be "described as an outstanding lay Christian document tinged with the philosophy of the day. The spirit and inspiration of this great political Christian document is basically repugnant to making human society stand aloof from God and from any religious faith. Thanksgiving and public prayer, the invocation of the name of God at the occasion of any major official gathering, are in the practical behavior of the nation, a token of this same spirit and inspiration."[55] In the Declaration of Independence too Maritain noted what the Catholic historian must be trained to see in the Founding Fathers' right to the "pursuit of happiness," "a slogan which, if well understood, denotes a series of implications" not just for the temporal "prerequisites of a free life" but for that higher freedom of "spiritual transformation" that perfects man in the supernatural order. The Catholic historian must realize that the Church's ancient teaching of the dignity of each person, because he or she is created in the image and likeness of God, is the only real justification for the "democratic state of mind" and the "democratic philosophy of life."[56]

The "energies of the Gospel" also had much to do with the "mutual respect and tolerance" of the American people, their remarkable "sense of fellowship." The United States was "the only country in the world where the vital importance of the sense of human fellowship is recognized in such a basic manner by the nation as a whole."[57]

But Jacques Maritain was too deep a thinker, too much the premier Catholic historian not to see the danger of what he called "temporalized religious inspiration in a nation or a civilization," whether in the absorption of the City of God into the medieval City of Man, or in its extreme form as the Voegelian "decapitation of God," the "mysticism of contracted existence," and the rise of the Hegelian and totalitarian God-state.

> The risk of that religion itself might become temporalized, in other words, so institutionalized in the temporal structures themselves and the temporal growth itself of a given civilization, that it would practically lose its essential supernatural, supra-temporal, and supra-national transcendence, and become subservient to particular national or temporal interests.[58]

At the very time Maritain was writing, the American sociologist Will Herberg, an orthodox Jew and former Marxist, was warning about the reduction of Protestantism, Catholicism, and Judaism to what he called "The American Way of Life."[59]

For Jacques Maritain—and the same was true for John Courtney Murray and Christopher Dawson—the past must never be canonized and made into an absolute. Whether viewing the Christian Middle Ages or the founding period of the United States, the Catholic historian in his Augustinian realism must not founder in the nostalgic attempt to reclaim some golden past. The Protestant Reformers tried to do just that, and the consequences for Christianity—a dynamic historical religion—were disastrous. It is in the present that we meet Christ. The divine liturgy, in the timeless words of Johannes Pinsk, "overcomes the historical gulf which separates us men of the Twentieth Century from Christ's life and work in Palestine." The purpose of the liturgy is that we should enter consciously, with body and soul, with all the activities of our life and work, into the work of Christ. That and only that, is what is meant by the phrase "to celebrate the liturgy."[60] Maritain, Murray, and Dawson roundly condemned the "deification" of history, especially in the post-Protestant Hegel. For the tombs of our ancestors are made empty by His Resurrection. We are saved by Christ, by faith and the Sacraments (the *opus Christi*)—not by the past.

The Declaration of Independence and Salvation History

The "outstanding lay Christian document," the Declaration of Independence, as Maritain adumbrates, yields another deep meaning for the Catholic historian. The legacy of ancient and medieval thought about the sacraments, particularly about the Eucharist, is transparent in the Founding Fathers' "right to life." None of the three thinkers we are discussing here, as far as we know, drew out the full, historic, sacramental meaning of this classic phrase. It seems that it was never their purpose to do so. Still, there is no doubt in the mind of the present writer that each of them would have agreed with the meaning of the Declaration's phrase in terms of what is ultimately the only history worthy of the name, salvation history.

The phrase "right to life" in the Declaration has clearly taken on new meaning to millions of Americans since the legalization of abortion in the United States, and this is a vivid example of how words and people interact according to changing times. One doubts, in fact, that Maritain and Murray in the 1950s would even have been able to anticipate that the Supreme Court of the United States would soon remove protection from the unborn. For all their wisdom and insight into what St. Paul called the "mystery of iniquity," it seems that even these brilliant men would not have been ready for the evil that was in store for the Christian West.[61]

But to return to the point that we should now make explicit, that the Catholic historian should be a kind of counter-deconstructionist in seeing beyond a text such as the Declaration of Independence, the fact that by the "right to life" the Founding Fathers were referring to supernatural as well as natural life. This may not have been Thomas Jefferson's meaning and that of the small number of Americans whose thought, in Maritain's words, was "tinged" by Enlightenment naturalism. But it was the meaning of the overwhelming majority of people who read and approved the Declaration of Independence as a "new gospel of liberation and hope." For they, like their forefathers, were still "one in their desire to create a Christian commonwealth."[62] The Americans, the Catholic Alexis de Tocqueville was later to write, "combine the notions of Christianity and liberty so intimately in their minds that it is impossible to make them conceive of one without the other."[63]

Maritain, Murray, and Dawson all believed that America and Europe must recover that "higher spiritual order" so that they might survive the secularization of modern culture, with its "nihilistic personalities." Murray described them as the new barbarians in Brooks Brothers suits. Spiritual order was the "ultimate foundation of human society," as Edmund Burke and others had recognized, "and no society which denies it or loses sight of it, can endure."[64]

The Spiritual Order of the American Founding

The recovery of spiritual order, all would have agreed, required what Fr. Delp had characterized in his prison journal as a "minimum of transcendence."[65] Dawson put it this way: There could be no real spiritual order, no religion worthy of the name, without a "sense of the Transcendent" and an appetite for the Transcendent that can only be satisfied by immediate contact—by a vision of the supreme Reality. A religion that "remains on the rational level and denies the possibility of any real relation with a higher order of spirituality, fails in its most essential function, and ultimately, like deism, ceases to be a religion at all," Dawson argued in repudiating the Pelagianism of Jefferson and Paine.[66]

But this was not the case with the Founding Fathers. The Catholic historian in America, fully aware of the historical reasons for Protestant minimalism and widespread anti-sacramentalism, especially in Puritan New England, must see that the "right to life" of the Declaration is really in the ontological, higher spiritual order, the right to the Absolute Transcendent, the right to Christ, the right to Life Himself in the Eucharist.

Roman Catholics in Maryland and Anglicans in the South and the lower counties of New York naturally understood this according to their varying degrees of participation in the Church. And, of course, there was—as there is today—a whole range of subjective attitudes on the Real as opposed to the merely symbolic presence of Christ in the "Sacrament." But the fact is that thousands of the American colonists in what is now the United States belonged to churches in which the ancient truth of the Eucharist was in some way, however imperfectly, observed. The Eucharist, Christ's promise, "made at a definite time in history, in a certain place in the world, and testified by the writers of the synoptic gospels"—was recognized by a majority of Christians in all the churches. Christ's "supreme gift," true to His promise in time, continued to be offered to men and women, even though their understandings of the Sacrament were darkened by centuries of theological controversy.[67]

The churches, the visible communities of men and women made one by faith and Baptism and united with one another by the celebration of the Lord's Supper, preserved—in the only way they knew—the historic fact of the Incarnation, of "God among us." In the Protestant congregations, as the convert Isaac Hecker put it in the next century, men cried out for love, for that absolute and transcendent Love that is to be found in this world only in the Blessed Sacrament.[68] The anthropology of eighteenth-century Americans was still overwhelmingly Christian. Man was created in the image and likeness of God, was made for God, and his rights came from spirit rather than "nature" in the Jeffersonian and modern, positivist sense.

The Jesuit Murray, like Maritain and Dawson, saw this clearly and believed with them—and the Founding Fathers—that in the end only transcendent truths can protect us against relativism. He wrote in his highly influential book *We Hold These Truths* (1960) that our natural rights are "as inalienable as they are inherent. Their proximate source is in nature, and in history insofar as history bears witness to the nature of man, their ultimate source, as the Declaration of Independence states, is in God, the Creator of nature and the Master of history."[69] Fulton J. Sheen, another Catholic leader of thought at the time, who also possessed that "long-range vision of Augustine" that the historian must have, termed the great American charter really a "Declaration of Dependence," asserting a "double dependence: dependence on God, and dependence on law as derived from God."[70]

The same could be said of the Bill of Rights, Murray pointed out. It was "not a piece of eighteenth-century rationalist theory; it was far more the product of Christian history." And the anthropology of the great founding charters, like the history, was Christian. "The 'man' whose rights are guaranteed in the face of law and government is, whether he knows it or not, the Christian man who has learned to know his own personal dignity in the school of Christian faith."[71] This was the dignity of man created in the image and likeness of God that Murray, Dawson, Maritain—and the Founding Fathers—celebrated. This was and is the precious Judeo-Christian heritage that the American nation was founded to defend against the "nihilistic personalities" and "mass men" of modernity who put to death Alfred Delp, Maximilian Kolbe, Titus Brandsma, and millions of Jews, Christians, and others. This the Catholic historian must understand.

The American Founding and the Right to Perfect Life in Christ

Like the scribe in Jesus' parable, the Catholic historian must strive to be "learned in the reign of God" and ready "to bring from his storehouse both the new and the old" (Matthew 13:52). And the old, the ancient truth of the "school of Christian faith," is the "right to life"—the right to perfect, infinite Life in the Eucharist, which dignifies the human person beyond anything that man himself could even dream, "the transformation of man into God."[72]

The historian, "profoundly historical and profoundly Catholic," must realize "that what once was, must in some sense now be. Nothing is really lost, history is contemporary with the present."[73] The Declaration of Independence and the other American charters of freedom are still ultimately Christian and Catholic. The "rights" they guarantee, their very sources, lie not in immanence of nature, but in the transcendent God. The Man-God came to pitch his tent among men and to abolish forever the Gnostic conflict of time and eternity, to hallow the Eternal Father's name, and to beg men to do His will "on earth as in Heaven." The Catholic historian must help his fellow men come to understand that it is the Church Christ founded, the dispenser of the sacraments, that stands behind the rights to "life, liberty, and the pursuit of happiness"—and all the myriad rights that, according to the Declaration, belong to man and woman. The Catholic as historian must testify to the divine fact that, in one supreme, ineffable thing, the Eucharist, the world IS God, but only through His own divine priesthood and not through anything divine that creation possesses of itself.[74]

That is why Dawson urged in his *Crisis of Western Education* that the Catholic college should "not confine itself to the Christian culture of Europe, but should devote special attention to the problem of the Enlightenment and the way in which the doctrines of Natural Law and the theory of the limited state had the original roots in the Christian tradition." The Catholic historian, more than anyone else, has the great responsibility of keeping "alive the concept of Christian culture in a secular world."[75] And what is particularly relevant in reminding his contemporaries of the Christian concept of the Declaration of Independence is that Christianity does not so much create institutions directly in history. In the words of Jean Cardinal Danielou, it is a much more subtle process. Christianity works "alongside those which exist, purifying them of their excesses and bringing them into conformity with the demands of the spirit."[76]

Perhaps Dietrich von Hildebrand has said it best when he wrote that the Catholic teacher and student must be "metaphysically courageous" and fully "conscious of the advantage for adequate knowledge which he enjoys through revelation, and of the responsibility of giving to mankind in the way of knowledge what by reason of this advantage he is capable of giving to it."[77] If we are "metaphysically courageous"—and von Hildebrand is saying no more than the others—we must recognize that the "right to life" of the Declaration is ultimately sacramental and catholic. For the Catholic scholar, the "new man" transformed in Christ, as St. Paul says, "the consecrated intelligence in act"—will "see more deeply, more truly, and more broadly than his non-Catholic colleague. And such insight will not derive primarily from a knowledge of the Christian Fact and its theological corollaries, but from an interior illumination of the intelligence."[78]

The only Catholic signer of the Declaration of Independence, Charles Carroll of Carrollton, who had suffered a lifetime of persecution for the ancient Faith in native Maryland, was fully conscious of the deeper, sacramental meaning of the "right to life." The cousin of America's first bishop, John Carroll, and Daniel Carroll, one of the two Catholic signers of the federal Constitution, Charles Carroll was devoted to the Blessed Sacrament.

The longest surviving American Founding Father (he died in his ninety-fifth year), the Irish-American patriot had been formed in Jesuit schools and was as close to being a daily communicant of Our Lord in the Blessed Sacrament as conditions at that time allowed. Carroll was also a member of a Sodality of the Blessed Virgin Mary, having consecrated himself to the Mother of God while a student in France. He daily meditated on the sacred Scripture and Thomas à Kempis's *The Imitation of Christ*, and was quite fond of St. Francis de Sales's *Introduction to the Devout Life*, which he said "schooled him in the love of God."[79]

The Maryland Catholic and founder of a nation, so firm in his spiritual formation (as the Catholic historian should be), was forearmed against the oversimplifying temptations of the philosopher and prophet. Neither did Charles Carroll of Carrollton try to order in any final way the "irrational multiplicity and idiosyncrasy of the world of history," nor did he "attempt to anticipate the mystery of divine judgment, like the friends of Job—that symbol of humanity agonizing in the toils of history."[80] History for Carroll was not a problem to be solved, but a mystery to be lived, precisely the language of Gabriel Marcel, Maritain, Dawson, and others.

Fifty years later to the day he had signed the Declaration of Independence, Charles Carroll, the last surviving signer, rededicated the American Revolution and his part in it as a Catholic dedicated to Christ:

> Grateful to Almighty God for the blessing which, through Jesus Christ our Lord, He has conferred upon my beloved country, in her emancipation, and upon myself, in permitting me, under circumstances of mercy, to live to the age of 89 years and to survive the fiftieth year of American Independence, and certifying by my present signature my approbation of the Declaration of Independence adopted by Congress on the fourth day of July, in the year of our Lord, one thousand seven hundred and seventy-six. I do hereby recommend to the present and future generations the principles of that important document as the best earthly inheritance their ancestors could bequeath to them, and pray that the civil and religious liberties they have secured to my country may be perpetuated to the remotest prosperity and extended to the whole family of man.[81]

Thomas Jefferson and John Adams, also signers of the Declaration, were dead when Carroll wrote these stirring words of Christian recommitment to the great charter.

It was most fitting, most historically appropriate, that Charles Carroll of Carrollton, the Eucharistic signer and consecrated intelligence, the metaphysically courageous, the man of Faith, should be the last witness to the Judeo-Christian legacy of the American founding—and that Charles Carroll should remain as the last signer, the guardian of the fullness of revelation, "written in flesh and blood," in his acceptance of the God-Man's command: "Do this in remembrance of Me" (1 Cor. 11:24) In Francois Mauriac's striking phrase, the American founder Charles Carroll of Carrollton, loyal to the ancient Faith of the Apostles, helped Our Lord keep His promise in the Eucharist, "a promise made at a definite time in history, in a certain place in the world."[82]

Charles Carroll of Carrollton died on November 4, 1832, in his ninety-sixth year. Fr. Constantine Pise, an Italian-American Jesuit from Annapolis with a doctorate in divinity and the title "Knight of the Holy Roman Empire" awarded by Pope Gregory XVI, quoted his great friend as most satisfied in his life not with his political achievements and great wealth, but "that I have practiced the duties of my religion."[83] An attending physician described the scene as Charles Carroll lay dying and received the Viaticum in the midst of his grieving family and servants kneeling in a semicircle around his bed:

> The whole assemblage made up a picture never to be forgotten. The ceremony proceeded. The old gentleman had been for a long time suffering from weak eyes, and could not endure the proximity of lights immediately before him. His eyes were therefore kept closed, but he was so familiar with the forms of this solemn ceremony that he responded and acted as if he saw everything passing around. At the moment of offering the Host he leaned forward without opening his eyes, yet responsive to the word of the administration of the holy offering. It was done with so much intelligence and grace, that no one could doubt for a moment how fully his soul was alive to the act.[84] The American Founding Father's real life, his history, like the history of each one of us, or a country, or the world itself, attained its final intelligibility in his last Communion.

The doctor tried to make his patient take some food. "Thank you, Doctor, not just now," Charles Carroll answered from the depths of the experience of saints and his own Catholic mysticism; "this ceremony is so deeply interesting to the Christian that it supplies all the wants of nature. I feel no desire for food."[85]

As one who had been formed by the Jesuits in the sacred mysteries of the Catholic Faith, schooled in the Catechism of the Council of Trent, and as an ideal "knight" and "prince of the people" in St. Francis of Assisi's famous phrase, Charles Carroll of Carrollton could not and did not minimize the teaching of the Lord about the Holy Eucharist. "He that eateth My flesh and drinketh My blood hath everlasting Life" (John 6:54). The meaning of the words used by our Redeemer, Life Himself, could not be clearer. "The use of tense is important. Christ does not say that such a one shall sometime receive everlasting life. He says that he has it already. His Heaven has already begun, in the sense that the life of the Blessed in Heaven is not a complete change, but rather a consummation of this life of Eucharistic union."[86]

This is what the "right to life" meant to Charles Carroll of Carrollton, apostle of the Eucharist. His presence among the signers of the Declaration of Independence, the presence of a "metaphysically courageous," fully Christian, theologically articulate member of the faithful, placing all of his great temporal possessions and even his worldly life at risk, this is the real meaning of the American Revolution's defense of freedom."[87]

Another signer of the Declaration of Independence who understood its "rights" in the ultimate sense of its Christian context was the Pennsylvanian physician Dr. Benjamin Rush. Rush was not a Catholic. Indeed, like John Adams of Massachusetts and other signers of the Declaration, Rush was a strong anti-papist. But while it is true that Rush in his invincible ignorance shared the anti-sacramentalism of so many Protestant Americans at the time and rejected out of hand the ancient truth of the Eucharist, he believed nonetheless in the New Testament teaching that Jesus Christ is the "Life of the world," "the Prince of Life," and "Life itself." The "right to life," like the other "rights" asserted in the Declaration, must be understood as having its full meaning in the Christian perspective.

"If moral precepts alone could have reformed mankind," Rush parted company with Jefferson and the deists:

> the mission of the Son of God into our world would have been unnec-
> essary. He came to promulgate a system of doctrines, as well as a system
> of morals. The perfect morality of the Gospel rests upon a doctrine
> which, though often controverted, has never been refuted. I mean the
> vicarious life and death of the Son of God. This sublime and ineffable
> doctrine delivers us from the absurd hypotheses of modern philosophers,
> concerning the foundation of moral obligation, and fixes it upon the
> eternal and self-moving principle of LOVE. It concentrates a whole sys-
> tem of ethics in a single set text of Scripture. "A new commandment I
> give unto you, that ye love one another, even as I have loved you."

No doubt, Rush went on, natural reason yielded great truths. But it was "reserved to Christianity alone to produce universal, moral, political, and physical happiness."[88] "The rights" of the Declaration, clearly, must be perfected in true life and true love in Jesus Christ.[89]

The Enlightenment rationalism and naturalism of Jefferson and Thomas Paine had no part in Rush's conception of the nation he was building. The "right to life" in all its Christian fullness was his founding vision.

Even though Rush never attained belief in the Real Presence of the Eucharistic Lord in the preeminent "Sacrament of Unity," he rejected the God-decapitating minimalism of Jefferson and the others, which, as we have seen, was ultimately Gnostic. "The Son of Man is not come to destroy men's lives but to save them," Rush argued against any taking away of man's transcendent gift of life. Love and Life Himself commanded men to imitate God in doing everything possible "to preserve, restore, or prolong life."[90]

The new nation that Rush had founded, he concluded from the Revolution, was nothing less than a "prelude" to the "glorious manifestation" of the "Spirit of the Gospel," which was working through history to influence the "hearts of men." The "light of the Gospel" was rising "gradually on the world," and America was the place appointed by Divine Providence for that true Christendom that the Old World had failed to create. The prophecies of the Bible were slowly being realized in the American Revolution. The "triumph of the Gospel" could be seen everywhere that its influence reached; and it would not be long before the "kingdom of this world" would be transformed into the "kingdom of the Prince of Righteousness and peace."[91]

This was how Rush interpreted the "right to life" in the Declaration of Independence: the God-given privilege for man to realize his status as created in the image and likeness of God, to attain Christ, "The Way, the Truth, and the Life" (John 14:6). Christ was the "Life of the world," was Life Himself. Rush in his doctrine of Universalism rejected the existence of hell and believed that "the idea of only one Soul being lost either by a defect of mercy to redeem, or of power to save after redemption, is pregnant with despair, and contrary to the universal command and obligation to believe the Gospel." "All life is the effect of one infinite, transcendent, cause, Jesus Christ," Dr. Rush asserted in his *Three Lectures upon Animal Life* (1799). "Self-existence belongs only to God." "Truth is a unit. Man is passive in animal life, volition, and salvation by Jesus Christ."[92]

So, Dr. Benjamin Rush, one of the most profound Christian thinkers of the American Revolution, never came to believe in the ancient truth that the Eucharistic presence of Christ transcends time and space. He was never sacramentally one with the "natural and historic presence of Christ on earth."[93] He never knew, and this was true of the great majority of his countrymen, the fullness of sacramental Life in Jesus Christ. But Rush's deep Christian faith did enable him to pierce through, in some way, to the One transcendent Absolute and participate in true history. His Christian faith conquered the Gnostic myth of "contracted existence," if incompletely, and the United States for this reason truly became for him—and many others—a "Christian" republic.

Alexander Hamilton was not a signer of the Declaration of Independence, but he was a Founding Father whose influence upon the new Republic of the United States was immense by any standard. Hamilton's life and thought ranged from the political naturalism or Gnostic statism of his youth and middle years, when Caesar was for him the "greatest hero," and nation-building was his secular religion, to the sacrifice of his life in 1804 upon the dueling field of Weehawken as a serious Christian and a firm believer in the holy sacraments of the Episcopalian Church.

We have told the dramatic story of Alexander Hamilton's pilgrimage, "From Caesar to Christ" elsewhere.[94] Here we can do no more than to suggest how Hamilton's life—as in Leo Bloy's words a "Pilgrim of the Absolute"—may be seen as a kind of allegory for every American's, indeed, every man's liberations from Gnostic contracted existence and the achievement in time and space of the transcending fullness of sacramental reality in Christ.

For this is the real, historical, that is, evangelical mission of the Catholic Church in Protestant and post-Protestant America, as Jacques Maritain, John Courtney Murray, and Christopher Dawson could only glimpse that mission in their day.[95] This is the meaning of history, the Pasch, the breaking through to transcendent in Christ among us. This is the Catholic mission of helping to restore the sacraments, especially the Eucharist, to our fellow-Americans and to the world.

Raised a Presbyterian, Hamilton had his first contact with the Anglican Church as a student at King's College, now Columbia University. But there is little evidence that Hamilton was serious about Christianity until near the end of his life, and only then after much suffering of himself and his family. In fact, in his middle years as a rank opportunist and political strategist without scruple, Hamilton had a cynical and exploitative attitude toward religion.

Hamilton prided himself on Machiavellian realism, or at best a kind of philosophy of the state—in the French manner of Jean Bodin and the *Politiques*—that held that the only hope for man in this world lay in preventing factionalism by trying to force man into static political and financial classes and structures that could then be absorbed by the totally organized state into a "transcendent" unanimity. The Scottish philosopher David Hume, in the same Gnostic tradition, summed up Hamilton's attitude toward man in the middle years by writing that "reason is and ought only to be the slave of the passions and can never pretend to any other office than to serve and obey them."[96] The perfectly organized totalitarian state—immanence not transcendence, Caesar not Christ—was the only "redemption" for man in the world. Men are "rather reasoning than reasonable animals," and motivated by the pleasure principle, Hamilton used to say.

> "Take mankind in general," Hamilton is reported to have told his fellow delegates to the Constitutional Convention, "they are vicious, their passions may be operated upon. . . . Take mankind as they are, and what are they governed by? Their passions. There may be in every government a few choice spirits, who may act from more worthy motives. One great error is that we suppose mankind more honest than they are. Our prevailing passions are ambition and interest; and it will ever be the duty of a wise government to avail itself of the passions, in order to make them subservient to the public good, for these ever induce to us to action."[97] Clearly, in these years for Alexander Hamilton there was no "affirmation of Divine Transcendence and of the Incarnation" which, in the words of Jacques Maritain, alone can save the authentic "values of immanence."[98]

Hamilton's false "anthropocentric" conception of political emancipation, again in the words of Maritain, is in essence the "divinization of the individual" and must lead to "revolutionary totalitarianism, communist or racist" and "general slavery."[99] What turned Hamilton back from this degraded Gnostic philosophy of man and the state of his early manhood was his deep conversionary experience years later, when his son, Philip, was killed in a duel defending the father's honor, and Hamilton's lovely daughter, Angelica, grief-stricken, broke down and was considered insane for the rest of her life.

"Never did I see a man so completely overwhelmed with grief as Hamilton," a close friend remembered after nineteen-year-old Philip's death. "The scene I was present at when Mrs. Hamilton came to see her son on his deathbed (he died about a mile out of the city) and when she met her husband and son in one room beggars all description." Hamilton's wife, Eliza, was a woman of such deep Christian piety that she was known in New York circles as the "little saint." A devout Episcopalian, she had great faith and courage that seem to have withstood every trial, including her husband's womanizing. Eliza held the family together. As for her husband, completely shattered, he began after Philip's death in 1801 to read and meditate on sacred Scripture, and even often led the family in prayer.

Hamilton spent hours studying William Paley's *Evidence of Christianity* (1794), the most popular work of Christian apologetics at the time. No longer affecting the dashing military officer, he was seen by relatives and friends to take much more seriously the role of loving husband and father in the company of his family. It was as though the words of a poem he had addressed to himself as a boy in 1772 were being fulfilled, words he had written after surviving a terrible hurricane in the Danish West Indies. "What is become of thy arrogance and self-sufficiency? . . . learn to know thy best support. Despise thyself and adore thy God."[100]

As much as Hamilton tried to retire from politics, it was impossible for him to do so. His old adversary and Machiavellist par excellence, Colonel Aaron Burr, with whom he had once so much in common, was believed by Hamilton to pose the greatest threat yet to the new nation. Burr must be stopped at all costs. He was a "dangerous man, and one who ought not to be trusted with the reins of government"—and Hamilton said it publicly. It was this denunciation, reported in the *Albany Register* and other newspapers in the winter and spring of 1804, that led to the fatal duel, or "interview," on the banks of the Hudson that summer.

Hamilton kept the duel a secret from Eliza. In notes that he left for her and the children should he be killed, he explained that he had done everything he could, with honor, to avoid the duel with Colonel Burr. Hamilton threw himself upon "redeeming grace and divine mercy," and he hoped for a "happy immortality." "The consolation of Religion, my beloved, can alone support you, and these you have a right to enjoy. Fly to the bosom of your God and be comforted. With my last idea I shall cherish the sweet hope of meeting you in a better world. *Adieu* best of wives—best of women. Embrace all my darling children for me."[101]

In his final letter to Eliza the night before the duel, Hamilton told his wife that because of his Christian faith he was prepared "to expose my own life to any extent rather than subject myself to the guilt of taking the life of another." "Heaven can preserve me, and I humbly hope it will; but in the contrary event I charge you to remember that you are a Christian. God's will be done! The will of a merciful God must be good!" Then in a tender gesture of love for his dead son, Philip, and all of his children, Hamilton lay down next to twelve-year-old John and recited with him the Lord's Prayer.

On the same field at Weehawken where Philip Hamilton had fallen several years earlier, Colonel Aaron Burr, vice president of the United States, and General Alexander Hamilton met the morning of Wednesday, July 6, 1804. As Hamilton said he would, in his letter to Eliza and in a statement found in his desk after his death, he threw away his fire rather than risk hitting Burr. "My religious and moral principles are strongly opposed to the practice of dueling, and it would ever give me pain to be obliged to shed the blood of a fellow creature in a private combat forbidden by laws."[102]

Colonel Burr did not reserve or throw away his fire, as Hamilton had hoped he would. The ball struck Hamilton on his right side, and it soon proved fatal. As Alexander Hamilton lay dying in the bosom of his loving family, having laid down his life for a fellow man, one thing alone remained. He sent for the Episcopalian bishop of New York, Benjamin More, who was also president of Columbia College and rector of Trinity Church, where the Hamilton family worshipped. The dying man begged to receive Holy Communion, to receive the Eucharistic Host, to receive Christ "whole and entire" for the last time on earth, to complete his transformation in Christ.

"Do you sincerely repent of your sins past? Have you a lively faith in God's mercy through Christ, with a thankful remembrance of the death of Christ? And are you disposed to live in love and charity with all men?" "Yes, yes, yes. I have no ill-will against Colonel Burr. I met him with a fixed resolution to do him no harm. I forgive all that happened."[103]

The True Protagonists of History, the Saints

What matters in the early history of the United States, the real story, may be seen not in the constitutional crises over how to interpret the federal Constitution or whether there was a provision for a national bank, but in the spiritual order of Christianity upon which the new nation was founded—and which has alarmingly eroded away in our day. Real history, here as elsewhere, is "the deliverance through baptism of souls in bondage, and the greater glory of God in the Holy Eucharist: and the protagonists of this history are in truth the saints."[104]

Charles Carroll of Carrollton, as a well-educated Catholic Founding Father, represented the perfection of that sacramental Christianity. Dr. Benjamin Rush, although historically deprived of the wholeness of Christian belief, nevertheless spent his life seeking what had been lost over the Protestant centuries, the Real Presence of Christ in the divine liturgy of the ancient Catholic Church. Alexander Hamilton, in character with his all-or-nothing determination to build a great nation, not only sacrificed his life rather than kill another man. In his martyrdom—and there is no other word for it—he consecrated the new Republic of the United States to Christ, sealing it in his own blood and with his final Holy Communion.

Hamilton's martyrdom was the ultimate victory over Jeffersonian naturalism and the Gnosticism of the Enlightenment. "Thy Kingdom come, Thy will be done, on earth as it is in Heaven," he had prayed with his little son before the duel. It was the greatest gift, of his will and himself, that could give to his country—the "right to life," perfect life, in Jesus Christ.

It has been said that every person has a choice to make, whatever the century in which he, or she, lives. He or she can choose to be to be a "god" by his or her own devices; or he or she can accept the ineffable privilege offered to each of us by Our Lord to participate as a transformed creature in His Life, the Life of God, the Life of the Second Person of the Blessed Trinity. Alexander Hamilton, in the end, chose the latter and died with the hope that his fellow countrymen would also choose "true life" in Christ. "I have set before you life and death, the blessing and the curse. Choose life, then that you and your descendants may live" (Deuteronomy 30:19).

The Catholic historian must know, write, and teach that the "true protagonists" of the only history that matters are the saints, who make the choice for life everlasting. They alone ascend to Being. "In nothing less than this does the destiny of humanity consist, according to the teaching of the Catholic Church." Christopher Dawson wrote in 1920:

> Without losing his own nature, man is brought into an inconceivably close relation with God, so that he lives by the Divine Life, sees God with God's knowledge, loves God with God's love, and knows and loves everything else in and through God. . . . In the Sacraments, in the life of faith, in every act of spiritual will and aspiration of spiritual desire, the work of divine restoration goes ceaselessly forward. In that work is the whole hope of humanity.[105]

It is gold that the Catholic historian must discover in the past; it is this gold that he must give to those who come after him—not lead or copper.[106]

It is the whole treasure of reality, past, present, and future that he must take for his province—not the "fools' gold" of the Gnostics, those counterfeiters of man who are with us in every age. And in the end, defeated only in the sense that good men must be, he will throw himself exhausted into the arms of Holy Mother Church and command the past "to the infinite mercy of the heart of Jesus" and the future to "His Providence coming to us through the hands of the Mediatrix of all graces." As for the present, he must live it "with joyous abandon as little children playing or working under the eyes of their mother" (Jacques Maritain).

"In a world of shifting values," Monsignor Ronald Knox has written, "there is one fixed point on which our hearts can rest, one fixed star by which our intellects can be guided, it is the personal presence of Our Lord on earth, yesterday, today, and as long as earth endures."[107] Christ in time, on earth among men, in His sacraments—this is the meaning of history. ♦

Faith's Past, Hope's Future, Charity's Present: The Enduring Role of the Catholic Historian

Michael B. Ewbank

ETIENNE Gilson once remarked that within the order of written history every age is inevitably "medieval" in that it is between what has preceded and what is yet to come. Each is equally "modern" within the lived experience of events since human consciousness manifests informing characteristics that dominate within a defined yet flexible comprehension of time according to "modus dierum."[1] More than a mere play of words, this observation applies to all ages of human history, including our own, since the only time that would be an exception would pertain not to history, but to eschatology.

Gilson's observations highlight a chiaroscuro that is one with human temporality and that involves a dramatic interplay of free agents with dynamic yet consistent natures that constitute the created universe. Within this complex matrix there are diverse points of departure that justify different understandings of history.[2] Jacques Le Goff implicitly confirms this when he affirms that "the study of philosophies of history is not only part of any reflection on history, but necessary for any study of historiography. This is true . . . to the extent that the ambiguity resulting from the double meaning of history as the unfolding of the time of men and societies and as the science of this unfolding remains fundamental."[3]

Such is buttressed by John Lukac's judgment that "the greatest Western historians have always understood that a sane understanding of human nature literally preempts the need for a philosophy of history. Therefore, they knew, too, that save for certain specialized branches of research, there is, strictly speaking, no such thing as a historical *method,* even though history has become a principal, perhaps the principal, Western *form* of thought."[4] In other words, there is no reductionist, uniform historical method, and thus "in order to agree, two historians must share in common the same mental categories, the same cultural basis, the same affinities," because "the universality or the generality, the validity, of concepts used by historians are not so much relative as dependent . . . on the validity of the philosophy, implicit or (preferably) explicit, which made it possible for him to elaborate them."[5]

Regardless of the manner of inquiry and style of articulation that a historian uses, his work is fundamentally a combination of fact and interpretation dealing principally with what is contingent, unique, and individual. Understood in the light of principles articulated by a thinker such as Aquinas, whose insights into the metaphysical constitution of reality integrated and deepened those of his predecessors, history englobes, as Hegel remarked, both a subject comprising the study of events and eventualities in the social world in its actual becoming. To accomplish his task the historian must be the master of a multiplicity of intellectual *habitus,* for though aiming at full demonstrative certitude concerning the full range of things that can fall under his consideration, he can only approximate this attainment concerning history as a totality. Aquinas's principles confirm the fact that if one considers the possible elucidation and explanation of the totality of temporal duration, then "history" can never be a science, yet it remains that the historian may enter into a course of working through the manifold of singulars and of the order of things: a process made possible, conditioned and regulated by the knowledge which is the divine providence; yet the latter as term can never be achieved in process. This is what men call a calculus.[6]

This is not to deny that the historian attains certitude appropriate to his discipline and the implementation of his autonomous methods. Such ultimately rests upon some actual testimonial vestige of the past. More often than not, by imaginatively and intellectually penetrating the subtle webs of interrelations of facts and probabilities, which include testimonies of credible witnesses concerning overt actions and covert motives of the human heart, the historian discerns dominant or recessive tendencies in the contrapuntal drama of events that are effects and reciprocal contributing conditions for human choices.

Seeking to sound the germinating potentialities of historical actuality in relation to the future in that today is tomorrow's yesterday, the historian must attend to what Jacques Le Goff calls the *"histoire de mentalites."* Such does not imply a view of history in terms of Enlightenment presumptions of inevitable linear progress, especially since "inertia is a crucially important historical force, and it belongs less to matter than to human minds, which often evolve more slowly. While they use the machines they have invented, men keep the mentality of earlier days."[7] Although Le Goff equivocates somewhat in contrasting matter and mind, he does approximate an insight popularized by Herbert Marshall McLuhan concerning men's propensity to match concepts dominant in an earlier era to experience that is actual in "rearview mirror" fashion.[8]

While never aiming at a spurious "futurology," the historian may hope to discern probable configurations of emerging order by means of a reasoned hermeneutics of actuality. As such, this is subordinated to the principal finality of every historian as a living being of flesh and blood, namely to assist himself and others to better judge things human and divine. Such does not transform the discipline into moral didacticism, nor does it preclude engagement in the pursuit of historical knowledge as an end in itself. But the nature of the activity finds its ultimate finality only in contributing to greater attainment of practical wisdom and comprehension of the human's true destiny.

Wisdom always brings order to what is known, is to be done, or is to be made. Since deliberating well about what leads to the good life ranges from individual, through familial, to political dimensions of prudence, the possessor of practical wisdom must necessarily possess good memory, since prudence is grounded in experience. But the coherence of experience is attained via memory as "presencing" things past for the sake of forging a future in the crucible of present actuality. Both individual and corporate prudence inevitably involve prevision or foresight; and this requires docility to, counsel from, and caution in terms of what memory makes actually present, whether such memory be one's own or others'.[9] Such is a proper effect of the historian's achievement, but it arises from disciplined meditative reminiscence achieved only by a being that can reason and search for order within temporal existence.[10]

These considerations are critical for any historian, but especially a Christ-faithful who is bequeathed the central explication of the mystery of history: "Sacred history presents us with *facts*. As such they are not subject to our reasoning, and human reason can only, in the last analysis, proclaim their 'contingency,' or else fall into illusion by substituting an 'explanation' of its own making. Yet if the mind persists in looking for some intelligibility in history, it can only be found *beyond* history, in the mystery of God, of that divine freedom which, however contingent its works seem to us, and must seem, is nonetheless 'the wisdom of God.' "[11]

Although there is some consensus regarding the state of agony of that Hydra which is "modernity," there are divergent views concerning its nature. Leo Strauss judged the modern project to contain at its core the assumption that "philosophy or science was no longer to be understood as essentially contemplative and proud, but as active and charitable [and] cultivated for the sake of human power."[12] Eric Voegelin contended that the seeds of modernity were germinating as early as the twelfth century, when advocates of an inner-worldliness prefigured eventual closure to transcendence for human consciousness.[13] Yet, even Voegelin's emphasis upon the "divine ground of being" as the common referent for all symbolizations of transcendence by human consciousness has been alleged to mirror that dominant contemporary "evolution from an original myth to a new psychology, that is, to a gradual interiorization of what was once believed to be the real."[14]

Vivid depictions of modernity's temporal trajectory are sometimes found in narrations that offer inductive insight into the nature of the age. "The twentieth century, is now over. It was a short century. It lasted seventy-five years—from 1914 to 1989. . . . The nineteenth century lasted ninety-nine years, from 1815 to 1914. . . . The eighteenth century lasted one hundred and twenty-six years, from the beginning of the world wars between England and France (of which the American War of Independence was a part) until their end at Waterloo. The seventeenth century lasted one hundred and one years, from the destruction of the Spanish Armada in 1588 (of which the establishment of a united France was an important consequence) to 1689, the year after the so-called Glorious

Revolution in England, when the main threat to England became France and no longer Spain."[15] And again, "Many of the main features of the Modern Age, which began around 1500, have come to, or near to, their end: the expansion of Europe; the conquests of the white race; the colonial empires; the Atlantic at the center of history; the predominance of sea power; liberalism; humanism; bourgeois culture; the predominance of urban and urbane civilization; permanence of residence; the respect for privacy; the Newtonian concept of the universe and of physical reality; the ideal of scientific objectivity; the Age of the Book."[16]

This seismic reading of human history justifies a reasonable inference that "not until centuries from now, when a new feudalism will have formed again, with the rise of new barbarian chieftains, when a future Otto the Great may be an uncultured but extremely intelligent combination of Rock Star and Gang Leader" may there arise constitutional hereditary monarchy to guarantee lawfulness and liberalism.[17] Nonetheless, "there is reason to hope that the New Dark Ages may not last hundreds of years; and there is reason to believe that their darkness will not be uniform."[18]

In contrast to the plurality of historical analysis of modernity's nature, one finds greater consensus regarding symptoms that indicate its tenuous stability. "The ideal of leisure differs on every score from today's and tomorrow's free time."[19] "Mechanical thinking never shrinks from violating what is dead. If the universe were really of that lifeless submissiveness which mechanical thinking presupposes, then to try to perfect technology would be quite a safe undertaking. . . . No matter where in nature technology applies its mechanisms and its organization, it simultaneously organizes the resistance against its own compulsion, and the force of this resistance hits man with hammer like precision, with the balancing exactness of a pendulum in those clockworks that measure lifeless time."[20] The human history "of time and number since Plato and Aristotle has never centered purely on moments and quantities, it has always been a matter of duration and quality too. . . . What is new about the modern age is not the uniqueness of events or the changeability of structures. . . . In the modern age, it is only the acceleration of historical change, far beyond human comprehension, which has increased."[21] Man has "become mobile, more mobile than he ever was. This mobility is a sign of progressive mass formation, which means the same as technical progress. It is one of technology's characteristics that it releases man from all non-rational bonds, only to subjugate him more closely to the framework of rational relations."[22]

Arguably, however, instruments for development of a new order are already borne within in the same dynamic matrix. "Technocracy has been whipped by having succeeded so brilliantly. Depersonalized functions no longer exercised by persons take care of depersonalization by eliminating it. The analytic mind—at its best coldly brilliant, at its worst, fanatical—reiterates a violated nature and a shattered humanity. If analysis forms the moment of pure work within the spirit, then synthesis is its moment of reflection in which man looks back on work done, on information marshaled before the bar of mankind presided over by a judge at leisure. "Speculation regarding the potential for a new technological culture bonded symbiotically with residual local ontological cultures depends upon the validity of a distinction between two species of technology, one essentially mechanical, which principally achieves its ends by executing violence to nature's processes, and the other electronic, principally subsuming the mechanical and accomplishing objectives by bonding *techne* with light's potential illuminating scrutiny." As a consequence, "electronic media are independent by involving [man]: but mechanical technology, while dependent upon man, progressively attempts to escape this dependence. The results, of course, are antithetical. The electronic involves man more and more as it approaches its perfection. The war between these two technologies—the older approaching fullness at the very moment of its immanent obsolescence even while it mingles with the newer—has produced an intolerable tension in the psyche of western industrialized man."[23]

Can the fullness of "Catholic" history be effectively elucidated and communicated within such an arena of contenders for human intentionality?[24] If the McLuhanesque axiom is correct that the "medium is the message," need the central content or message of this plenary history be altered, as many Catholics, both lay and cleric, seem to have believed? Or, is the challenge rather to adhere to the splendid adage of Vincent de Lerens, *"Non nova sed nove,"* not what is novel, but in a novel manner?[25]

In a certain sense, historical consciousness always antecedes historical event, which only becomes formally historical by entering consciousness.

In this originative sense, history neither exists nor is intelligible apart from a tradition, for "tradition" refers to those transmitted memories through which human consciousness may articulate experience.[26] As such, alterations of traditions and symbolizations inevitably resonate in the order of historical continuity, for though decisive and energetic efforts may be made to preserve what must exist for the conservation of a society's corporate identity, "a change in externals, in things in and of themselves non-essential, most probably *can* and *will* threaten the true preservation of the essence of tradition, so that one who too quickly cuts away or denigrates the so-called 'outer' traditions does something quite problematical." Yet, blind conservatism that puts disproportionate weight on non-essentials can hinder reformulation of an original heritage that must be handed down.[27] Lived experience constantly evidences the fact that some features flow from the very nature of a thing's being, while others are only incidental.

Obviously, the designation of "Catholic" when qualifying history implies a view of reality illuminated by the Catholic faith. This must impart an intrinsic character to one's understanding of history's events knowable through natural cognition under the sustained guidance of divine revelation. Certainly, the content of revelation or dogma cannot enter as an explicit premise in the historical reasoning of a given historian, for a Catholic historian must remain a genuine historian, fulfilling all requisites demanded by the canons of his discipline and its subsidiary sciences. However, the range of his concern comprises the totality of history, understood not as an abstract concept, but as a body of inclusive and comprehensive judgments about specifics. Such can be the aim of any true historian, but it must be thus due to a distinct motive for the conscientiously Catholic historian: "All history is the history of the path toward salvation, the path towards God or the loss of God," since "history is for the Christian first of all universal history. . . . There is no reality so clear or difficult to emphasize as the universality of history, because being itself is universal and history presupposes being."[28]

Even though different intra-historical orders are radically open to progress, the Catholic historian can never prescind from the fact that the central achievement of creation is situated in our past with the Incarnation and Resurrection of Christ. Such is deeply encoded within the Catholic's sense of history, since prior to Christ the fundamental dogmas, or articles of faith, were not yet complete, but were prefigurations that implicitly contained later articles. In relation to dogmas articulated after Christ, what is explicit stands to what is implicit as conclusions made from premises since "complete explication of the articles of faith is through Christ."[29] In the theatre of time, surprises and intrigues there will be, but they concern that vast panoply of supporting actors and props, since the central dramatic action has been performed and it remains forever the measure of all other human action.

Any Catholic historian assenting to the Creed as containing "all the truths which the faithful must believe," takes upon himself that universality of concern that englobes all places, times, and conditions of mankind.[30] This capacity to profoundly understand *res humanarum* is one with the awareness that the deepest longing of the human heart is to pertain to that unity of charity in which all men are conjoined with one another and God in mutual love; of hope in which all are secure in seeking eternal life; and of faith in which all believe the same truths, even though this does not necessarily imply uniformity of articulation.[31]

These trans-political, foundational goods are tacitly aspired to by the temporal city in all its configurations throughout the ages. "The series of metamorphoses of the City of God. . . . is the history of an obstinate effort to make of the eternal city a temporal one, substituting some conceivable natural bond as the unitive force of this society." The Catholic historian as historian is unique in manifesting the patient divine comprehension that human society needs to "accept from the Church that perfect unity towards which it tends and which it is incapable of giving itself."[32] Of course, this "perfect unity" is only approximated *in via* and will never be fully manifest until all is revealed in Trinitarian Beatitude. Without appropriating this truth, a historian might ply the trade and be a decent, even devout, follower of the Faith, but not a "Catholic historian" in the fullest sense of the phrase.

Ultimately, fidelity to what has been called the "homogeneous evolution of Catholic dogma" grants the Catholic historian an abiding focal reference to judge events to be interpreted as well as the quality of his own elucidations.[33] Such should inoculate the historian from any restrictive a priori

understanding such as would condition one tainted by rationalism, positivism, or Gnostic assumptions, since this historically conditioned retrospec-
tive comprehension of the explication of history's original revelation does
not enter as a formal explicit component in the Catholic historian's ability to
read history in the light of inclusive principles.[34]

Only a fully elaborated Catholic history, ever in process so long as time
endures, would seek to synthesize into unity all true histories, no matter
what aspect of human temporal endeavor they consider, whether biographical, political, economic, ethical, artistic, philosophical, theological, empiri-
ological, or technological, for all that occur within the purview of sacred
history. Depicted with broad strokes for the young and unformed, elaborated with greater and greater detail for those mature and knowledgeable,
the aim of Catholic History is nothing less than a full depiction of history
in terms of the Church's divine origin and mission, including both the
accomplishments and the failures of her human personnel. In short, the
aim in regard to this awesome and mysterious subject is, insofar as humanly
possible, a presentation of the fullness of historical truth.

The goal to "re-presence" to future generations an ordered symbolization of the temporal extending from echoes of the original ordering of
Genesis to anticipative prefigurations of Apocalypse through a diligent
concern with specific personages and events is obviously replete with chal-
lenges. However, such attention to specificity in the elucidation of history
can never be antithetical to contemporary experience on the level of fundamental pervasive lived actuality, for all scientific and technical innovations imitate in some truncated fashion the omnipresent teleological activity of nature.

This inbuilt finality of rationalized technology to do more with less
and less, what some term "etherialization," is the constant latent objective
of the technician. Though metaphysically impossible to actualize in its
fullness, such implicitly mirrors, albeit in limping fashion, the very "fiat"
of Genesis, in which the Trinity makes creation be *ex nihilo*. In practice,
whenever a proper utilization of innovation is actualized, it ultimately
finds its veiled rationale in terms of some compensation for a loss endured
by man in his very nature. In a profound sense, the achievements of technological creations are but clumsy, primitive adumbrations of those gifts

that will be granted to resurrected enfleshed souls enjoying beatitude: impassability, or a preservation from corruption; subtlety, or the ability to penetrate physically the totality of the material order; agility, or capacity to be where one wills; and clarity, or the possession of luminous comprehensive transparency.[35] These vestigial shadows of what should be due to man in his regained and uplifted integrity, however, turn into threatening phantoms if moral and spiritual integrity is not proportionate to the power possessed.

In this sense, Marshall McLuhan's reflections on the nature of technology as being an extension of man's powers and faculties to aid in what theologians have long acknowledged as a legitimate dominion over matter were correct, in spite of the uneven quality of his analysis. In a posthumously printed work, McLuhan sought to inductively establish the validity of four fundamental generalizations regarding the very nature of all such extensions: Every technology extends or amplifies some organ or faculty of the user; each contributes to some "closure" in relation to some previously established equilibrium in sensibility, since intensification of one sense accompanies diminution of another; each leads to a reversal of its characteristics or effects in some manner; and each permits the retrieval of an older medium.[36] By "enhancement," McLuhan refers to the intensification of a situation or configuration of the senses, as well as of turning an element of the surrounding experiential ground into figure. "Obsolescence" refers to the displacement of a former situation or figure. "Retrieval" refers to the process by which what has been rendered obsolete is revivified through a novel ground. And "reversal" involves alteration of figure and ground ratios.[37]

McLuhan's reflections are undoubtedly valuable and insightful. His guiding interpretative model was based on Aristotle's understanding of a fourfold order of causality at work within nature, even though McLuhan's applications were not perhaps always as nuanced and analogical as those of Aristotle and Aquinas.[38] Nonetheless, he did grasp the reciprocal and simultaneous interrelatedness of these basic causal orders: material or componential, formal or structural, efficient or agentival, and final or objectival. Moreover, he conscientiously acknowledged human creation as containing virtualities that are more often than not unforeseen by their makers. Finally, he diligently kept his attention upon man as an intellectual being who must engage himself with things via the senses, and due to this he was remarkably attentive to how any technical extension of man's cognitive powers can affect their equilibrium, whether in terms of direct, originative experience or of what is elaborated and subjected to constructural mediation. We never merely sense, imagine, or intellectually intuit or reason. Rather, all of these simultaneously are in act in our cognition, with distinct proportions or ratios of each order of powers being dominant within intentional awareness at any given instant.

Because of this, McLuhan emphasized the impact of diverse forms of electronic technology as varying in terms of being principally auditory or visual. His intention was to highlight how the aural-oral and visual modulate man as a sensing-perceiving-imagining-remembering being. In regard to what are euphemistically called electronic technologies, whether analog or digital, or whether the application be television, hologram imaging, or computers, we confront first and foremost extensions or "externalizations" of the central nervous system, and correspondingly, of the capacities of what thinkers such as Aquinas called the inner sense powers of integrating perception of varied external sensation, of imagination as presencing the perceived, and of memory as presencing of the perceived as past.[39]

Actualization of these inner powers of cognition inevitably affects understanding, for they together serve as the mediators for intellection and reflection, since intelligible content or concepts are ultimately derived from and developed through the order of phantasm-symbols, which partake of the material order. St. Thomas is convinced of the importance of this act. Although he certainly acknowledged that intellectual cognition does not remain limited to phantasm, he nonetheless follows Aristotle's judgment that it is within phantasm-symbols that men intellectually grasp intelligible truth. This is so not only for natural cognition, St. Thomas adds, but for revealed knowledge as well.[40] Further, once said powers are affected, there is spontaneous actualization or determination of the concrete power that discerns immediacy of pleasure or displeasure, benefit or harm, and that accordingly is the immediate cognitive cause for the actualization of the emotions or passions.

Epistemology, the dependency upon the actualization of imagery in media such as television, hologram imaging, and the computer, confirms the status of man as being a bodily knower due to noetic relation of understanding to the image.[41] To the degree to which dependency on these instrumentalities become "terminal," men indeed can come to ape angelic knowledge, for an angel is where he acts, and his action is his cognition and desire. As we know all too well, without sufficient virtue to maintain temperance in utilizing these devices, any man is able to be terminally restricted to "what" here-and-now-is-being-imagined.[42]

McLuhan was reported as once stating that if we were fully aware of how greatly innovations such as television and computers impact our lives, we would shut them off and ponder whether their perceived benefits are worth their accompanying effects. Others view such instruments as fostering what is intrinsically evil in moral order.[43] "Techno-anxiety" is certainly not without foundation. Heidegger feared that digital texts might subsume his own work. "Maybe history and tradition will fit smoothly into the information retrieval systems which will serve as resource for the inevitable planning needs of a cybernetically organized mankind. The question is whether thinking too will end in the business of information processing."[44] It is reported that even Jacques Maritain expressed similar concerns in his declining years.[45] In contrast, Walter Ong, following in the wake of insights offered by McLuhan, has insisted that the electronic age can sublate previous oppositions between the oral aural and visual culture, between synthesis and analysis, between intuitive simultaneity and linear revolution.[46] If one abstracts from ludicrous and delusional dreams of future implementations espoused in the public forum concerning potentialities latent in new technical innovations, Ong's judgments seem to be not naïve, but temperately optimistic. Many persons are overly preoccupied with the possibility of future generations' being subjected to solipsistic worlds of conjured images and immersions within private universes of sensual hedonism. One may seriously doubt that such will become pervasive for the majority of possessors of technological power. Rather, most utilizations will tend to remain subservient to man's enhanced abilities to discern the inner intricacies of the natures of real things in order to alleviate real necessities.

It is a fact that electronic digitization has permitted technical interfaces of the audio-visual that not only will enable individuals of little talent to produce for the mere sake of production, but also will assist the recovery of past cultural achievements for the sake of what is in jargon called "repurposing."[47] While the quality of any achievement realized through electronic "inspiration" of past attainments will depend upon the capacities of its producers, it is possible that the "electronic text will also serve as the vehicle for displaying all of Western literature in a new light. Since much of this literature is oral in origin and nature, and self-consciously rhetorical, and since electronic text is both oral and rhetorical to a degree, 'repurposing' can reveal to us aspects of our greatest works of art—literary, artistic, and musical—that we have never noticed before."[48]

These instruments will never guarantee that their users will be of one spirit with that which is turned into content. But inevitably, the user himself is noetically one with content in knowing it. Still, even if such developments occur, there will be certain enduring limitations intrinsic to the electronic text that are distinct from those encountered in dealing with printed texts. For while texts, even great ancient and medieval ones, may be transfigured into a new "interface" with the reader and made available through instant access, such does not cinch comprehension on the part of the human receiver. "Hypertext" extractions, which lift terms and phrases out of their full contexts so that occurrences may be compared in a new light, though valuable as a sort of "epochal" deconstruction, can, if relied upon too greatly, lead to disorientation and incomprehension in relation to the profound sense of a text as a totality. This danger, however, is not limited to our own time, since one could easily point to hastily contrived improper comprehensions in previous eras wherein the rich complexity of our patrimony was reduced to monochromatic caricatures in manuals aiming at simplified homogeneous presentations of history.

The electronic web that extends human consciousness via the perceptual order has, indeed, subsumed into its orb the awareness of the need for dominion over all of mechanical technology, so that a hoped-for symbiosis with nature can be maintained. It has altered the understanding of privacy, for better or worse, and in turn shaken the rationalistically defined procedures and structures that condition modern democratic republics. Adjustments have occurred and continue to occur in regard to work, free time, and the understanding of the nature of leisure. And important shifts have occurred in the manner in which we understand subjectivity, consciousness, and the mythic.[49]

However, we are witnessing only the germination of these tendencies.[50] Analog technology is being subsumed by digital technology.[51] While analog technologies, such as have dominated television, film, and telephone, have in common the need to be application specific, they demand an amazing array of ingenious devices that are not truly compatible.[52] These tend of their nature to reinforce centralization and monopoly, since "analog signals mostly tie the receiver to the transmitter in a lock step rendition of the signal," being the "appropriate medium for a world of few transmitters and many receivers."[53] Such favors the centralizing ideological mentality so akin to autocratic minds and tyrannical wills guided by ideological essentialism that seeks to impose by fiat of a juridical power uniformness of feeling, thought, and action.

However, the unfolding future promises a prevalence of digital technology that will accelerate the conditions for a flourishing of diversification, as well as of autonomous and heterogeneous centers of power set over against the centralized monopolies of power, whether these concern the material or the spiritual orders. Such will encourage, as George Gilder noted, a multitude of analogical incentives and pluralization within what may become an ever thinner homogeneous, univocal cultural overlay. In this, historical reality will confirm the prophetic vision articulated in the Decree on Ecumenism of the Second Vatican Council: "All in the church must preserve unity in essentials. But let all, according to the gifts they have received, maintain a proper freedom in their various forms of spiritual life and discipline, in their different liturgical rites, and even in their theological elaborations of revealed truth."[54] This transition will without doubt be plagued with notable dangers. Aside from prognostications of "cyber-terrorism" and "logic bombs" that may increasingly imperil modern centralized states, the future portends a neutralization of all rationalistically ordered institutions and homogenized centralized states that have been held in a tenuous balance of force and counterforce. In certain of the latter there may arise traces of tapestry of ancient nations seeking to reclaim sovereignties possessed prior to the establishment of the post-Enlightenment political topography.[55]

There is no blueprint full-blown from the mind of Zeus for the Catholic historian speculating about the future. Yet, many of the observations that Christopher Dawson made concerning the nature and crisis in Western education some thirty years ago have been confirmed with a renewed intensity. His recommendations for specific content in programs for the study of Christian culture would, if "repurposed" according to the potentialities of the new electronic technologies, be a remarkable step toward transmitting Catholic history to the future, so long as it is borne in mind that the book itself as a semiotic technology will be subsumed and modulated according to the dynamics of electronic cognitive technologies.[56] The book in its anterior realizations will serve a subsidiary role to the intensified assistance of the oral-rhetorical in the unfolding electronic future in which articulation of reminiscences will be significantly, though not necessarily substantially, modulated by the dynamics of instruments that extend the sensible cognitive powers.

Truly creative historical action transcends mere deconstruction or reconstruction to realize a novel "togethering" of contemporary achievements and previous attainments. Again, if we consider the deepest intentions of the fathers and theologians at the last great council of the Church we can discern somewhat the profound sense of discretion they hoped would be instilled in Christ-faithful in order to manifest the truth of the Redeemer to a new age. In exploring the implications of the end of the Constantinian Era, M. D. Chenu presented a profound fundamental contrast between comprehension of the legitimate profanity of the world and a hyper-sacramental view. The first, he argued, is implied in the principles of St. Thomas Aquinas, with the latter in the Augustinian orientation of St. Bonaventure.[57] Chenu centered his reflections on the fact that for St. Thomas Aquinas "the [creature's] goodness is the cause of its reference" toward God, whereas in the highly explicated symbolic theology developed by St. Bonaventure and the tradition he represented, it was vice versa.

For St. Thomas sacramental symbolization is one with the simplicity of the execution of sacred actions. He insists upon the fact that humans need the sensible to maintain an awareness of and form notions of the trans-sensible, yet such acknowledgment of the necessity and importance of the incarnate symbolic order, both for the individual and for society, must not imply any depreciation of the implicit reference of the created nature in its very own proper operations and ends to its source in the Creator. Aquinas's principles therefore do not imply a necessity for a predominant veneer of sacramental symbolizations to guarantee the natural operations of creation, nor for a rationale that justifies a juridically insulated clericalist caste that performs supplementary sacred actions to assure that creatures truly achieve what their own natural powers properly enable them to attain. For Thomas, however, natural actions are virtually sacramental if executed in accord with their proper finalities, and sacred actions are sacred by virtue of re-presencing rituals by the historical Christ with simplicity and dignity.[58] This realism of sacred action purified of obscure historical features was what many theologians and fathers of the recent council sought to attain, since it would eventually assist Christ-faithful to become more aware of their active common participation in Christ's royal, priestly, and prophetic characters, as well as become more mature daughters and sons of the Eternal Father, engaged as true coadjutors of the Creator and spiritual leaven in an era wherein expansive technological dominion over nature would explicate virtualities of the divine delegation in Genesis. The implications of all this inevitably become manifest in how the Church determines to develop or permits to atrophy certain rites that develop throughout history. A rite discerned no longer to be accessible to the *populus Dei*, though it may have been a vital narrative "figure" in a previous cultural context, cannot, even with contrived efforts to sustain it, effectively serve as a cultural ground within contemporary actuality to form faithful capable of fully integrating the sacred rituals and their implications into their engagement with the secular. A rite that codified sacred rituals into a coherent unity meshed within allegorical additions in the past may offer a tissue of aesthetic extrinsicist *vestamenta* within a new context, but it can also encourage the delusion that the interior perfection of its performers is attained principally by memorized rubrical actions, especially if such had developed into predominantly repetitive, marvelously symmetrical and textured aesthetic visual unity.

Extrapolated from historical context and absolutized, justification of conserving adherence to a rite of such formalized beauty will require a montage of contrived romanticized rationalizations, since true integration of natural and supernatural virtues presupposes rites transparently accessible to actuality, so that the New Testament priesthood of all the faithful is brought into maximal intentional community in conjunction with the ordained priesthood. By symbolizing the sacred character of the rituals that pertain to the entire *congratio fidelium* with dignity, simplicity, and full intelligible accessibility, one better ensures the inculcation of the natural political virtues within all participants through true interpersonal communion in a manner that implies no exclusive or dominant possession of sanctifying grace and supernatural virtues by the ordained priesthood, which exists to serve the priesthood of the faithful.[59] Such neutralizes the erroneous rationalization of a segregated pseudo-aristocratic or autocratic privileged clericalist class ipso facto in possession of superior knowledge, wisdom, or natural or supernatural virtues, a topic that is still worthy of investigation since it is the profound basis for many misunderstandings behind the polemic of so-called "traditionalists" and "progressives" who do not comprehend the finalities of the Second Vatican Council.[60]

The Vatican Council's Constitution of the Sacred Liturgy and its succinct Decree on Instruments of Social Communication are intriguing not only due to their proximity of promulgation in early December 1963. The second emphasized moral diligence concerning the content communicated in all mass communications, but also suggested that at least some Christ-faithful attain greater understanding and expertise in these semiological technologies "for the good of human society whose destiny is daily becoming more and more dependent on their right use."[61] Yet there is a thread binding this concern with all the reflections on the sacred liturgy as the central action of the entire Church, wherein one should encounter rich simplicity, brevity, lucidity, and transparent intelligibility so that "the intimate connection between word and ritual in the liturgy can become clearly apparent."[62] In fact, what the Church intended concerning the liturgical renovation is exemplary in indicating what true historical retrieval or appropriation must involve.

True retrieval of what was an earlier ground or cultural surround in a prior era so that it may perform as a figure or meaningful symbol within the present is commonplace. Consider the numberless aspects of secular history's retrievals of the past extending to the archaic.[63] Paradoxical interface and tension between the most vital endurable elements of ancient heritage and contemporaneity has always marked great creative eras in which Christ-faithful profoundly affected temporal institutions and events. Such suggests that the Church will fare best in the emerging era in which centrifugal dynamisms will displace centripetal features of the recent past by encouraging adaptable, venerable, archaic attainments that best promote spiritual unity capable of maintaining profound diversity of cultural manifestations. The more profound the spiritual and moral unity realized, the greater the diversity of integral cultural realizations sustained within that unity, an axiom that is antithetical to the totalitarian uniformist.

Frederick D. Wilhelmsen insisted that the emerging era will be dominated by what he felicitously termed "neuronic man," who is won over not so much by sharply reasoned issues, but more by connotative images, who "no longer exits outside the limits of his own technology," and for whom "anarchy is the symptote."[64] *Christifideles*, in truth, must be fully engaged in the evolutions and devolutions that occur under these altered conditions of social order, and they would be well-advised not only to comprehend profoundly the theoretical and practical aspects of their patrimony's past, but as well that of the emerging order. Regarding the former, we must avoid the proverbial temptations to gloss events and personages from our patrimony with romanticism and sentimentalism, and concerning the latter we must not substitute precipitous global moral condemnations for intelligent engagement and sober comprehension. We may hope that eventually some Christ-faithful will invest energies and resources in these evolving instruments that extend the power of the symbolic image in a manner that equals or surpasses those who are so accomplished in exploring the virtualities of these augmentations of human cognitive powers.

Christ-faithful in what are ambiguously called the "Middle Ages" attained unforeseeable heights in the arts and sciences, laying methodical foundations for their future development in the Renaissance and Modernity. Ironically, history as an autonomous discipline was never a prevalent component in formal teaching during the Middle Ages.[65] Yet our medieval predecessors did these things and more, first of all by living according to faith, even though all did not live as saints. A central issue of our time is whether history informed by the bespeaking of this culturally complex patrimony presenced to our contemporaries may analogically influence human endeavors anew. If this is possible, it might be said one day of each in service to the Lord and King of history and humanity that she or he "realized that the seeds of [their] actions would one day burgeon, but unlike the seeds sown in terrestrial fields, at no specific time or place and in no predestined shape, but in some place somewhere, and under some form impossible yet to imagine."[66]   ♦

Nature, Culture, and History

Rocco Buttiglione
Translated by John F. Crosby

WHEN we undertake to reflect today on Christian social doctrine, we do it in a definite social and cultural context in which there is a ferment of desires and hopes, fears and problems, all having a precise historical form. A defect with which the social doctrine of the Church has oftentimes been charged is that it lacks any historical dimension, that is, that it proposes and propagates programs that are derived from the eternal and immutable nature of man and that are valid for all times and for all purposes. At times, there has been a hidden agenda behind this charge, and at times it has seemed to have an appearance of truth. Since we want to study the possibility, the usefulness, and the meaning of the social doctrine of the Church in the contemporary world, we can begin in no other way than by settling accounts with this objection in a radical manner. And the best way to do this is to locate our effort within an understanding of our time, or rather within *a tentative interpretation of contemporary history.*

But before proceeding in this direction, refuting with the facts the objection about a lack of historical sense and laying, so to say, our cards on the table, it is necessary to give some attention to the problem of the historicity of Christian social doctrine from a methodological point of view that is more general and necessarily more abstract. That is, we have to face up to the decisive question as to the relation between nature and history. We have to do this in the most fundamental way possible, even if we are compelled to limit ourselves to the basics. The nature of our subject will require us to return again and again to this point; it is nevertheless necessary that we clarify here in principle the way in which we intend to deal with the problem.

Those who accuse Christian social doctrine of being abstract have in general thought that there is no such thing as a *human nature* from which general ethical principles could be derived that are valid at all times and in all places. They have set a kind of evolutionist and historicist way of thinking in opposition to the tradition of natural law to which Christian social doctrine appeals in one way or another. However numerous and profound the points of contrast between Catholic social thought and the natural law doctrines of the seventeenth and eighteenth centuries (I am thinking, for example, of John Locke), it is entirely evident that in the way of arguing, in the way of posing problems, to say nothing of many particular solutions to them, these doctrines are much closer to Christian social doctrine than to the evolutionist-historicist forms of thought. The rupture between Catholicism and modern social thought occurs, in fact, only in the eighteenth century, with the formation of the great systems of evolutionist and historical thought. These maintain that man is radically made by his circumstances. His supposed "nature" is his freedom, by means of which he possesses the power to create himself. For classical social thought, by contrast, man is necessarily subject to his own nature. Nature assigns to him certain potentialities that he has the task of developing as well as he can in the course of his existence. All that a man can accomplish is only an actualization of the potentialities with which he was originally endowed.

This way of thinking has two supremely important consequences. First, it implicitly supports the religious sense of man—it was not I who made this set of potentialities that I am; I have not given them to myself, but I have received them from another. Man is therefore always at least implicitly led back to the thought of the Other who has placed him in being.[1] Secondly, man finds immanent in his nature the laws of his development and of his history. From this point of view man presents himself to us as a *being essentially finite*, similar to every other animal, indeed in a certain sense similar to every other being in creation. The potentialities constituting man belong to the world, and hence man himself, who has these potentialities, belongs to the world. The affirmation of the evolutionist-historicist position puts into question both of these consequences:

Man creates himself, and hence, in order to understand himself, is not led back to any other being than himself. On the other hand, man has the liberty to change the world, to undo it, and to reshape according to his own measure the whole of existing reality. Nature is a mere presupposition that ought to be surpassed, abolished, entirely transformed by the creative activity of man.

In the formation of the evolutionist-historicist attitude, there are above all three factors at work:

1. The experience of *the transformability of nature* by means of human work, guided by science and technology. Man had always transformed nature, but in repetitive ways, acting as his ancestors had always acted. Technological advances and change were very slow and were hardly being consciously perceived. Now man discovers that he is lord of nature, and this in a vaster and profounder sense than he could previously have ever imagined.

2. The experience of *the transformability of the orders of society.* The English Revolution, the American Revolution, and above all the French Revolution show that not only the mode of production, but also the mode of organizing the common life of man is not subject to laws of a nature that always repeats itself, but rather can be (or seems to be able to be) freely devised by man.

3. The experience of personal interiority, which becomes more intense at the beginning of the modern period. Perhaps in connection, at least partially, with the development of the capitalistic market, man perceives more profoundly his own individuality and does not let himself be absorbed by the community of the family and the neighborhood in which in the past he used to be incorporated; he feels his own success or his own failure to be in his own hands, and he feels as a result *the lord of his own destiny* in a manner almost unknown to previous generations.

The claim, however, of creating oneself is hardly tenable if made with respect to the single individual and the human race. It takes on a certain plausibility only if the subject of such creating is the whole human race.

This fact confronts the evolutionist-historicist thought with an inevitable contradiction. On the one hand, this thought sinks its roots at least in part in the Augustinian tradition, which affirms the transcendence of the human person with respect to any given natural order. On the other hand, this transcendence cannot be attributed to a single existing human being, but to the humankind in its abstract generality. We encounter here the unresolved and the unresolvable problem of the relation between universal and particular. As man realizes his own absolute freedom in the continuous creation of the world, the universal ought at the same time to realize in itself the aspiration of the individual for freedom and for happiness. If, however, this does not happen (and empirical experience, for the most part, attests that it does not happen), the evolutionist-historicist thought is on the whole constrained to take the side of the universal, degrading the sufferings of the individual, or of all the millions and millions of individuals who taken together constitute the human race, to the level of a disagreeable accident that is ultimately insignificant in the realm of history.

This is the scandal of idealism, against which the young Marx violently protested.[2] But it is necessary to say that the very same scandal, only worse, is found in Marxism itself, which considers the right of the individual to be a negligible quantity, which can be sacrificed to the advancement of history presenting itself as *revolution*.[3]

If we turn back to the problem from which we started, that is, the criticism that the social teaching of the Church is ahistorical, we see that this criticism is vitiated at its root by the historicist point of view in which it is situated. Nevertheless, the error of historicism is not yet enough to free us from that criticism and to overlook its relative validity. Man is not only a historical being because, great as is the variability of his circumstances and his capacity for adapting to them, man draws all of his energy for transforming the world from the set of forces and from the physical, psychic, and spiritual attitudes with which he was originally endowed. From this there results a series of physical, emotional, and ethical bonds that he is not free to break without destroying and annihilating his very self.[4]

When this Promethean ideology of the 1800s tried to realize itself, it showed its own limit: The ecological disaster (and we include in this the disaster of cultural ecology) is precisely the result of an attempt to dominate nature *in an arbitrary manner*, not recognizing the limit that is imposed on the dominion of man by the nature of things and by *the nature of man himself.*[5]

At the same time, however, we must not forget that man is not only nature. Inherent in the nature of man is a certain capacity for self-transcendence, by which man does not simply do the same thing again and again, but is capable of recognizing, finding, devising something new in the succession of human generations. This human capacity for transcendence is directed toward God but at the same time is directed toward the world of things. The highest law of human nature does not bind us (as happens in the case of animals) to an unchangeable destiny, but binds our creativity and our capacity for changing ourselves and our world to a dialogue with God, in which this capacity is given to us. This is one of the points on which the Vatican Council II, in the Constitution on the Church in the Modern World, has laid great stress.

In this way, we see how fundamentally unjustified the charge is that Christian social doctrine is ahistorical; but, at the same time, we see how reductive the response is that has been given to this charge. One has responded often enough that *there exists a human nature and hence eternal principles of an ethical character, which ought to be respected in every and any situation.* There is here an essential truth: The innocent man who suffers under an unjust oppression is not going to let himself be convinced by some evolutionist-historicist sophism of the historically legitimate character of the rule that condemns him to death.

However much the historical conditions vary, there nevertheless exists a fundamental content of the words *liberty* and *dignity* that is not subject to historical change and that remains an indispensable point of ethical reference. And yet the evolutionist-historicist objection can be refuted only if one is capable of indicating and justifying *the way in which* the vindication of justice becomes concrete, meaningful, and politically, socially, and culturally real. If value in its essential form (its *eidos*) does not change, its reflection in the history of the world changes as it is refracted in thousands of various ways. Precisely because man in fact has *the power to create himself and his own world,* for good as well as for evil—either responding to the vocation that God offers him through finite beings and through history or rejecting all of this—precisely because of this we need a kind of topographical map to find our place in the world; we need a map of orientation that helps us to discover value in its historical and social form.

The evolutionist-historicist doctrines had wanted to abolish the heaven of principles so as to immerse themselves in events and to study their internal evolutionary laws in the conviction that the course of history would lead by its nature to the good, or rather would itself be good. Diametrically opposed to this was a certain rigid traditionalism that had tried to *defend the eternal principles against history*. The real task now is rather to try to direct the course of history according to the fundamental truths constitutive of the human subject. However much these may be embedded in the history of the world, man can *intuit them in all their purity*; but instead of contemplating them he is sent into the history of the world to search for ever fuller and more adequate forms of their realization.[6]

In a certain way, this movement characterizes the history of Christian social doctrine from its very beginning. If in fact we look at the encyclical *Rerum novarum*, with which one usually dates the beginning of the social doctrine in the modern sense, we see how it undertakes to reaffirm the principles of Christian social anthropology precisely in a historical era of rapid transformation and revolution in all the traditional areas, whether social, political, economic, or juridical. The task now, after the Second Vatican Council, and after the encyclicals *Laborem exercens, Sollicitudo rei socialis,* and *Centesimus annus*, which in a certain sense represent the Magna Carta of postconciliar Christian social doctrine, is to take up again this task with a greater methodological awareness.[7]

We can say that between the level of principle and that of *praxis*, there is another level, which is that of *the understanding of contemporary history*.[8] If man is the agent of history and the builder of society, and if, on the other hand, human history is not a formation of the semi-naturalistic kind assumed by the philosophies of history in the nineteenth century, then it is inevitable that one's hypothesis of how to construct one's own history and world will come into conflict with other hypotheses of other individuals and groups. The understanding of the creative character of human action in the world makes us thus realize the reality of the struggles in the history of the world, or rather the reality of the world as struggle.

Does this mean that we here come up against the Marxist conception of history as the history of class struggle? The point is important, and we will have to return to it later, but already at this stage in our reflection we can respond with a decisive no. The struggle of which we are speaking is about the meaning of the world and for the meaning of the world; it is the struggle for truth, for justice, and the good. But it is an important fact that the understanding of the historicity of man requires us to assume this dimension of struggle, which is a struggle in the positive sense of a building-up (and thus the word *struggle* is less appropriate than the word *work*), but it is also the struggle to defend one's own right to build up, and it is a peaceful struggle, conducted with the arms of dialogue and of culture, aiming at convincing the others to participate in one's own work of building up.

While there are numerous projects according to which it is possible to build up the world and history, *the world is one, and the history of man is one.* It is just because of this that each can realize his own project of life only *together with others* in a common effort and on the basis of mutual recognition.[9] We are in need of an interpretation of history precisely to be able to understand the historical struggles of our time and to be able intellectually to form a judgment about them.

What is the difference between this stress on the importance of *an interpretation of contemporary history* and the position that has been maintained concerning the necessity of a *cultural mediation* between values and history, or rather concerning the necessity of a *socio-analytic mediation* as we find it for instance in Marxism, for the purpose of being able to bridge the gap between theory and practice?

Here we clearly encounter the problem of the theology of liberation. Without wanting to give an exhaustive assessment, we will limit ourselves here to a few points. In the first place, we have to recognize the existence and the relevance of the problem. Antonio Gramsci stressed that the true problem of Catholic social doctrine is not so much the general adequacy of its principles as rather the fact that it functions politically as kind of a backup.[10] He means that it exists to give a pretext for saying in moments of crisis that Catholics, too, have a social doctrine; but in reality Catholics are not capable of acting effectively so as to put it into practice. Once the critical moment has passed in which they made use of it, especially to distance themselves from the Socialists, they put it again in mothballs.

This observation of the great Communist philosopher is important because it introduces into our scheme a dimension of concreteness that is often lacking in the ecclesial discussions of the theme of *cultural mediation* and of *socio-analytic mediation*. It is in fact evident that the weakness which Gramsci points out is not an exclusively theoretical weakness that could be overcome by a better theological and philosophical elaboration. As soon as he poses the problem of who is the subject of understanding history, Gramsci clearly indicates that this subject is not the isolated intellectual. Not that the support of the intellectual is unimportant; it is even decisive on certain occasions. It is, however, not sufficient, and above all does not have the capacity to originate. The subject of which Gramsci thinks is a collective one that interprets history because it is in history and because it makes history. The subject Gramsci is thinking about is clearly the party.

Now where does Christian social doctrine find an analogous subject? Would the subject be the Church as such or, better, the Church understood as a hierarchical institution? This would be difficult. As Gramsci observed sharply, the hierarchy as such tends to get involved in politics only when the very existence of the Church and her freedom of action is at stake.[11] One has often rebuked the hierarchy for this tendency, but such is altogether understandable. Christian social doctrine becomes concrete when it generates judgments within a social setting concerning concrete situations, that is, when it gets involved in the struggle to define what is, concretely the just thing in the situation. The more this happens, the more action requires a charism that is not of the hierarchy, requires responsibilities that are typically lay, and implies the assumption of risks that the hierarchy is unprepared to take. However much in these recent years, largely under the influence of the constant preaching of the Pope on the theme of human rights, there has been on the international level an unexpected revival of the figure of the bishop who is *defensor civitatis*, or defender of the city (think of Poland, the Philippines, Chile, Nicaragua, etc.); nevertheless it is impossible, and not even desirable, that the hierarchy intervene in civil controversies unless there is at stake some direct and obvious attack on the Church herself or on fundamental human rights.

According to another hypothesis concerning the subject of Catholic social doctrine, the involved are some Catholic party or the party of Catholics.[12] There is no doubt but that in certain historical circumstances, the Catholic parties have been concrete subjects of the development and practice of Christian social doctrine. A balanced evaluation of the experience of the Christian Democratic parties has to admit that, if certain requirements of social security, stability of employment, fair compensation, and the like have to some degree been realized in the countries of Western Europe, and if, on the other hand, democratic political reformers have asserted themselves to avoid civil war between the dictatorial ideologies of the right and of the left, then the merit should certainly be ascribed to the Christian Democratic parties as well as the social democratic ones. If the Communist project of Gramsci failed in Italy, this is due in large part to the political subjectivity that Italian communism at a different moment in the history of Italy was able to express by means of the Christian Democratic Party.

And yet the Catholic party does not seem to be the adequate subject of Christian social doctrine. First of all, it is problematic for a Catholic to think that the primary social historical conveyer is the party, even if it is entirely understandable that Gramsci thought this. In him, *politics takes over the very first* and political action is a world-transforming praxis of the highest kind. The project of social transformation has therefore as its center of gravity the battle for political power, which begins in the factory as the struggle for power in the factory (politics is in this view the terrain on which the questions of economic structure are posed) and which is carried out as a contest for control of the structure of the state.[13] This is coherent with a general conception of man that looks for his roots and the ultimate principles of his behavior in the economic sphere. But things look different if one searches for the roots of man in the sphere of culture, above all when the word *culture* is interpreted according to the particular meaning that it receives in light of the encyclical *Laborem exercens*.[14]

Culture means here in fact not a collection of abstract ideas, but rather *the cultivation in man of his humility*, the capacity for recognizing values and committing his life for them. Culture is also the inner meaning of work understood as a specifically human action. If one looks for the roots of man's being at this level of depth, then one necessarily has quite another conception of the principles on which it is necessary to act in order to transform society and in order to render human life more human.

Political action does not lose importance in this view, but it does not occupy the commanding position. The problem here is not to organize a front line of attack to seize power in the conviction that this will change men, but rather it is to set in motion a process of education by which men, changing themselves, also change the conditions of their life and learn to cooperate for the realization of truth, of justice and the good, at the political level as well as at all other levels of existence. The difficulty of *being in the truth* takes precedence over the problem of seizing power.

Sociologically, the conception of Gramsci presupposes centralized structures of power that are easily identifiable and are available to control by means of planned action, which in their turn organize and dominate civil society. In this respect, despite the great flexibility and aristocracy of his thought, Gramsci remains a Marxist, indeed, a Leninist.

The other images of political life take it for granted that power should be decentralized, not controllable from a single central point, but entrusted to the responsibility of a large number of social subjects, each of whom is empowered in his own realm with autonomy. In this view of things it is not necessary *first of all* to take over the seat of government in order to change human life, and power is exercised primarily by giving concrete witness, that is, by being present in the various realms of life in which the life of the nation is organized, and being present for the sake of forming its ethos.[15]

From this point of view, there seem to be strong objections to considering a Catholic party as the subject of Catholic social doctrine. And by the way, this too seems to have been grasped by Gramsci when he welcomed the birth of the Italian Popular Party, thinking that it would be the form in which Italian Catholicism would commit political suicide. In fact, he thought that if Catholics enter into politics as a party, they will be forced to think so much in terms of politics that they will lose sight of their religious motives and will in the end recognize either the failure of their political experiment or the uselessness of it for their religious faith. Gramsci is not far from recognizing a contradiction or at least a tension existing between the party as such and the principles of Catholicism.[16]

The party as such, of which the Leninist party constitutes the supreme realization, tends to absolutize itself and to see its whole source in itself, thus expelling from itself the religious dimension. Without wanting to deny the historical merits of the Christian Democrats in Italy, nor the reasons for the political unity of Catholics in the history of our country, it seems as if the fate of this party partly confirms the intuition of Gramsci: Just think of a Dossetti who abandons politics to save his faith, or think of those who have continued in politics, but a politics that was ever more deprived of any transcendent reference.

In saying that the subject of Catholic social doctrine is not the party, however—in order to introduce a qualification here—we do not mean that the Catholic parties in certain circumstances cannot be useful or even indispensable. We simply mean that they are not thought of as the subject of social doctrine, but at most as only one of various articulations of this subject.

Once we have rejected the idea of the Church as the one who primarily works for the realization of Catholic social teaching and have rejected the idea of the Church's delegating a Catholic party to do this, the question remains whether it is even possible to find a social subject that is the bearer of this social doctrine. Perhaps we could propose the hypothesis that the subject of social doctrine is lay Christians, more or less organized in their associations and movements, who constitute, broadly speaking, *a cultural and social movement in the life of their country.* When we speak of movements here we are not speaking in organizational terms.

Let us not forget the question from which we started: Who is the subject of the interpretation of history that renders the social teaching of the Church a force in history? We have responded that this subject is a presence in a social setting that we call a movement. Such a presence is a given that is recognized; it is not something that is devised. There is a way of being in a social setting that is itself a judgment, even if only inarticulate and implicit, on what is good and what is bad, what is justice and hope in that situation. This is a given that is accepted and from which we begin, recognizing it and following it out.

This specific charism of a movement, which is being a concrete incarnation of the Church in a definite social setting, is measured of course at bottom by its fidelity to the Magisterium. But this implies a specific gift and responsibility proper to lay people, even if freely developed in a close collaboration with the hierarchy. The cultural elaboration follows upon the event of this presence, or rather is an aspect at the center of this presence. In this way, the Christian event becomes history; and insofar as it is the subject of history, it acquires the right to interpret history.

We are now in a position to see clearly the error of those who stress one-sidedly the moment of *cultural mediation.* They forget the famous and ever valid axiom of Vico: *verum et factum convertuntur,* truth and deed are convertible. This axiom is susceptible of various interpretations, some of them frankly unacceptable. But one that certainly is shared is the one that stresses the necessity, for every hermeneutical operation, of a *Sitz im Leben,* of a commitment in the world of social life, or, as we said above, a presence.

One interprets a reality only if one takes a position within it; one knows and understands a historical situation only if he is situated in it and shares the vital principles of it.[17] But to share them, it is necessary to formulate them according to one's own subjectivity, accepting the conflict with others and with different interpretations. Even if in the course of the conflict one's own position has to change and be substituted by another more profound one that is better able to recognize the valid reasons of the adversary, it nevertheless remains true that one could not have arrived at that understanding of the reasons of the other without the act of placing oneself in the situation and identifying oneself as the subject in it. If what I have said is true, then the error both of the thesis of cultural *mediation* and of the thesis of *analytic mediation* is this: that one fails to think of the Church as subject in the situation and fails to think of movement as the lay form of the presence that concretizes the Church in a given social setting. As a result, either one remains in a state of extreme abstractness and is not a real force in history— and this is the case with cultural mediation—or else, without noticing it nor intending it, one ends up assuming the point of view of some different historical subject and then forming an idea that corresponds to it.

In both of these cases, in the end the social doctrine of the Church becomes impossible, because the movement that goes forth from principles toward reality does not meet a movement that comes from reality toward the principles. Social reality, if not read from the point of view of a historical subject to whom it belongs, does not reveal those points of contact that enable the affirmed truth to become history. One inevitably subjects oneself to another historical project, which, it is thought, will guarantee for those values dear to the Church, and even guarantee for the Church itself as an institution, a certain limited sphere, if not of self-realization, then at least of survival.[18]

We have now clearly laid out our position on who the subject of Catholic social doctrine is, and laid it out in contrast to the position of *cultural mediation* or of *socio-analytic mediation*. This, however, does not resolve the problem that we posed regarding the relation between nature and history, even if it indicates to us a methodological condition of fundamental importance for work toward this end: the immanence of the Church or of a movement understood as the presence of the Church in a social setting, which renders the Christian event history.

It is just this immanence that generates a historical sensibility, which is another factor distinguishing us from the position of socio-analytic mediation. This latter position is in fact more attentive to the material structures in which man finds himself living than to the integrated historical process of the formation and growth of his culture. The difference between a simply socio-analytic point of view and our historical viewpoint does not lie in that ours is supposedly totalizing and the other is not. Both are totalizing, but in different ways. In the one case, attention stops with the social and material conditioning within which man finds himself living. The difference also does not lie in that the scope of the analysis in the one position is simply synchronic where the other admits of a diachronic dimension, that is, it does not limit itself to describing the social situation at a particular moment but considers a more or less extended span of time.

What is decisive rather is that the socio-analytic mediation is in a position to offer only a history of human conditioning, but not a history of freedom. It is not methodologically capable of perceiving the eruption of something new in history, hence of perceiving the ethical dimension. Our historical-cultural point of view, to the contrary, sees in history the struggle of freedom with human conditioning, the effort of man to gain for himself bread and at the same time to save and to affirm his own dignity, transcending his own conditions of existence and at the same time recognizing their rights and fulfilling his obligations toward them.

The historical perspective that we have thus indicated or sketched out is distinguished from historicism because it *presupposes an anthropology.*[19] According to this anthropology man, the agent of history, is not a product of history itself, but has his own independent structure that is put to the test in history, which tends toward its proper fulfillment and at the same time is always in danger. It is just the fidelity to anthropology that saves history as the history of man, preserves it from the structuralistic overthrow to which it is inevitably condemned when it assumes a *historicist* dimension. If in fact one assumes that man does not have proper essence, it is necessary to admit either that his freedom creates the world or, when this thesis runs up against reality, that man's freedom simply does not exist, and that man is simply the result of the conditionings to which he is subjected. History leads us back, then, to anthropology. If history articulates the various social sciences, anthropology grounds the possibility of history itself; we have, therefore, need of *an anthropology capable of articulating the unity of nature and history, showing both the historicity proper to human nature and the existence of a natural substrate in man that is the condition of any possible history.*[20]

Here we encounter the anthropology of Karol Wojtyla, who shows how the relation with the other, action performed together with others, is a constitutive dimension of human subjectivity, which however does not mean that the individual subject and his personal responsibility get lost in some collective action or collective subject. This opening to inter-subjectivity is at the same time an opening to the reality of human work, that is, to the factor by means of which man modifies his natural environment and builds history. Wojtyla provides us with the foundational elements of a philosophy of human praxis, which allows us to think coherently about both the immanence and also the transcendence of truth and justice in history. This corresponds from a practical point of view to the categories of *movement* and *presence* elaborated in this study.[21]   ♦

Christianity and the Philosophy of History

Robert A. Herrera

HISTORY as a transmittable record of events first came to light during the third millennium B.C.[1] The term itself was probably introduced by Herodotus and later taken up by Thucydides. Polybius expanded its boundaries by weaving a tapestry glorifying Roman imperial conquest. Nevertheless, history was not accorded great importance in the Greco-Roman world. Aristotle, for example, maintained that poetry was superior to history as it extracts a universal idea from disparate events.[2] Plotinus viewed historical events as incidents in a play, contrasting them sharply to the authentic life, that of interiority, the drama of the return of the soul to God.[3] The purpose of history, as Ranke indicated, is to reveal the past as it truly happened.[4] The philosophy of history uses this as its point of departure, "what truly happened," but does not stop at this point. As Pieper has indicated, the philosophy of history inquires if the events mean something over and above the merely factual.[5] It poses the question of ends, of finality. And in so doing it reveals its relation to theology. This distinguishes it from history proper, which eschews eschatology and imposes a plot of time, interpreting events through this prism.[6] While history can look back several millennia, its philosophy is a recent development, the term probably first employed by the Abbe Bazin in his *La philosophie de l'histoire* (1765) and used widely only after its adoption by Voltaire.[7]

This essay was previously published in *Reasons for our Rhymes* by Robert A. Herrera (Grand Rapids, MI: Eerdmans, 2001), and is reprinted here with the permission of the author.

The foundational charter of both disciplines is found in Scripture, the first verse of Genesis: "God at the beginning of time, created heaven and earth" (Genesis 1:1–2). Biblical creation shattered the pagan conception of an eternal universe parceled out by an infinity of cycles.[8] Entailing linear time, a vast horizon of novel events is opened, extending far beyond the dreams of the ancient chroniclers. Even Herodotus, celebrated by Cicero as the "father of history," in his superb nine-book epic in Homeric style, remains imprisoned in a circle.

The noncreative deities of the ancient world stumble. Looking toward the future, Aristotle perceives a whirl of events that repeat endlessly. His Unmoved Mover is no more than the final cause of motion and desire in the universe. A true autocrat, it cannot control or even know of human and cosmic affairs, ensconced within the supreme beatitude of self-contemplation.[9] Plato, when he refers to the gods at the beginning of the *Laws* or the ending of the *Apology*, merely refers to those popular deities, the "gods" of the Athenians.[10] The pagan hierarchy, which descends from the Divine Cosmos to the gods, then to intermediary beings *(daimones)*, and finally to man, is rejected. In the hierarchy to be imposed by nascent Christianity God reigns supreme, followed by man, and, at a distance, the demythologized cosmos.

The God of Scripture is a living being, not a mere principle, one, not a multiplicity, for Christians an *Unum* (one reality) not an *Unus* (one person). The eternal cycles are abolished, replaced by linear time with beginning, middle, and end. Time reaches its apogee in the Incarnation, to which and from which flow historical tides. And these follow the divine script "by the deliberate will and plan of God" (Acts 2:23). A lengthy process reflected in Wisdom literature reaches its climax in the splendid hymn of praise to the Logos-God of the Gospel of John (John 1:1–18), which leads to the enthronement of Christ as the Lord of History. In the words of Hebrews: "in this final age, He [God] has spoken to us in the Son whom he made heir to the whole universe and through whom he created all orders of existence" (Hebrews 1:2–3).

Apocalyptic, both prior to and following the Gospels, had a role in the formation of the philosophy of history.[11] The surviving apocalypses, both Jewish and Christian, from the Book of Daniel to the Sibylline Oracles span a period of some four centuries (200 B.C. to A.D. 200). The paradigm is provided in Daniel: The monstrous figure composed of four metals (Daniel 2:7) has fascinated exegetes for centuries. Moreover, Daniel provides an eschatological division of history beginning with the Babylonian Captivity and divided—based on a prophecy of Jeremiah (Jeremiah 25:11–12:29)—into seventy weeks of years. This, in turn, is divided into three periods of seven, sixty-two, and one week, after which the end will come.[12] In the Christian era, the Epistle of Barnabas provided a cosmic-week interpretation of world history looking forward to the second coming of Christ when the time of the "wicked one" will be destroyed.[13] This is also encountered in Enoch 1, 4 Esdras, and the Book of Jubilees.

Apocalyptic is rife with examples dividing mankind into sheep and goats, the elect and the reprobate. In Enoch 1, God separates the "children of light" from the "children of darkness," as does the Apocalypse of Abraham. Qumran's Rule for the Final War describes the final apocalyptic struggle between the "sons of light" and the "sons of darkness." The masterpiece of the genre is the Book of Revelation (Apocalypse). Even prior to the onset of Christianity the utopian aspect of apocalyptic influenced the secular domain, inspiring novel social structures, as evidenced by the Qumran community.

The doctrine of the Incarnation linked Christianity indissolubly with creation, linear time, and temporal progression. Augustine's anguished cry that Christ will not again be crucified resounded throughout the centuries. Events simply do not recur. But the doctrine of the Incarnation also initiated a less auspicious trend. As Xavier Zubiri has indicated, the instant the Logos is identified with Christ, speculation launches on a wild career in which the Logos, the essence of God, ends in the essence of Man.[14]

This "wild career" is paralleled by the succession of theories reasonably grouped under the umbrella of the philosophy of history. The Divine is transmogrified into the profane, God into man, by a grotesque alchemy. The God of Scripture pales into a mere concept, generating God-substitutes that suffer decomposition before fading away. Each stage is accompanied by a different vision of the end. It is the philosopher's task to come to terms with these variations, to impose a plot that will fixate that which, in itself, is dynamic and fluid.

It should be noted that the waning of biblical sentiment is accompanied by the reduction of historical sense. Such threatens to lead to the loss of history itself. The awesome God of the Old Testament and the Pantokrator of the New Testament is replaced by Providence, which declares its independence, and attains an impoverished autonomy, only to be ousted by its secular surrogate—Progress. The classical world picture—eternal universe, infinite number of cycles, and so on—makes a brief, halting reappearance during the Renaissance. It is not until Nietzsche in the closing decades of the nineteenth century that a major effort is made to reinstate the pagan cosmos by absorbing linear time into the cyclical whirl.

St. Augustine's *City of God* arguably is the best introduction to the philosophy of history.[15] A stunning mural is created by the convergence of historical, philosophical, and theological insights. For Augustine the basis of history, that which determines its route and directs it toward End-Times, is the ongoing struggle between two cities or pyramids of loyalty. The two cities correspond to different spiritual inclinations. The City of God *(Civitas Dei)* is centered on God, with all else placed on the periphery. The Earthly City *(Civitas Terrena)* is centered on created things, with God banished to the periphery. This struggle encompasses the whole of history. The Earthly City will predominate until End-Time, when direct Divine intervention will bring about the definitive victory of the City of God. This theory in its totality set the stage for speculation and provided the paradigm followed by later thinkers and found to some degree in minds as disparate as those of Vico and Marx.

However, no matter how strong Augustine's influence, speculation on the philosophy of history would be subject to variations.[16] A case in point is Orosius, Augustine's sometimes guest at Hippo, who followed the route taken by Origen and Eusebius. He maintained that the Roman Empire was the divinely established vehicle for the advancement of Christianity, a major factor in fulfilling the Divine plan. Closer to Augustine were those who followed his inspiration through the optics of either the Pseudo-Denis or Boethius.[17] History was interpreted as either a fall from a Golden Age or an ascent through stages of increasing perfection under the tutelage of the Divine Pedagogue.

Both Hildegard von Bingen and Joachim of Fiore were unique in that their theories were anchored in visionary experiences. To some extent these "experiences" helped formulate the content of their thought as well as the method to expound it. Hildegard saw history moving in a descending spiral that reaches its watershed in the "effeminate age" *(tempus mulieribus)* and then plunges by degrees to the chaotic Age of the Grey Wolf. Gerlob of St. Emmerman took the opposite tack. History is an ascending spiral that progresses in accordance with God's pedagogical blueprint.

It was Abbot Joachim who departed radically from Augustine's path by proposing that a higher level of human existence—the age of the Holy Spirit—was to appear and would perdure until the catastrophes of end-times. History is interpreted from the perspective of the Holy Trinity. It begins with the Age of the Father, moves to the Age of the Son, and culminates in the Age of the Holy Spirit, each Divine Person grounding a "status," or age. Joachim's novel addition, the Third Age, would be marked by a superior spirituality permeating all areas of human endeavor. It would be primarily reflected by a greater insight into the meaning of Scripture. Joachim traces the path of history from the moment of creation to the borders of the Age of the Holy Spirit. His works were energetically adopted by the Franciscan Spirituals and later incorporated into the radical ideology of the Joachites under the esoteric title of the Eternal Gospel.

A thought-egg was placed in the consciousness of the West that is still present in the hinterlands of the contemporary world. Joachim's speculations produced a tidal wave of religious, social, and political unrest that influenced the Age of Discovery and is reflected in Columbus's *Libro de las Profecías.*[18] The Joachites, who expected universal renewal, joined with the residues of the Latin Averroists, who advocated a theology-free domain of thought and opened the door to the modern world.

Utopianism melded with desiccated reason and antiquarian hubris to produce the Renaissance. The Magi of the Age, such as Pico della Mirandola, Giordano Bruno, and Tomasso Campanella, envisioned a utopia brought about by means of social alchemy. The alchemist took transubstantiation as his model. While he attempted to convert base metals into gold, the philosopher-magus endeavored to transform a nasty, brutish society into a veritable paradise.

The philosophy of history again took wing after the hermetic interlude of the Renaissance. But this did not prevent the majestic YAHWEH from being replaced by Providence, at best an anemic surrogate. Providence then falls from its high station and takes on an autonomous status. The transition is reflected in the difference between Bishop Bossuet and Giambattista Vico. Bossuet reflects the Augustinian heritage, although in a debilitated manner. He marks the "sacred ordering" between sacred history *(historia sacra)* and secular history *(historia profana)*. They intertwine and march in step in their journey to the end-times.

Vico elaborates a theory that bears a faint resemblance to that of Abbot Joachim. It has a triadic structure; humanity develops in three stages. It follows a set pattern that, though cyclical and immutable, is none the less finite and directed by Providence. The "Age of the Gods" is followed by the "Age of Heroes," which is then succeeded by the "Human Age." A relapse of sorts then takes place. The process begins anew. Furthermore, the workings of his system pertain to secular history, as *historia sacra* is restricted to a narrow, though privileged, enclave that is excluded from the natural operations of history.

Hegel marks a turning point. His impressive system, often bordering on the grotesque, revolves around a central notion that extends to all of reality. He traces specific clusters of ideas that permeate an age, impinge on other ideas, and form vast symmetries. The center of his thought—the nodal point—is the Absolute of which the adequate idea is the Idea of Freedom. History, for Hegel, is the development and manifestation of the idea and reality of freedom. It advances dialectically, which is to say, it advances according to a rhythm in which affirmation (thesis) is followed by negation (antithesis), culminating in elevation (synthesis), all of which is covered by the term *Aufhebung*. As Hegel repeatedly affirms, his system is a theodicy, a justification of the ways of God to man.

At first it may seem that Hegel has restored sacred history to the privileged position it occupied in Augustine's *City of God.* All of history is no less than the formation of the Absolute, the resolution of its self-alienation. Although a religious tone pervades Hegel's thought, the theological is completely subservient to an omnipotent Reason that constitutes reality and determines the course of history. Theology, consigned to the inferior level of imagination, can only "picture" a content that reason can know. History does not end in an indeterminate future but in the present actuality of the Prussian State. Eschatology has been abandoned. Secular history *(historia profana)* has become "sacred." The decks have been cleared of all possible opposition.

Hegel's system harbors a notion of progress that provided the point of departure for several different variations of the theme. But it also arose from other directions. Adam Smith grounded progress on the acquisitive instinct, and Condorcet, following Turgot, on the cultivation of the sciences. It was Auguste Comte who first elaborated a comprehensive theory of progress that held a philosophy of history at its core. Many sources influenced him to move in this direction, including Hegel, though Abbot Joachim and Saint-Simon—whose secretary he was—deserve pride of place. Comte proposed that history proceeds according to "the great fundamental law of Order and Progress," moving through three stages or epochs: the mythological, the metaphysical, and the positive or scientific. At first humanity seeks absolute knowledge, aspiring to delve into the very heart of reality. His explanations recur to the gods, ultimately to one sole God. In the mythological stage the gods are replaced by concepts, mental abstractions. No longer satisfied with the otiose methods of the past, mankind advances to the third, and highest, stage, the positive, that of scientific knowledge. This three-stage process is linear and cannot be repeated.

Comte maintained that the troubles plaguing his age, the unsettlement following the French Revolution, was due to the intermingling of the three stages. When the positive stage has triumphed completely, the "telos" of history is accomplished and the epoch acquires the stability of proper order. However, this is only one side of the coin. Society requires a social agglutinate. Comte proposed the creation of a new religion, the religion of the *Grand Être*, humanity. It reproduced certain aspects of medieval Catholicism. The metamorphosis of the secular into the sacred, the world into the Church, latent in Hegel, now becomes overt. The façade of Christianity is discarded.

The cult of progress became an integral part of the public orthodoxy. It boasted of thinkers, propagandists, and even martyrs. Only the horrors of the twentieth century were to force an agonizing reappraisal. The last great proponent of the cult of progress, whose importance transcends this limited aspect of his thought, was Karl Marx. History, he urges, is marked by a succession of class struggles, which move dialectically toward the ultimate goal of human renovation. Strictly speaking, history has yet to begin as it follows in the wake of the proletarian revolution and the subsequent resolution of contradictions. Only then will the realm of freedom be attained. Like Hegel, Marx believed that history was a vehicle of progress. Unlike Hegel, however, Marx's system is monolithically atheistic. Spirit does not supersede Nature. History is incorporated into Nature.

While the heirs of the French Revolution enthusiastically embraced the cult of progress, the adherents of the ancien regime, influenced by selective readings from Augustine, presented theories of inverse evolution. The French Traditionalists, the Comte de Maistre and de Bonald, were followed by the Spaniard Donoso Cortés, who considered that history, at least after the sixteenth century, exhibited a progressive decline. This, he believed, was generated by the corruption of religion, the loss of authority, burgeoning technology, and the excesses of liberalism and Socialism. A similar though less pessimistic view is found in the works of Orestes Brownson and in Brook Adams's *The Law of Civilization and Decay*.

The philosophy of history reaches an impasse with Friedrich Nietzsche through his theory of the eternal recurrence time and again swallowed into the vortex of the eternal cycles. The question may be asked: *"Circulos vitiosus Deus?"* Out of the decaying rubble of Christianity, the "foul religion"! In with a religion bonded to the earth, a life-affirming religion. Nietzsche's "death of God" theory, while it opens the door to novel speculations, closes the door to the philosophy of history. In his view, the end of history is marked by the definitive triumph of the "last men," the mediocre masses. Spengler, who spoke of the masses as the "radical nullity," took up this notion.

In the wake of Nietzsche and fin de siècle decadence Providence is dismissed and progress degraded into mere good fortune. It becomes a truism, a stale political slogan. History appears to be devoid of meaning. As Tolstoy wrote Nazariev, "history is nothing but a collection of fables and trifles, cluttered up with a mass of unnecessary figures and proper names."[19] The visions of prophets and the speculations of thinkers are lost in the quagmire of mass culture.

The early twentieth century witnessed the return to Christian eschato-logical theme with Soloviev and Berdyaev, the latter affirming that redemp-tion will in fact be redemption from history. In terms that recall the effusions of the Joachites, he maintains that the next stage of human existence is likely to involve a "spiritualization" of humanity, a notion similar to Toynbee's "etherialization" and Teilhard's "hominization."[20] The ghost of St. Seraphim of Savoy and the spirituality of the transfiguration looms in the background.

Soloviev began by advocating a "theogonic process" that would birth the Kingdom of God on earth through the free union of humanity and the world with the Absolute Principle—God.[21] Through the passage of time history wends toward God-Manhood, the Body of Christ expanded into a single divine-human organism. Soloviev discarded this optimistic view when he encountered radical evil. He then turned to traditional Christian eschatology. The building up of humanity now is transformed into spadework for the advancing empire of Antichrist.[22]

Posthistory is the latest rung in the chain of historical speculation. Kojeve provided the spark that ignited it in a series of lectures he gave at Paris between 1933 and 1939 on Hegel's *Phenomenology of Mind*.[23] The gist: Hegel was right. History had stopped at Jena. The French Revolution generated the modern bourgeois state, beyond which it is impossible to progress. This is to say, history has ended. Life will continue but without seriousness or meaning. Humanity will continue, but one-dimensional: alike in attitudes, interests, and judgments, not far removed from animality.

A similar view was popularized recently by Fukuyama. The liberal rev-olution has triumphed. Capitalism has proven to be the only viable eco-nomic system and democracy the only viable political system. As they are, Fukuyama insists, completely satisfying it can be affirmed that history has come to an end.[24] If this is true, humanity has entered into a malevolent caricature of the traditional Millennium, condemned to plod along a beaten path, condemned to plod along a beaten path.

Whether the philosophy of history is to be borne away on the treadmill of a neo-pagan universe or return as an important sign of the times, there is little doubt that the Christian enjoys a privileged place. Because of the Incar-nation he is firmly bound to the doctrine of creation, linear time, and there-fore, history. The Christian whose faith has not suffered from doctrinal seepage occupies a unique perch. From this vantage point he can impose a plot only partially of his own making on the course of millennia, melding the chilling multiplicity of fragile events sliding into nothingness into a significant mural.[25]   ◆

Christian Philosophy, Christian History: Parallel Ideas

Glenn W. Olsen

OVER a long life, Etienne Gilson (1884–1978) often used, defended, and refined the expression "Christian philosophy."[1] The phrase, which he seems first to have used in 1924 in regard to his study of St. Bonaventure, occurs in more than one of the English titles of his books, indeed sometimes even when not in the title of the original French.[2] Almost from the first, it was met with hostility, especially with the complaint that "Christian philosophy" was a contradiction in terms.[3] More than a decade after his death, Gilson was still being accused of "extreme confusion," albeit by a less-than-expert critic.[4]

Clearly, Gilson's thought about the nature of Christian philosophy deepened with time, and one can easily be led astray by some of his more summary statements. For instance, his foreword to the *History of Christian Philosophy in the Middle Ages* says Justin Martyr and Nicholas of Cues mark the beginning and end of the period covered in this book. These are writers not usually included in histories of philosophy, presumably because of the strongly religious orientation of their thought and the difficulty of separating that which is philosophical in them from that which is theological. If the defenders of the purity of reason already have their suspicions raised, Gilson does nothing here to calm them. He immediately gives a definition that may seem to leave unclear how philosophy and theology are to be distinguished: "We call Christian philosophy the use made of philosophical notions by the Christian writers of those times. . . . [T]his book . . . is primarily concerned with the history of philosophical ideas even though, as is generally the case in the middle ages, philosophy is only found in a theological context." The unconvinced could argue that this definition applies equally well to any systematization of revealed theology as to philosophy, and for that matter describes what is called philosophical theology. That is, the definition seems to present an amorphous notion. Only the reader careful enough to notice that if philosophy can be used in a theological context its own integrity must lie elsewhere will not be misled by such summary statement.

In general, Gilson seems to have been intent on making two separate but related claims: (a) that philosophy in any period reflects larger cultural preoccupations, and (b) that both historically and intrinsically "philosophizing under the influence of Christian faith" profoundly enriched philosophical thought, helping human reason to deal more adequately with age-old problems that so-called unaided reason had been unable to penetrate sufficiently.[5] Because the contribution of the present paper lies elsewhere, we cannot explore Gilson's justification of his second claim here, but his *Christian Philosophy* amply illustrates the proposition that historically Christian theology deepened the understanding of such philosophical ideas as being, essence, cause, and participation.

Philosophers took exception to both Gilson's claims, especially the second. Indeed, certain writers made Gilson sound plausible to almost anyone by taking "Christian philosophy" as involving only the first claim. Thus David Knowles presented Gilson's position as commonsensical:

> Every group or school of thinkers has a social or cultural or confessional background, and . . . this leads it to focus its attention upon certain fields of the great area of thought available for development. A group of Christians, working in a fully Christian society and for purposes that are largely theological, will naturally direct its attention to subjects, such as the existence of God, the immortality of the soul, human freewill, and the like, which come inevitably into the forefront of its interests.[6]

Now in fact the history of philosophy has often been pursued by those who are not commonsensical, so even Gilson's first claim, and Knowles's ever-so-reasonable presentation of it, has been so far from undisputedly received. Some words on this are in order, for the question bears on the possible parallelism between Christian philosophy and Christian history.

Secular minds, the kind who against most of the evidence have tradi-tionally presented the history of, say, Greek philosophy in isolation from Greek theology and religion, let alone the Greek stage, not understanding the intimate historical intertwining of all these areas of cultural expression, have bridled at the very idea that a philosophy could be religious, let alone Christian.[7] For their own reasons Protestants, too, having learned from their sixteenth-century masters the denial of natural theology and the analogy of being, commonly have not seen how a body of thought could at once be linked to reason and to revelation without betraying one or the other. Even Catholics, at least initially, also gave much resistance to Gilson's first claim, for habituated to the two-story textbook universe of reason and revelation many attributed to Thomas Aquinas, and common to the history of philosophy and theology since at least the time of Chris-tian von Wolff (1679–1754), they had as much difficulty as Protestant Christians understanding how a subject could at once be philosophical and Christian. Philosophy was the realm of unaided reason, and thus by definition could not be Christian. Only after the great debates roused by such books as Henri de Lubac's *Surnaturel*, which of course initially itself aroused opposition and condemnation, some of this leading to refinement of de Lubac's own views, could most Catholic thinkers begin to recover a patristic and medieval way of looking at things in which grace, while for-mally distinct from nature, was present at the foundation of nature itself.[8]

Gilson, somewhat unnervingly playing to the stands, presented St. Thomas as an "existentialist" to make the point that Aquinas's emphasis was on "esse," the act of being, rather than on essentialist categories. But no more than any other Thomist did Gilson propose a confusion of rea-son, the sum of those things knowable from sense experience, with certi-tude by deduction, and revelation, the sum of those things known by trust in God's revelation. His first claim or observation, rather, was that philos-ophy is not normally neutral in regard to its historical setting, but imbibes from the culture in which it works itself out things exterior to itself that nevertheless give it shape. If philosophy is practiced in a Buddhist culture it takes a different form than if matured in a Christian one, and in both cases this occurs even if no content from the larger culture is intruded into the philosophical enterprise.

Philosophy inevitably develops differently in a polytheistic environment than in a monotheistic ethos. In the former, because there is no first cause in an Aristotelian sense, no Aristotelian monotheism, the government of the world is, so to speak, by committee, by the gods. Although the gods will be of various degrees of power and influence, and likely there will be a chief god, by definition no god by him- or herself will control the universe in the manner of the Jewish or Christian God. The direction or drift in things will at the most be the sum of the various gods' negotiations and competitions with one another, for Hera will scheme against Zeus. Such a larger cultural pattern of thought, especially if developed in a world that assumes that the material order has always been, and therefore is not an effect of any god, discourages philosophy from fully understanding certain subjects, such as freedom of the will, intrinsically its own.

This observation exactly parallels Stanley Jaki's observation that certain environments, especially Christianity, have fostered science, while others have retarded it.[9] Although there will likely be some sense of and discussion of freedom of will in a polytheistic culture, this can hardly be the center of reflection. If on the other hand philosophy develops in a monotheistic culture, the problem of freedom will be forced by cultural considerations from periphery to center. If God is creator rather than maker, that is, the source of everything rather than of, at most, simply what order there happens to be, the problem of human freedom becomes acute. If God is the source of all, is there any intelligible sense in which man can be the source of anything? How can a choice be called his? In sum, the larger cultural assumption of monotheism will cause philosophy to reconsider its position, now feeling much more acutely the problem of how humans possibly can be free.

Gilson's point was that, even when philosophy understood as the realm of unaided reason is alert to protecting its boundaries from intrusion, which is rarely the case, inevitably the larger culture shapes its interests, determining which problems will be deemed philosophically central and which peripheral. If a culture has gone through a monotheistic period, further, philosophy will out of habit keep the problem of the individual and of freedom at the center of consciousness long after the formal props for such concern have disappeared. In a formerly Protestant country, ethics will remain "Protestantism by other means," that is, have a content that continues to reflect the assumptions of Protestant theology long after Protestantism has lost its place at the center of the culture. The same is true of formerly Catholic countries, or formerly Marxist countries.[10]

Gilson was interested in the afterlife of "Christian philosophy," in the ways that philosophy in our own apparently secular times still reflects Christian assumptions; but his use of the term was primarily developed in regard to the period in which philosophy formed in a Christian matrix, namely the Middle Ages.[11] His argument was simply of a historical nature, that, since the rise of Christianity, philosophy in the West has necessarily taken on the shape of Christian preoccupations. This was most true in the period in which Christianity took the form of Christendom, but it is more than residually true to the present.

This paper cannot explore the richness of Gilson's second claim with the space it deserves: He seems more than amply to have justified it, even if we stay with the single work *Christian Philosophy*. Fortunately, the nature of this second claim, that "philosophizing under the influence of Christian faith" profoundly enriched philosophical thought, has been partly anticipated in the exposition of his first claim. The question to be addressed in the remainder of this essay is whether, under the form of either of his claims, there is an idea of "Christian history" parallel to Gilson's "Christian philosophy." A consideration, both preliminary and central to that and all that follows, must first be addressed.

The person using the term "Christian history" will likely meet less resistance than Gilson initially encountered, because the expression "Christian history" has long been employed with various commonly accepted meanings. It has the air of familiarity. Most obviously, and here the parallel with "Christian philosophy," while real, can deceive, that is, most people are willing to allow labeling this or that historical experience by the name of a shared religion. Jews can have Jewish history and Muslims Islamic history. If all that is at issue is whether there have been concrete historical phenomena that have taken their shape under Christian influence, this can be granted. "History," because it includes everything that can be shaped into a narrative, seems less an autonomous body of knowledge than philosophy, and while there may be reluctance to acknowledge Christianity's coloration of any part of philosophy, "history" seems to encompass so much that we may readily allow various religious currents within it. Indeed, and this is the heart of our preliminary consideration, history seems only to gain a certain definition by ordering "everything that has happened or claims to have happened" by some set of principles exterior to itself, that is, by introducing some principle of selectivity by which the real can be discriminated from the unreal.

Some illustration is in order. As long as we stick to the Aristotelian definition of history as (to give the later Latin convention) *narratio singularum,* which we can translate as "the narration of specific things," we can avoid, or not even feel the need for, the definition of "history in general" or "universal history." No pretense need be made that somehow the historical materials are dictating their own interpretation (although the historian may feel this to be the case), for clearly each history is the result of a principle of selection that decides to include certain materials and exclude others. Although the decision to write the *History of the Peloponnesian War* depends on that war having taken place (for history, *pace* Simon Schama, is wed to events in a way literature is not), and on there having been a previous history of Athens, Sparta, Persia, and so on, the decision to choose this war as the narrative framework of a history clearly lies with Thucydides. So too does the decision to see the war as instructive about future politics, so instructive that speeches may be crafted (the reader is fairly warned) that represent no reality other than what should have been said on some occasion to make the instructive point. That is, Thucydides's decision to use the war to instruct future generations would have collapsed if the only causal explanation of the war was one over which humans have little or no control, namely as the work of the gods.

If the war was nothing more than the result of divine initiatives, no science could be developed on the basis of its study. If an understanding that could be useful for politics could be produced, it would be because something other than divine causation exists. Thus Thucydides turned to the study of those causal relations open to human examination, to the study of "secondary (interworldly or horizontal)," rather than "primary (divine or vertical)," causation.[12] The gods did not have to be denied, but they had to be ignored in favor of study of those things humans can understand and therefore anticipate, above all politics and human psychology. Beyond observing that interworldly causal relations do exist, Thucydides does not justify constructing a world of men rather than gods, he simply does it, for his principle of selection necessitates such a world. The centering of history on politics and war and human character in subsequent ancient historical writings is not something solely dictated by the so-called raw facts, although these things had to exist for a dialogue between the historian and the historical record to take place; this centering was one result of what these historians and their audiences considered to be real and worthy of portrayal.[13]

Clearly that there had been a Peloponnesian War made possible an essentially political principle of narrative selection, just as the idea of Rome made possible a narrative built on the course of empire. Augustine's ability to write a narrative of something not fully observable, his own spiritual development, and his equally novel construction of a narrative around a not fully empirical entity, the City of God, show that politics was not a necessary narrative basis, and that indeed the historian was free to choose his story.[14]

Gregory of Tours (ca. 538–94) manifests the dangers and possibilities of this freedom, and the degree to which, except for exceptional thinkers like Augustine, narrative has been hitherto dependent on politics.[15] With the collapse of the Empire in the West, Gregory is not at all sure what his story framework should be, and his mimesis tends to be of chaos and disorder. Political history fails him, because politics had failed his times, and it was not yet clear what story other than a political one could be told. He lived in an age when slowly *heilsgeschichte*, a narrative built around the spread of salvation, was replacing politics as the perspective from which to read history, or rather was wedding theology and politics.

Bede (672/73–735) is the witness to, if not a successful marriage of the two, at least a tolerable concubinage, and in him we find a new historical framework in which primary and secondary causal explanation, revelation and politics, coexist.[16] History now is universal not simply in the long-established Jewish and Christian sense of God's great deeds in time done ultimately for all, but as it would be for centuries, a this-worldly narrative, specific in time and space, of the spread of salvation "beginning from Jerusalem." History is ultimately the chronicling of the salvation of the human race (though, Bede, unlike some of his contemporaries, saw no need to go back to Adam and Eve before taking up the newest stage of the story), but immediately it is the story of how the most recently converted people has joined its history to universal salvation history, a *Historia ecclesiastica* in which a "church" is at the same time a "people."

Karl Lowith correctly argued that there is no universal history without Judaism and Christianity. That is, the notion that all mankind shares in the same history, a linear history moving toward a goal, appeared historically only with the Judeo-Christian tradition.[17] All histories outside this tradition, even that of Rome, were less than universal and never—the Stoics came closest to being the exception—saw the whole human story as one story. Lowith also showed powerfully the manner in which, once given birth by Judaism and Christianity, the idea of universal history has persisted to the present, whether in liberal progressive form or in Marxism.

The Christian sanction for such an idea may be rejected, but the idea is kept. Perhaps the greatest philosophical figure to embrace a secularized form of the linearity of history (albeit in the shape of dialectic) was Hegel, who saw in the one story of mankind the gradual emergence of freedom. Marx a little later, Lowith argues, may be viewed as a secularized Jewish prophet, and Marxism as a form of Judaism. Marx's view of history, beginning with a propertyless, harmonious, benevolent world (Eden), proceeding through class struggle (history), and ending with the heaven of the withering away of the state and of private property, the restoring of Eden, is a form of "Jewish history" (with heavy Christian overlay).

Such views are not dead. Although in the United States old Christian ideas more commonly take progressive and meliorist forms, only a few years ago Francis Fukuyama, apparently with a straight face, returned to a Hegelian form of the question whether there is a direction to the history of mankind.[18] Fukuyama developed the double sense of history's end already present in Hegel. If there is a direction in history, an end in the sense of a goal, must it not follow that as we near that goal history in some sense disappears, has an end in the sense of no further development, and we remain permanently in some best state of life? Fukuyama suggested that the logic of modern science and what he, following Hegel, calls the struggle for recognition, the desire of people to leave their mark on history, have led to the collapse of tyranny and the victory of capitalist liberal democracy, the end, in both senses, of the historical process. Here, as with Hegel or Marx, we have the possibility of conquering time itself, an end of the historical process within history.

But Fukuyama retains a doubt. Will man be content in his last state, or will it prove a delusion, banal rather than satisfying, something to be fled for the satisfying terrors of history? Will liberty and equality produce a stable, ended, society, or lead inevitably to the quest for reentry into time? We need not linger over Fukuyama's undigested views. But the questions he poses illustrate rather well a kind of bastardization of Christian patterns of thought, now made the subject of some end of history imminent to the historical process itself.

Christianity, according to Lowith the most self-conscious and honest of the historical traditions on these matters because acknowledging that its views come from revelation and not from history, at least fitfully sees that its principle of historical narrative is not some inevitable framework dictated by "the facts," but an a priori by which the facts are organized. Only with Christianity's stepchildren, Hegelianism, Marxism, progressivism, did a certain forgetfulness about where the framework had come from occur, with the resultant delusion that history itself was about freedom, class struggle and its overcoming, or progress. It takes little reflection to see that many of the main components of secular presentation of history to the present, above all the idea of progress, are hardly intelligible without the Christian matrix that formed them.

Our preliminary but central observation, therefore, is that "Christian history" is a very useful phrase to articulate both the truth that all historical narrative rests on principles of selection brought to the historical record, and the truth that therefore all "history" will be organized by an adjective, whether "Christian" or something else. The Enlightenment ideal of a secular, simply worldly, history is a lie and a deceit, if its claim is that it is the only true history. Also a deceit is the closely related positivist ideal of self-interpreting facts. Like Marxism in Marxists' refusal to stand with the Christians and honestly acknowledge that their principles of interpretation rest on acts of faith, such notions are noticeable for their lack of self-consciousness

or self-understanding. In spite of all the recent attacks on the idea of historical objectivity, all attempts to say "my history is as good as yours," many of
which embrace a relativism as flawed as the naive objectivism they replace,
the Enlightenment heritage is by no means dead.[19]

Thus the modern historian, if he is to remain respectable, must, as
much as Thucydides, treat divine intervention as something other than it
claims to be. By saying for instance, that since a priori miracles cannot
occur, and that when they are met in the historical record they may safely
be explained as something else, one makes possible a safe and comfortable,
an enlightened and bourgeois "history."[20] My point is that without a priori starting points, history has virtually no shape at all, is infinitely mal-
leable or amorphous. One great merit of the idea of "Christian history" is
that it underlies the a priori nature of all historical interpretation, its
dependence on something other than a bare historical record. Now we can
turn to the claim not simply that Christianity has historically been more
honest than its competitors about what it is doing in interpreting history,
but that the a priori, the Word, it uses is superior to, more illuminating of,
man's situation in history. In a single essay one cannot be exhaustive, and
must largely speak by way of examples, making comparison not to theoretical alternatives to Christianity, but to actual alternatives today.

Nothing better illustrates the ways in which Christian theology can
deepen the understanding of history than its formation in the individual
historian of what I will call a Christian sensibility. Just as in the case of
"Christian philosophy," the claim is not that nothing is understood without viewing the evidence from a Christian perspective—obviously a great
deal is—but that a much richer sense of reality is communicated by taking
especially Christian anthropology, a Christian reading of what man is, to
heart. Above all this avoids all the silliness involved in the idea that history
has laws or is a science in any very rigorous sense of that word. A Christian perspective nurtures humility, a sense of mystery, and the gravest
doubts about all claimed historical patterns.

The chief knowledge that the Christian historian brings to history is
the glory of God. As Paul already said in the first two chapters of Romans,
some sense of this glory is open to all humans, that is, it is not specifically
Christian. But the Scriptures immensely deepen our natural sense of God's

glory by an account of His great deeds. From the scriptural record the believer discovers that the very creation was aimed at man's dominating the world and cooperating with God in co-creation.[21] The Scriptures tell us how God formed a people, that He wishes all to be saved, that He sent his only son to redeem the race, and that the Paraclete is now present in the Church. Although no clear picture is given of either the course of history after the New Testament period or of what the end is to which God is leading the race, the New Testament encourages hope as the appropriate human response to this revelation, confidence that God in His good time is accomplishing His will. As Julian of Norwich tells us Jesus told her, "all will be well, and all will be well, and every kind of thing will be well."[22]

A sense of the glory of God calls forth in the historian a sense of the mystery of history, of the mystery of God's ways. Even in the Bible, where, for Israel and the earliest stages of Christian history, we have presumably our clearest statement of what God is doing, it is all very mysterious. Constantly human expectations are overturned. The younger brother is preferred. The last shall be first. Jesus says God Himself is not simply King, but characterized by lowliness and service. Christ is at once Suffering Servant and Judge, dying Redeemer and Victor over death. Indeed it is the picture of Jesus in the Scriptures that is the heart of mystery. One reason there are so many Jesuses in later portrayal is that He escapes all easy categorization, is always so much more than any one human picture can make Him.

Certain things follow from this. Although I have some sympathy with all the attempts, from Orosius in the fifth century past Bossuet in the seventeenth, to write a Christian history in the sense of recounting what God continues to do in time, I am as suspicious of these as was Augustine of Eusebius, the founder of the genre. Even the best flatten the mystery. Some distinctions are in order. The Christian believes that he has certain kinds of insight into God's will, formed by the scriptural account and the reflection of the Church. Thus the Christian follows Genesis in believing that humans have been made to rule the earth, he follows Exodus in believing that he has been given commandments to obey, and he follows Matthew in believing that he has been called to some form of perfection. In some measures the Christian knows what it is to do God's will, and what it is to violate it.

Presumably, therefore, he can say something truly when he says "Here God's will is done," or "Here it is not." Such knowledge, though enough to guide a single life, falls far short of being able to "read history" from God's side, to tell us what God is doing in the present. We know something of what He wishes done, but hardly anything of how His will works. From Creation through the death and resurrection of Christ, the coming of the Spirit of Pentecost, and the earliest Christian mission the Scriptures themselves give a reading of history, of certain events that are central to history's interpretation. But there is nothing comparable to this once the New Testament account ends. It is not that nothing at all can be said, for as Eusebius showed, ecclesiastical history can be written.

The history of attempts to continue to respond to God's will, the history of ecclesiastical institutions, the history of the spread of the Gospel, the history of reflection on the Gospel, all these things are possible. We might also say, to jump to the modern period, that Hegel is possible, that is, that one may take a theme deriving from Christianity, such as the spread of freedom, and using this as one's principle of selection, write its history. Here the possible theologies of history are endless and include, for instance, a reading of history according to liberation theology. They are as good as their principles of selection are adequate to capturing the whole Christian message.

Augustine's doubts about Eusebian history were not doubts that one could write ecclesiastical history at all, but doubts that one could with any certitude specify God's will, for instance, saying that Constantine's reign represented the culmination to which history has been moving. The Christian believes that God is always at work in history, but Augustine did not see that this gives specific information of the kind Eusebius retailed. Augustine believed God is at work in everything, constantly bringing good from evil, but danger lay in the unqualified claim, made about any historical force or party, "this is the will of God." Everything in time, every individual, as well as the Church itself, is mixed, composed of good and evil. Therefore while some timeless principle, say the first commandment, may express the will of God without reservation, nothing born of time can be anything but mixed. Moreover, because everything is in some sense the will of God, the question, if one is to write a Christian history in the manner initiated by Eusebius, is not whether God is working in all things, but how he is working. Here, beyond such things as chronicling the keeping of the commandments or tracing the spread of the Gospel, Augustine thought the Christian has no "methodology" for discovering God's ways.

He himself had felt the call by God in the garden, what Gregory the Great (590–604) was to call the goad of the Spirit and Calvin in the sixteenth century a sense of vocation. Julian of Norwich, around 1400, thought Jesus spoke to her. Such things could tell one what to do with one's life, might even as at Fatima in the twentieth century give some specific prophecy, but again did not give the kind of information by which a reading of one's times could be attempted with much confidence. One might even, in the spirit of Herbert Butterfield, go a little further and doubt that even on the relatively simple question of one person keeping one commandment, a historian can "read hearts," that is, know enough about a single human being to render a certain judgment on motivation.[23] What indeed does it mean to trace the spread of the Gospel?

The historian can count baptisms given, communions taken, and saints reformed. Yet, important as these are, the deepest movements of the Spirit seem out of grasp. The theologies of history and Christian histories, therefore, are best read as speculative attempts to guess what history might be about, and attempts to dig below the surface. They, though not unimportant, are always inadequate. We return to the point that "Christian history," looking at history from the vantage point of Christianity, first should foster a sense of mystery, rather than Christian histories. In some degree, all the great Christian histories obscure God's nature, make things too clear, too easily take sides, or see only one side.

This said, Christian history—here the parallel with Christian philosophy is exact—understood as the examination of history in the light of Christianity, can give a more adequate and very differently textured account of human events than that normally found in academic history, which is still very much the child of the Enlightenment. A Christian anthropology is quite different from an Enlightenment anthropology, and the two result in different histories. I remember that Arthur Schlesinger, Jr., a quintessential liberal son of the Enlightenment, said after serving in the Kennedy White House that he, the author of many stout volumes on various aspects of the American presidency, now realized that the history of no presidency could be written.

By this I supposed he meant not that nothing could be said, but that now that he had experienced how presidential decisions are made, he understood that what the historian considers documents are poor evidence of what took place. It is not just that the documents may contain disinformation and obfuscation, but that the heart of decisions taken is likely and intentionally not found there at all. I cannot see that this momentary insight much affected how Schlesinger continued to view history, but it shows that even a non-Christian writer momentarily saw the benefit of writing "Christian history." By that I mean that the narratives of the Enlightenment commonly deceive by their suggestion that a historian can confidently chronicle great human events. In contrast, the narratives of Christianity—of Augustine's, not Bossuet's, form of Christianity—profoundly enlighten by suggesting that, since God is the author of history and his purposes are largely hidden, all history is mysterious and chronicled only in hesitation. They communicate what life, seen through a glass darkly rather than by a futurologist in a department of sociology, is really like. They are never confident about reductionist explanations, "explaining" things as "really" issues of power, class, or gender. They suspect all the simplifying, non-mysterious accounts of the Marxists, liberals, social historians, and feminists.[24]

These seem hardly human at all, accounts written in great hubris, as if one had found the key that unlocks the mystery of life. Certainly, as Anthony Burgess has shown, one does not have to be a practicing Christian to see the rightness of the doctrine of original sin, of man's cross-grained nature. There are, even in academia, historians with a sense of human complexity. But the assertion that at the heart of man there is a mystery grounded in the struggle between good and evil is the lantern held before the Christian historian. He or she does not expect life to be something that can be successfully planned, something in which there is much connection between what we want and what we get. This could be so only if we are the authors of history.

The doctrine of original sin points in two ways, articulating both mankind's degradation and grandeur. We are not simply sinners, but sons of God, called to divinization. We can plan, and our plans do not always go astray. They achieve their goals sufficiently to encourage us in keeping to the course. Even according to the rules of the Enlightenment, the study of history well pays our efforts. Much more than this, there are moments in life of transcendence, of surpassing grace. This grandeur in life, the glory of God that runs through things, seems also not present in much historical writing. The favorable implications of our cross-grained nature are as much missed by the sons of the Enlightenment as the unfavorable. That is, just as the tragedy and limitations of human life, its lack of control over the future or failure to understand its own times, commonly are not at the center of academic history, which in treating even subjects for which there is "no exit" tends to retain an air of optimism, neither is the sense of genuine goodness in life often communicated.

Granted, striking and variegated goodness is less common than mediocrity or active evil. But it is almost as if the secular historian does not know what to do with the goodness—or the strangeness—he comes across. Again, we tend to get a flattened history not attendant to the striking differences between people. I can only guess that egalitarian premises have so influenced modern historians that they tend not to be alert here. Moralizing abounds, Hitler gets condemned, but little attention is given to the forms of heroic goodness that are encountered in everyday life. Christianity, by contrast, with its sense of the unique mission given to each person, makes one suspicious of theories that see humans as interchangeable or equal and predisposes one to sympathy for hierarchical systems, thus for noticing the great differences between people. I will not belabor the point, but part of the sense of mystery Christian history fosters is an awe before the extraordinary goodness—always so far as we can judge—one sometimes meets in the historical record.

The very categories of "development" and "progress," constantly used by the children of the Enlightenment, will be deeply suspect by the Christian historian. Although he will see how such notions trace their lineage back to Christian ideas such as Providence, he will also see that they radically flatten such ideas and again pretend that history can be read as a clear story. Thoughtful examination of history in fact raises the gravest doubts about whether there has been general progress. Meditation on a theology of history such as that of Hans Urs von Balthasar should lead to a questioning of the general presentation of history under the category of "development."[25] I do not mean that we can or should get rid of all mechanical and organic metaphors of change, but that, if one examines any substantial part of the historical record, such metaphors seem to capture only a small part of what is happening.

Taking just the biblical record as an example, the category of the unexpected, of the jump or quantum leap, but also of the about face, is at least as important as any developmental category. One can know all there is to be known about the development of Hebrew thought and be unprepared for what the book of Isaiah says. And how much silliness has been written in the eminently justifiable search for development in the New Testament, say from a low to a high Christology? Not everything should be forced into the mold of development. In this case it would be better to see the New Testament writers as something like the Elders of the Apocalypse, who are often placed with the Gospel writers on Romanesque tympana, sitting, chatting, perhaps, with their instruments in hand, ready to make music, with Christ in the middle. There is high and low from the beginning in this assembly, this choir of the blessed, points of view as well as development, differing perspectives as far back as we can see. Each evangelist sees a part of the mystery: Four are better than one.

The Savior Himself seems hardly bound by the categories of time and space at all, and moves in and out of our world. Categories of development and, especially, of progress, convey very little of the whole. The Christian historian studies with this always before him. Further, he knows that, like his Enlightenment brother, he first sees the surface, the literal sense of Scripture or, so to speak, the human nature of Christ. But he believes this is far less than the whole: The literal sense of Scripture opens on the spiritual sense, the human nature of Christ is wedded to the divine.[26] In sum, although history is more amorphous than philosophy, "Christian history" stands to the one as "Christian philosophy" does to the other, both as historical reality and as sobering insight. Gilson thought "Christian philosophy" made its own case, that any fair-minded person could see how Christianity had historically deepened philosophical perception. "Christian history" makes the same claim about understanding history. ◆

PART

II

God at the Center
of History: A Purview
of Permanence

Banning the Supernatural: Why Historians Must Not Rule Out the Action of God In History

Warren H. Carroll

SCHOLARLY history as written today, and for the past forty years, has banned everything supernatural as though it were an intellectual plague. The very possibility of action by God in history has become academically taboo. This prohibition applies not only to miracles and apparitions, but even to the power of prayer. So universal is this ban, so chilling its effect even on the minds of historians who personally believe in the supernatural, that its imposition has gone virtually unchallenged the past forty years. Indeed, in all honesty I must say that since I began writing scholarly Catholic history fourteen years ago I have found no other contemporary historian who writes in defiance of this ban.

This situation cannot be allowed to continue. For our Christian and Catholic faith is preeminently a historical faith. We believe that God, the Creator and Sustainer of the universe, entered history, incarnate as the man Jesus Christ, at a particular time and place. No other religion has ever claimed that. In G. K. Chesterton's words:

> Right in the middle of all these things stands up an enormous exception
> . . . nothing less than the loud assertion that this mysterious maker of the
> world has visited his world in person. It declares that really and even
> recently, or right in the middle of historic times, there did walk into the
> world this original invisible being, about whom the thinkers make theories

This article was previous published in *The Catholic Social Science Review*, vol. 1 (1996) and is reprinted here with the permission of the author and the *Review*.

and the mythologists hand down myths; the Man Who Made the World. That such a higher personality exists behind all things had indeed always been implied by all the best thinkers, as well as by all the most beautiful legends. But nothing of this sort had been implied in any of them. It is simply false to say that the other sages and heroes had claimed to be that mysterious master and maker of whom the world had dreamed and disputed. Not one of them had ever claimed to be anything of the sort. Not one of their sects or schools had ever claimed that they had claimed to be anything of the sort. The most that any religious prophet had said was that he was the true servant of such a being. The most that any visionary had ever said was that men might catch glimpses of the glory of that spiritual being; or much more often of lesser spiritual beings. The most that any primitive myth had ever suggested was that the Creator was present at the Creation. But that the Creator was present at scenes a little subsequent to the supper parties of Horace, and talked with tax collectors and government officials in the detailed daily life of the Roman Empire, and that this fact continued to be firmly asserted by the whole of that great civilization for more than a thousand years—that is something utterly unlike anything else. . . . It makes nothing but dust and nonsense of comparative religion.[1]

If that is our faith, we should never allow ourselves to be persuaded or pressured to consent to any field of study—especially history—being declared off limits to it. Rather we should say, with Dom Prosper Gueranger:

> History ought to be Christian, if it is to be true: for Christianity is the truth complete; and every historical system which disregards the supernatural order in its explanation and evaluation of the facts, is a false system which explains nothing, and which leaves the annals of humanity in chaos and a permanent contradiction with all the ideas that reason forms on the destinies of our race here below.[2]

From the first Catholic historian, Eusebius of Caesarea, through St. Augustine's magisterial *City of God*, to Caesar Baronius, the first modern Catholic historian, and Bossuet's *Discours sur l'histoire universelle*, and on down to the middle of this twentieth century with the works of Belloc, Chesterton, and William Thomas Walsh, strong and indeed mighty voices were always heard telling history from the Catholic viewpoint, which puts God and His Son and the Church He founded at the center of history. But the last great avowedly Catholic historian, Christopher Dawson, was much more cautious, seeking academic acceptance as he was for his presentation of Christian culture; and since Dawson, even Catholic historians have generally accepted, without even a protest, the academic ban on the supernatural, which consequently now reigns supreme.

Let us look at seven examples of how it works.

The first concerns the great Old Testament prophet Isaiah. A hypothesis elaborately built up over the past hundred years and now generally accepted by both Scripture scholars and ancient historians holds that there were two, or possibly even three, Isaiahs. Though this hypothesis is defended by linguistic and literary-critical arguments with which I am not fully competent to deal, even a cursory reading of the works of its advocates shows their principal premise to be that prophecy which actually predicts the future (and which therefore, if more than mere coincidence, must be of supernatural origin) cannot occur. A writing that names, as Isaiah does, a deliverer 175 years in the future (King Cyrus of Persia) must, by definition, have been written after that deliverer actually came. In a rare recognition of the fact that Catholics believe God does know the future and sometimes reveals this knowledge to men, the *Jerusalem Bible's* Introduction to the Prophets states:

> Almighty God could, of course, have conveyed the prophet into the distant future, severing him from his own time, transforming his imagery and cast of thought. This would mean, however, a duplication of the author's personality and a disregard for his contemporaries—to whom, after all, he was sent—for which the Bible provides no parallel.[3]

This astonishing statement not only disregards the continuity of history (why would Isaiah's personality be "duplicated" by receiving a revelation?) and the self-evident utility of prophecy that comes true, but is flatly wrong in asserting that such prophecy is found only in Isaiah. Jeremiah correctly predicted the fall of Babylon; Daniel correctly predicted the eventual total ruin and desolation of Babylon and Tyre; Jesus himself predicted that within the lifetime of some of his hearers the Temple of Jerusalem would be totally destroyed, as it was forty years later. But reason and even common sense must give way, it seems, in the face of anything or anyone challenging the ban on the supernatural.

No such simple solution as multiplying the prophet is available for scholars studying the New Testament from the anti-supernatural position. The Gospels in particular are full of miracles, and above all point to the Great Miracle, the Incarnation itself, crowned by the Resurrection. The extraordinary, long-continued, and still vehement campaign against their authenticity as history constitutes the second and most important example of scholarly prejudice against the supernatural.

It is understandable, though very sad, to see Catholic historians and teachers overwhelmed by the blizzard of destructive criticism of the New Testament in general and the Gospels in particular, seeking refuge in the dictum that the Gospels were not intended to be history, but works of faith. Of course they were and are more than histories, but they are not less than history. The events they describe really happened. They pass all the critical tests historians apply to contested early documents. Internal, external, and manuscript evidence prove at least two of them (Matthew and John) to have been written by those apostles, who were eyewitnesses.[4] The four Gospels confirm each other on all major points, while differing enough in details to make it clear they were not copied from each other. The chronological systems by which Luke and John date events at the beginning of Christ's public ministry, beginning at completely different starting points, converge on precisely the same year, A.D. 27–28.[5] Their story is independently verified by a non-Christian source in the Old Slavonic edition of Josephus's *The Jewish War.*[6]

But if one accepts the Gospels as authentic historical documents, confirming and reinforcing one another, they are more likely to command belief in the supernatural events they describe. So it is that any arguments challenging their authenticity become academically correct, while those sustaining their authenticity are not to be heard.[7]

A third example of the rejection of the supernatural in modern history is provided by the extensive historical literature on St. Joan of Arc. We are fortunate in possessing an unusually large volume of contemporary documentary evidence on St. Joan, notably the complete transcript of her trial for heresy in 1431, which led to her conviction and death at the stake. The fundamental issue in her trial and in her mission was whether it was in fact of supernatural origin. Her prosecutor, Bishop Pierre Cauchon of Beauvais, assembled an enormous staff consisting of a cardinal, 6 bishops, 32 doctors of theology, 16 bachelors, 7 doctors of medicine, and 103 other associates, all to prepare questions for and to interrogate this illiterate nineteen-year-old peasant girl, who was not allowed a single counselor.

The principal purpose of these 165 prosecutors was to prove Joan a fraud and impostor, or at least a psychologically unbalanced person suffering from auditory hallucinations. By universal agreement, they failed. Most modern historians writing of Joan lack the will or the courage to affirm a belief in the objective reality of her "voices," but the best of them firmly reject all alternative explanations of them, which logically leaves no choice but to believe she spoke the truth. The fashionable and fanciful psychological and physiological explanations bear almost no resemblance to the real Joan, whom we know so well from the memoirs of her contemporaries and especially from her trial transcript.[8]

The fourth example comes from the early life of the great Queen Isabel the Catholic of Spain, when she was still only a princess of Castile. In 1466 the Marques of Villena, the most powerful nobleman in Castile, pressured Isabel's hapless and incompetent half-brother, King Henry IV, into ordering her to marry Villena's own brother, Pedro Giron, a man of the vilest reputation. Villena even persuaded the Pope (Paul II) to agree to the marriage by dispensing Giron from his obligation of celibacy as a soldier-monk of the Order of Calatrava (though he had hardly been known for observance of that obligation). Isabel, just fifteen years old, her father dead and her mother insane, had nowhere to turn for help or protection, but to God. And to God she went.

For a full day and night she was on her knees, praying, over and over, that God would not let this obscene union happen, but would prevent it by taking either Giron's life or hers. Giron was riding northward to claim his bride. He would arrive and marry her in less than a month. But on the road, immediately after her day of prayer, he sickened, and in three days he died.

There is no lack of contemporary documentation of these events. All the major chroniclers of the time mention the planned marriage, Isabel's reaction, and the death of Giron following so swiftly upon her prayers.[9] One modern historian commenting on the manuscript of my biography of Queen Isabel, which includes an account of these events, with a brief reminder of the power of prayer, said it made him "very uneasy." The great taboo had been violated.

The fifth example—actually a group of examples—concerns the modern apparitions of the Blessed Virgin Mary that are authenticated historically: Our Lady of Guadalupe in Mexico in 1531, Our Lady of Lourdes in 1858, and Our Lady of Fatima in 1917. These apparitions were accompanied by some of the most spectacular visible miracles since Christ was on earth: the portrait of Our Lady of Guadalupe, which may still be seen in Mexico City, whose survival and composition cannot be naturally explained,[10] which was followed by nine million baptisms of Indians in the next fifteen years; the spring opened by St. Bernadette Soubirous at Lourdes at the Blessed Virgin Mary's command, with its hundreds of carefully investigated, scientifically verified miracles of healing;[11] and the "dance" of the sun in the sky at Fatima in Portugal, on October 13, 1917, which was seen by thousands of people and cannot be naturally explained, after the Blessed Virgin Mary had warned the Fatima children on July 13 that the evil coming out of Russia would sweep the world and bring much suffering to the Church.[12] But one will find little if any reference to these events, well authenticated as they are, in general histories of Mexico, France, Portugal, and the West; if a reference is made, it is always condescending and superficial, without any indication that apparitions and associated miracles could actually have happened. The report on the nine million baptisms in Robert Ricard's history of the conversion of Mexico makes no mention of Our Lady of Guadalupe.[13] Until the appearance of my *1917: Red Banners, White Mantle*, no history including substantial material on World War I, the Communist Revolution in Russia, and other political events of 1917 had mentioned the apparitions at Fatima.

The sixth example concerns not the action of God, but of the Devil— if possible even more a taboo subject among late twentieth-century historians than God. It is the death—or, rather, the repeated failures to die—of the so-called monk Rasputin in Petrograd (now again St. Petersburg), then the capital of Russia, in December 1916. Rasputin had gained almost complete personal ascendancy over the mind of the Tsaritsa Alexandra and through her, over her weak husband Nicholas II, last of the Tsars. Rasputin's domination and known evil character destroyed much of the popular respect for the Tsar and thus helped bring about the Communist Revolution in Russia. Unable to break Rasputin's grip on the all-powerful Tsar in the midst of a world war, a group of Russian patriots decided that their only recourse was to kill Rasputin. Through almost all of the night of December 30, they tried to do so.

The events of that horrifying night are amply documented. We have two firsthand accounts by eyewitnesses, Prince Felix Yusupov and Vladimir Purishkevich.[14] There was also a written report on the autopsy of Rasputin's body when it was recovered from under the ice of the Neva River, read and commented upon at the time, though it has since disappeared. Rasputin had eaten three cakes and drunk two glasses of Madeira wine, each containing a lethal dose of cyanide—one of the fastest-acting and deadliest poisons known—prepared by a doctor. He had been shot near the heart and in the neck, both wounds later pronounced mortal by medical examiners. He had been beaten over the head with a two-pound lead weighted stick, and his head was broken by impact with one of the supports of the bridge over which he was thrown into the Neva River, bound hand and foot. By then he had died six to eight times. But he was still alive and breathing and struggling to escape under the water and the ice, before his lungs filled with water and he drowned.

Rasputin's previous behavior as well as his survival of so many deaths that night strongly indicate demonic possession. Though most historians writing about Russia during 1916 and 1917 refer to Rasputin's death, and some describe it at length, not one even mentions the possibility of demonic possession.[15] Yet the evidence for supernatural action is so strong that only one historian, Richard Pipes, tries to offer a rationalistic explanation. He cites the statement in the vanished autopsy report that no poison was found in the body, declaring that this shows that no poison had been administered (but a power capable of blocking the action of cyanide could do so by removing it as well as simply neutralizing it) while ignoring the report's avowal, also vouched for by those who read it prior to its disappearance, that the body did have water in its lungs and hence that Rasputin was still alive when he went under the ice.[16]

The seventh and final example brings us almost to the present day: the fall of the Soviet Union and its Communist system of power, which Alexander Solzhenitsyn once called "inhumanly strong," devised by Lenin and apparently unbreakable. As late as the beginning of the year the Communist collapse began, 1989, not a single authority on the Soviet Union— and from a lifetime during which I have done much work in Soviet studies, I knew of most of them—ever thought that this system would fall so soon, so quickly, with so little loss of life. It is very hard to find any natural explanation to account for it. I believe it to have been a specific answer to prayer—the prayers especially of the Slavic Pope John Paul II, and of the millions of Catholic and Orthodox Christian victims of the system whom it had imprisoned.

At one critical moment in the last stage of the collapse, the failure of the August 1991 coup to overthrow Gorbachev and restore full Communist power in the Soviet Union, an important incident occurred that appears to have been the direct result of the power of prayer. On the third night of the coup, its makers sent helicopters to land on the roof of the Russian parliament building where Boris Yeltsin and his supporters held out against them. Tens of thousands of people had surrounded the building with a human chain that soldiers, trucks, and tanks would not cross. But they had no anti-aircraft weapons. Nothing could stop the helicopters from landing on the roof but a downpour of rain. Fr. Gleb Yakunin, a survivor of the Soviet prison camps, a devotee of Our Lady of Fatima, stepped forward and prayed for rain, and a downpour of rain came. The helicopters did not land on the roof of the parliament building.[17]

General Konstantin Kobets, chairman of the Russian parliamentary commission building, was convinced that this rain came in direct response to Fr. Yakunin's prayer. But no Christian historian has dared to suggest even the possibility. It was left to journalist David Remmick, a Jew, to speak of "the blessed rain" on this extraordinary occasion.[18]

Reviewing these examples, and the state of mind they reflect among both non-Christian and Christian historians, is not intended to suggest that Christian historians should fall into the opposite error of undue credulity. There are many more spurious apparitions and alleged miracles than genuine ones. Historians must apply all genuine critical standards of scholarship when dealing with these reports. But the arbitrary a priori assumption that apparitions and miracles and the Incarnation itself could not have happened, that historical events never transcend the natural order, is not a critical standard. It is a flagrant bias that ought to be firmly rejected. Jettisoning this prejudice is a reasonable and fair position to demand even from non-Christian historians. For the Christian historian it is nothing less than a duty. In the hard-hitting but just words of Dom Gueranger:

> The Christian has not only a duty to believe, but also a duty to confess what he believes. This double obligation, founded in the doctrine of the Apostle [Paul] (Rom. X, 10), is the more binding in ages of naturalism, and the Christian historian ought to understand that it is not enough for him to declare his belief, in passages here and there in his book, if its Christian character then immediately disappears.[19]   ♦

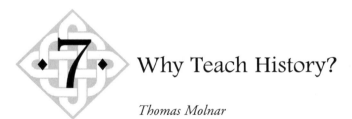

Why Teach History?

Thomas Molnar

O N two recent occasions, in 1993 and again in 1994, publishers in France requested that I send them an essay for books of which the collective titles were, respectively, *On the Right of the Father* and *Why Do You Believe in God?* I am the only non-Frenchman in both volumes (each about three hundred pages); thus I had the opportunity to read a total of some 170 responses, as it were, from outside. The respondents belong to the intellectual class, with writers such as Gustave Thibon and Jean Raspail, army generals, well-known lawyers and jurists, bishops and theologians, businessmen and journalists, artists and housewives. The only connecting link is their Catholicism; otherwise they are active or in retirement, are serving the public as professors or ambassadors, with much travel behind them, or are well-rooted parish priests.

I am not addicted to statistics nor to polls, but it was easy to cull from the entries a general impression of the near totality of the obviously honest answers. The overwhelming conclusions after reading through twenty-eight long interviews (the first volume) and through a hundred and thirty-four answers (the second volume), with few overlaps between the two books, was the following. These believing and mostly practicing Catholics attributed their faith and the integrity of their lives to three factors, hardly noticing the fourth factor that sprang to my eyes from the lines. The first faith-shaping influence is the *family*, its joined faith and practice, its unity, its heart-warming atmosphere. The second driving force is *schooling*, which, far from undermining belief, strengthened it through intelligent and subtle teachers. The third was the encounter with one or more *priests* who introduced the child or adolescent to profundities of the faith, but to the same extent, to a wide horizon in which religion and the life of the Church made additional sense, by awakening the young curiosity and answering its questions and doubts. Almost entirely the 162 responses developed these themes, before turning to individually nuanced life-spans characterizing personal experiences.

The fourth inducement that none mentioned, but that I found with increasing delight, is the broad area of what may be called "cultural reference." Whether Michele Morgan, the great actress (you remember her from films with Charles Boyer and Jean Gabin), the much younger Dom Gerard, abbot of St. Madeleine Benedictine monastery in the Provence, or Yves Congar, the theologian, the respondents practically meet in their knowledge of literature, art, history, and a number of auxiliary disciplines. Let's be clear about it: They do not show off their knowledge; it is absolutely natural to them that, next to religion, they were taught as young persons all that an educated man or woman must know. And now they use this knowledge not as the sign of anything, but as a matter-of-fact reference in conversation, interview, memory, and the writing of a short essay.

I venture to say that their religious sensitivities have developed in a parallel way to their educated culture, one helping the other, enriching it, deepening it. I repeat: They are not aware of their culture, and for the time being they concentrate on the origin and nature of their faith; they express the contents of their soul together with the contents of their mind—a harmonious and organic ensemble we used to call a cultured person.

The prominent part of this faith-and-culture (although I am reluctant to use this formula) is, without a doubt, the intimate acquaintance with *history*. I do not mean only dates and battles, the usual caricature reference, although that too is essential, for example to situate St. Anselm and Pascal, the Septuagint and St. Bernard, the reasons why Romanic architecture metamorphosed into Gothic, or what do the Council of Trent and the baroque inspiration have in common. I mean history as an ocean in which all people and events swim or are anchored like islands. There is no solid knowledge and thus education, nor culture and Christian culture, without a very thorough foundation in history.

One of our better Catholic colleges here in America, misled by the idolatry of the Great Books, years ago decided it would not teach history in its "core curriculum" because this discipline is not "scientific" according to Aristotle. Scientific or not, history is an essential part of education. Can we imagine St. Augustine without the history that is also his life: consciousness of time, growth and decrepitude, accumulated wisdom, discernment, taste? And a propos of the *Confessions* or of Newman's *Development of Dogma*, is there any better proof that without the comprehension and the internal living of *times* we are like ephemeral insects, or worse, machines, not living and remembering and projecting, but crawling on a dimensionless surface?

For a Catholic, history is a vital element of his faith. Paul VI reminded us—and the ignorant, malevolent contemporaries—that the Christian religion is a documented part of history, a fact constantly denied by the erudite, who anyway despise history and certainly the "past," irrespective of their puny ambitions. While the now fashionable religions wrap their origin in obscurity and their raison d'etre in myth, Christianity is present in Roman imperial records, in the testimonies of people near and far, in internal evidence. How else do we gather certitude if not *also* from history?

Why then must one argue that the teaching of history is the first building block of intelligent manhood? Simply put, because we live in a Utopia whose first condition of building is that history is denied, everything starts from scratch, *hic et nunc* with social sciences, condoms, and lesbian armies. All these initiatives are shamed by historical knowledge; the latter must therefore be erased together with the rest of the record. We are told (for example by a Richard Rorty) that the past cannot teach us anything; man is a floating individual thing, just right to be part of the consensus. Even less: Man is a condensation point of some electromagnetic fields, at a crossroad of chance, events with no more inner life than a computer. Indeed, history is then nothing more than an echo of the Big Bang, a faintly captured murmur of the spaces whose silence so frightened Pascal's freethinkers.

It is strange that teaching now in post-Communist Budapest, I can take it for granted that my students know a great deal about history, the world's and their own nation's. They even know enough to pinpoint the ideological tricks by which the Communist authorities tried to present a false history, rewritten for their own Utopia. Yet, these authorities did not think for a minute to deny history and its relevance; they respected history, being aware of the requirements of the human mind to situate itself in the current of time. Many times I find, in discussion with the remnant of Marxist students, that their knowledge of history is precise, up-to-date, even fertile, and with some modifications, explains events if not adequately, at least intelligently. Thus one can teach them, re-presenting history according to different standards than the ones they are used to. New discussions follow that are usually fruitful.

Nothing of the sort in this country, which seems to have given up its national consciousness, exchanging such for a collection of conformist habits. Yet, there is no history without the nation whose unified being it expresses. There is no planetary history either, only juxtaposed national histories, or the history of well-profiled institutions, nuclei of a vigorous idea and its unitary unraveling. No wonder that we teach less and less history, and that Catholic schools follow the general trend. For something to be taught and learned it must be worthwhile. Not only in time, also as a meaning, a symbol, as an object of admiration.

In proportion as the Church divests itself of the external signs of its universal presence at the heart of history, its significance in time also collapses, because this significance used to be sustained by symbols, monuments, great ceremonies, and the mystical dimensions of liturgies. All of these are today veiled, if not denied and called an embarrassment. Why should Church history be taught when the "other" history is also underplayed—television is interested exclusively in the given moment—and thus the marvelous interaction between history and the superadded sacred history cancelled? The element of wonder and marvel that ultimately justifies what we want to learn and undertake is absent from history and its teaching. We may deplore it, but concrete proposals are in my opinion wasted without an underlying historical consciousness, present in teachers, students, and society around them.

A desacralized society first discards its history because history in itself has something sacred in it, namely the *past*, which is unchangeable, thus awe-inspiring. Particularly is this the case when the society in question, ours, regards itself as above history, a luminous point in the darkness, a terminus of old aberrations and a beginning of a planetary, even cosmic, adventure, the locus of the Big Bang. A certain Dr. Richard Gott, of Princeton University, recently suggested with a straight face that since planet Earth is polluted and (historically) bloodstained, mankind ought to move to a new location in "our" galaxy! How do you expect Dr. Gott's (the well-named) students to register for history courses, that is, for the story of a degraded and shelved temporary place of settlement? They would prefer Astronomy or Space Travel 101, which tells them about an extremely hypothetical future in a truly Utopian curriculum.

In short, the study of history needs a favorable intellectual atmosphere and a respect, not to say reverence, for things old, not because of the number of years that have marked them (although that is a non-negligible factor), but because man is inseparable from history, unless he is brainwashed and artificially separated from the roots where his being is immersed. The question is really this: Without such an atmosphere of reverence, which we are unable to create by any magic or by promise of heaps of dollars for an illusory "reform of education," can we realistically envisage a revival of history teaching? Not unexpectedly, only under the aegis of the Church could such a thing be undertaken. The Church is the only institution in this society of future-orientedness that is rooted in the past and whose vocation is to regard *man* and *mankind* in a historical framework. Church history displays the unity of faith; it not only chronicles an uninterrupted message with clearly contoured messengers, it also reaches from the first couple to Judgment Day and beyond. Every act in the mystical body is indelible; one leads to the other in responsibility and freedom. This chronicle is at all points intermingled with a mysterious counter-chronicle, that of sin and evil, without giving in to them, yet taking them into consideration and offering reintegration. Through this history—not only a dry chronicle but events with meaning—one is treated to a daily lesson of understanding human motives, passions, sacrifice, suffering, and glory.

I had a professor of Roman history at the University of Brussels who told us he should not teach us since we are too young for the lessons of history. Before the age of forty, that is, when experience has accumulated, history is viewed as too aloof, irrelevant, abstract. At the time, I hardly

understood; by forty I thought he had been right; now I disagree in retrospect because my alleged un-historical mindset at twenty-four was also
part of my process of maturing. I know now that I too had a "history" and
that any lack of receptivity at the time *was* an aspect of that history.

Once we agree that the only reasonable teaching of history must be
the initiative of the Church—or at least the spirit of Catholicism—the
next question is whether we can do it by imitating what the Church did
when, overnight, it became the administrative and intellectual guide of the
Roman empire. The answer is, we cannot. The Church schools themselves
were a continuation of the *paideia* and the *humanites*; the foundations
were Plato, the Stoics, and Cicero and the poets and rhetoricians. Augustine himself was a rhetor; he acquired his knowledge and curiosity in the
Roman schools. The Church had an old master in pedagogy and the
admiration for old truths that neither Augustine nor Jerome would give
up. Augustine's exclamation before his North African coast at sunset car-
ries an inimitable echo to our days: "I know that Nature is un-redeemed,
but oh how beautiful it is!" The perfect integration of paganism and
Christianity.

This state of mind we do not possess, nor the time that Church schools
had at their disposal up to the scriptoria and the cathedral schools of
Charlemagne and Alcuin. Nor did we inherit, admiringly for the past, our
past, the foundations for the trivium and the quadrivium that *paideia* and
humanitas had left as a legacy. So we must begin in the atmosphere not of
humble paganism with which we may have so much in common, but in
the atmosphere of a triumphant and arrogant paganism: liberalism, technology, Utopia. Yet the task is clear. If we want educated Christians, we
must begin with "monasteries." Not the existing institutions, themselves
tempted by radical secularization, but small schools, one class, with voluntary candidates of all ages. Look at the sects: New Age feminism, earth-
worship, orgies. How easily they recruit and train, although their "classes"
of sensitivity are ephemeral and will collapse in short order. Why not set up
schools teaching history, developing unashamedly with no federal funds
and authorizations? They could feature voluntary classes, not sporadic and
precarious, but institutionalized ones. Teaching history, they of course
would be creating the receptive mind by investing the senses with art,

music, monuments, symbolic expression—linking all that to the life of faith, wonder and admiration. No jealous and envious side-glance to the sciences, psychology, sociology, and the incomparable greatness of our centuries of technical progress would be present. History would be seen as a human dimension, the unraveling of God's plan in a forever transformed world, with themes as in a symphony pulled together the way the conductor and orchestra do, humbly following the composer's partition.

I do not say that this is all we must do to return history to ahistorical sensibilities, to children of twenty-first-century America. But it would be a beginning of making the ground fertile again. America desperately needs good examples, not bigger television screens, not more dollars, not the organization man's promises and profits: good examples, links with the past, with reverence, so that the child should not have to remain a cultural outcast, constantly lied to, misguided toward false idols, blocked and stifled by outlooks on commercial entrepreneurship.

This is not the place for an outline of programs. But one thing is obvious. What destroys the little history teaching that goes on here and there is the shallow offering of a course or two that follows the scrapbook approach: a little "history" of Rome, another bit of the "history" of Japan's industrialization, or the "history" of the Third World since decolonization. This is not teaching but primitive indoctrination, ultimately *fun*. History, as we said, is about time, permanence, and change. It can be assimilated as a continuity, a *reprise* again and again on several levels, in different registers. History begins at the beginning, ends today (no "end of history" tomorrow); it must be approached quasi-catechetically: all of it so that the atomized mind of the young in our society should at least be told that history is about God and man, with nothing to skip, nothing to ignore. It is on historical consciousness that we can build the rest of the curriculum and can educate civilized man and woman. Nothing less suffices. ♦

Things Hidden since the Beginning of the World

James Hitchcock

As with so many aspects of Catholic higher education, the disappearance of "Catholic history" in the past thirty years, while justified as a sign of a new intellectual maturity, was in fact the opposite—a panicky impulse motivated by insecurity before the larger secular culture.

The ideal of historical "objectivity," first formulated by the "scientific" historians of the nineteenth century, was always misleading, in that such objectivity, implying the complete absence of personal feeling on the part of the scholar, would be possible only with respect to subjects that the scholar found uninteresting, even perhaps trivial. Almost by definition an interesting and important subject calls forth a personal response from anyone approaching it.

More realistically, many scholars now believe that their ideal ought to be honesty, a personal response that nonetheless strives to use evidence with scrupulous fairness and to reach conclusions based on the evidence, even though those conclusions might make the scholar uncomfortable.

In fact almost all great historical scholarship has been biased in certain respects, that is, based on the historian's point of view, although often (as, for example, with the "Whig" interpretation of English history) not recognized as such by the historian himself. As Herbert Butterfield, one of the most astute historians of historiography, has put it, even an overtly polemical approach to history sometimes reveals aspects of the subject neglected

This article was originally published in the journal *Touchstone*, and is published here with permission of the author.

by others.[1] Even someone who is regarded as a crank may by his single-mindedness focus attention on things no one else noticed.

Even as Catholics were surrendering the right to have their own history, that is, a history overtly informed by a Catholic viewpoint, the legitimacy, indeed the inevitability, of this kind of scholarship was being urged as normative in the secular academy. Black history, women's history, homosexual history, and numerous other kinds are now enshrined, each resting on the privileged assertion that only persons who belong to a particular social group can adequately understand that group's history and that scholars outside the group are irredeemably insensitive or prejudiced. The claim of women's history, for example, is that all of history needs to be interpreted from a feminist perspective and that those who do not are morally irresponsible and intellectually deficient.

The continuing intellectual immaturity of the Catholic universities is revealed in the fact that, almost without exception, they have embraced this approach to scholarship even as they have systematically expunged all evidence of a "ghetto mentality" with respect to their own religious past.

Liberalism defines itself in terms of intellectual "openness," and thus is required to give evidence of its sincerity through repeated public acts of self-criticism. Perhaps the first great modern Catholic historian was Lord John Acton, who was also one of the fathers of modern liberal Catholicism, and Butterfield noted how Acton's bias in his scholarship was against Ultramontanism, the Catholic historian distorting historical truth in the very act of demonstrating his "objective" detachment from creedal royalty.[2]

On one level, "Catholic history" proceeds from what Jacques Maritain called "connatural knowledge"—the understanding of his subject that a scholar possesses by virtue of its being in some sense a part of himself.[3] Maritain noted that, whereas a scientist is wholly detached from the physical world that he studies, a historian approaches his human subject in terms of his entire personal disposition. Great works of religious history have been written by non-believers, but they are required to make a prodigious imaginative leap in order to do justice to their subjects, whereas for the believer there is an immediate sympathetic comprehension of even the subtlest dimensions of religious history.

Thus, all things being equal, the believing historian should be a better student of religious phenomena, able to penetrate its inner meaning more profoundly. But of course things are not always equal, and the believer may be deficient in intellect, ambition, or diligence. A peculiar temptation for believing scholars (Hilaire Belloc, notably) is to deduce reality from their principles instead of studying the empirical evidence, a habit that more than once has embarrassed Catholics when a secular scholar discovers inconvenient information that the believer had neglected.

Curiously, what is still often called "the new social history," although it is now four decades old, despite the fact that almost all of its practitioners have been secular-minded, has had immense effect in revealing the pervasive influence of religion on history, since it strives to map nothing less than the entire fabric of a given society, and thereby come face to face with the ubiquitous role of religion. At the same time, such discoveries are problematical for the believer, in that they often show that there was an apparently wide gap between official teaching and actual popular practice, a gap a theologically and spiritually sophisticated scholar might be able to close on a deeper level.

Virtually all of Christopher Dawson's works were a meditation by a believing Catholic on the meaning of history. Yet few of them actually required the reader himself to be a believer. Dawson's faith made him extraordinarily sensitive to the powerful influence of religion on history, and he was able to reveal its workings in such a way that all but the most biased readers had to acknowledge it. Toward the end of his life Dawson's plan for a comprehensive educational program based on the study of "Christian culture" was merely a plea for what is sometimes now called religious literacy—that students at least be made aware of the influence of Christianity on history, even if they reject that faith in their own lives. It was a program, Dawson noted,[4] that would not necessarily require believing professors.

Once again the failure of the Catholic universities even to attempt an approximation of this is a sign of their immaturity, their failure to achieve a consistent and settled identity. This too may be endemic to a certain kind of Catholic liberalism—Butterfield noted that Lord Acton tended to treat religion almost exclusively in institutional terms, especially the involvement of the Church in politics, which Acton deplored. The founders of the

Catholic University of America, such as its first rector, Bishop John J. Keane, deliberately excluded "medievalism" from its curriculum,[5] and thus an area where Catholics were potentially well-equipped to exercise scholarly leadership was left to be developed by secular scholars such as Charles Homer Haskins at Harvard.

At the same time Catholic historians ought to avoid the trap of nostalgia, whereby the Middle Ages (usually) is presented as the high point of history, from which everything since has been a decline. To idealize a past historical age is itself heretical, the unrecognized assumption that orthodox belief is a guarantee against sin. Christian historians should not leave to their enemies the discovery of how often good has been perverted by self-righteous men, and the believer's very understanding of his faith ought to make him especially sensitive to this inevitability. The idealization of a particular era is also heretical in that it fails to recognize that the redemption continues throughout history.

The refusal to idealize any past age also serves the Christian by precluding the use of the present to judge the past. One of the central insights of the man often considered the father of modern historiography, Leopold von Ranke (a devout Lutheran), was that "each age stands by itself in the sight of God,"[6] that is, no age should be treated merely as a preliminary to what follows. Butterfield, unlike most liberal Christian historians, approached the history of Christianity itself in those terms, insisting that the greatest Christian contribution to history was its witnessing to the primacy of the spiritual and the imperative of charity.[7] In contrast to the current practice of "politically correct" history, he insisted, for example, that the saints retain their significance despite perhaps having been wrong about certain historical questions, such as the rise of democracy. Here again the wisdom of the historian and the wisdom of the believer, both recognizing the singularity of history, coincide.

Since history is an empirical discipline, there ought not to be differences over facts between believing and non-believing scholars. The same criteria for establishing the credibility of historical sources ought to be employed identically by both. Inevitably bias might affect the way they evaluate the evidence, but believing historians have a special obligation not to suppress or underestimate sordid chapters from Church history.

Butterfield observed that, like the physical sciences, the study of history began to make "progress" when historians ceased to look for ultimate explanations and concentrated on secondary causes, which led to an increasingly detailed study of those causes.[8] As Butterfield pointed out, both the scientific method and the historical method arose out of Western Christian culture. Men of faith have no short cuts open to them toward the same goals.

Practically speaking, a Catholic historian will manifest his personal faith, at least minimally, in his recognition that the role of religion in history is often slighted, that even those who acknowledge it often do not adequately understand it as a spiritual phenomenon, and that the decline of religious belief has empirically verifiable affects on a culture, many of which are measurably debilitating. (American history, for example, is often written as though Christianity never existed, except in instances such as Puritanism, where it is unavoidable.)

In a famous remark, Cardinal Newman said that experience seems to force the conclusion that mankind was implicated in some "primordial catastrophe,"[9] and this awareness too is one of the believer's special qualifications for the understanding of history. Specifically as a historian, the believer has no special knowledge of the exact nature of that catastrophe, but his faith allows him to understand that it did occur.

Butterfield proposed that the sense of sin is one of the believer's crucial contributions to the understanding of history. The Christian understands evil best, because he is part of it (Maritain's "connatural knowledge" again). Historical evidence alone cannot unlock the mystery of human nature, and without this knowledge of sin history itself remains a mystery. Butterfield noted that the historian and the Christian both begin by assuming the greatness of humanity, then proceed to offer negative accounts of human behavior. The historian's negative view of humanity is demanded by innumerable crimes of history, while that of the believer is reinforced by his faith. R. G. Collingwood, a secular scholar who was the rare combination of a historian and a philosopher of history, went so far as to say that the Christian doctrine of the Fall, by asserting that man alone is not sovereign over history, broadened the study beyond what the Greeks knew and thereby rendered it open to an awareness of impersonal forces.[10]

The Jesuit theologian Jean Danielou argued that history simply cannot be understood apart from sin, in the form of universal selfishness,[11] and this seems undeniable. Many secular-minded people employ the concept of sin, if not the word. However, those who deny that a tendency toward evil is basic to human nature simply cannot make sense of history, which then becomes endless, incomprehensible tragedy, since the story of mankind is to so great an extent the story of benign dreams somehow treacherously undermined and turned into evil. A sinless view of history could only be Sisyphean, the historian chronicling the endlessly repeated process whereby mankind approaches fulfillment of its exalted plans, only to see them destroyed in the end. Any doctrine of inherent human goodness must confront the massive and continuing evidence of James Joyce's "history is a nightmare from which I am trying to wake up."[12]

This daunting reality inspires an approach to history that is a perennial temptation to Christians, albeit not exclusively for them—history is a moral judgment. Butterfield, who was a Methodist lay preacher as well as a distinguished historian, argued strongly against this, noting that few things foreclose historical understanding more quickly than the pronouncement of moral judgment.

Acton, he noted, was especially prone to this, and it is by no means merely the temptation of the orthodox. Indeed contemporary historiography is awash with this kind of moralism, in which the past is endlessly ransacked for examples of alleged injustice to designated groups, so that appropriate condemnation can be pronounced (the dominant approach at the time of the Columbus quincentenary in 1992, for example).

Butterfield offered a theological reason for refraining from such judgments, the fact that all men are sinners and thus dare not set themselves up to judge others. Acton had a famous exchange with the Anglican Bishop Mandell Creighton, himself an important historian, over the latter's refusal to condemn Pope Alexander VI, whom Acton thought a wicked man representing a wicked ecclesiastical system. Butterfield observed that, apart from the question of whether the contemporary accusations against Alexander were accurate, Acton lacked sufficient knowledge of the pope's soul to condemn him, while for the same reason Creighton could not acquit him. (In fact he did not; he merely refrained from condemning him.)

Acton came to believe that all great men of history were wicked, in that virtually all of them used force and treachery to achieve their goals, and Butterfield responded that this may be true but is also unhelpful in understanding the past. (Acton's curious myopia led him to concentrate his attentions almost exclusively on men of affairs and not, for example, on the great saints of history.) Such moralism is perhaps inevitable in a certain kind of liberalism, which tends to assume human goodness and is endlessly sympathetic with what it deems to be the "progressive" movements of history, and then can only attempt to salvage meaning from the wreckage by pronouncing condemnation on those who appear responsible.

The historian's task, according to Butterfield, is to record and describe the deeds of past men, deeds that may be deemed wicked by those who read them, although it is not the historian's task to force this conclusion. In Butterfield's words:

> The whole process of emptying oneself in order to teach the thoughts and feelings of men not like-minded with oneself is an activity which ought to commend itself to the Christian. In this sense the whole range of history is a boundless field for the constant exercise of Christian charity.[13]

An obvious argument for Butterfield's counsel of perfection is the fact that condemning the deeds of men long dead can have no effect whatever; they have passed into God's hands. The danger of this, as Acton saw, was the blunting of contemporary moral sensitivity—if the wicked deeds of past men cannot be condemned, how can modern men be held to account and their wickedness thwarted? The Christian historian must live with this tension, but in exactly the way that every Christian must, enjoined not to judge his fellow man but without falling into moral agnosticism. The Catholic belief in human freedom proves to be one way out of this dilemma—since men can and do make responsible decisions, to understand all is not to forgive all. Historians can press to the limit their powers of empathy, without thereby becoming apologists for past wickedness.

Moral judgment is at the origin of Western historical consciousness, which grew not only out of the Greek but also from the Hebrew sense of history, as the Hebrews were driven by an urgent need to find some comprehensible purpose in the repeated catastrophes from which they suffered.

As has often been pointed out, they were forced to reject the seductive, even irresistible, hypothesis that suffering was simply God's punishment for sin, since they could see quite obviously that their faithless enemies repeatedly triumphed over God's people and that Israel's own infidelities could not adequately explain this. Making moral sense of history has preoccupied human beings ever since.

The study of history immediately confirms that evil men often flourish and the good are often defeated, with no reversal or vindication in this life. Indeed, this reality is almost a priori, in that the selfish wicked, who are usually calculating and clever, would obviously not embrace wickedness if experience showed that they would inevitably suffer punishment. The dichotomy of time and eternity is nowhere more evident than in the fact that justice often does not triumph in this world. Thus calculating people can choose to ignore the justice that may be visited on them in the next life, in order to prosper in this one.

Calvinism offers a logical explanation of this in insisting that all men deserve damnation and God cannot be blamed for bestowing free gifts on some. But among other defects, this view of history tends to moral agnosticism, in that the seemingly innocent are revealed as being as wicked as their persecutors, with no final distinctions to be made between Adolph Hitler and his victims.

Liberalism, including liberal Christianity, finds the triumph of evil particularly in need of urgent explanation, although, as noted, its view of history dooms it to continuous disappointment and frustration. Butterfield pointed out that Acton originally viewed providence in the orthodox Christian sense of God bringing good out of evil, but then moved to what is essentially a secular view that "progress" itself is the chief manifestation of divine providence in history. The fatal flaw in the liberal idea of progress is its unavoidable short-sightedness. Thus the evolution of the Greek *polis* might be justly celebrated as progress, but that achievement lasted for about only two centuries and was then crushed by new forms of despotism. Most liberals see the history of the past two centuries in terms of self-evident progress, yet no one would be so foolish as to deny the fragility of that achievement, vulnerable to being snuffed out by both physical and political disorders. The liberal view of progress offers no explanation of the movement of history over the centuries, and in fact forces the condemnation or ignoring of whole periods of history that are not "progressive" or settles for the trivial task of scanning bleak periods of history for small signs that the light of progress was dimly shining over them.

Butterfield believed that Christianity alone provides a resolution of this dilemma, through its doctrine of vicarious suffering, Christ himself the great exemplar through whom the sufferings of other innocent people can have meaning.

In this as in other respects, however, the believing scholar's personal faith cannot successfully be made an explicit part of his teaching and scholarship, except insofar as he explicitly makes himself into a kind of theologian. History does not prove beyond all doubt the value of vicarious suffering, and offers innumerable examples to the contrary. The triumph of Christianity can be seen as vindicating the sufferings of Christ, but the non-believer will persist in finding other explanations for this triumph. Rather, faith allows the historian to approach his subject with a certain serenity, as capable as any non-believer of being shocked and appalled at "man's inhumanity to man" but ultimately hopeful nonetheless. As Butterfield said, history is indeed the war of good against evil, but the exact progress of that war is hidden from human eyes.

From earliest times one of the great temptations of Christian historiography has been to deduce, from a general belief in divine providence, its specific manifestations in history. Whole theologies of history have been based on this, and each one has finally failed as a comprehensive explanation of historical events.

The belief that specific catastrophes are direct divine punishment for sin dies hard, for obvious reasons—the laudable desire to make sense of events but also the less than laudable desire to see one's enemies vanquished. For every wicked man who finally suffers his deserved fate, there are perhaps ten who die in prosperity, honored in their communities. Edifying stories of devout people saved from danger by divine intervention (a city spared the plague, an angelic visitor steering a child away from a precipice) fail to explain why countless other even more pious and innocent people have been allowed to perish.

Christianity can understand this quite easily on the individual level—suffering itself is redemptive, and God takes his servants when he wants them. It is, however, far more difficult to explain events in terms of whole societies, the very mystery with which Israel was forced to wrestle obsessively.

The ultimate Christian explanation is again in terms of providence, meaning that God finally brings good from evil. Without such a belief there could be no such thing as redemption, since even Christ's redemptive act would be repeatedly and successfully thwarted.

The temptation for Christians to discern the exact contours of providence in history is even more compelling than the tendency to explain evil merely as punishment, since it speaks to the basic question whether history makes any sense at all, whether God's goodness can be vindicated within the confines of his creation. It is, however, a temptation that believers, and historians in particular, must resist. It is bad theology and even worse history. At best its validity is limited to edifying speculation that believers might engage in as a pious exercise but that can never be assumed as true.

The fundamental barrier to a knowledge of providential history is the simple fact of human fallibility; genuine understanding of providence would require omniscience; the pattern of history could be fully seen only by someone above history.

An obvious obstacle is limited temporal horizons: If, as some early Christians believed, the Roman Empire came into being in order to prepare the way for the birth of the Savior, this was not at all evident to pious Jews longing for the messiah. They experienced the Roman incursion as merely another of those periodic mysterious catastrophes that fell upon them. But hindsight also does not suffice. An argument can be made for the providential role of the Empire in preparing the way for Christ, but in other respects the Empire was a formidable obstacle to the spread of the Gospel, mainly through persecution, which had the affect of strengthening the faith of many but of intimidating many others.

Once again this desire to discern the hand of providence is an especially strong temptation for liberal Christians, as exemplified in Acton's facile, even perversely false, view that modern "progress" is equitable with divine providence.

Maritain was not a theological liberal, but he was a political liberal, and he tended to trivialize his own philosophy of history by making a similar suggestion—that modern democracy is somehow the fulfillment of providence and vindicates the actions of God in history, a judgment that precisely illustrates the fallacy of providential history. When Maritain formulated it, shortly after World War II,[14] it was possible to see the American experiment in those terms, because the Church was flourishing in ways it had never flourished anywhere else, at any other time in history, and this was attributable in part to the democratic conditions that gave religion the fullest possible freedom. Maritain did not foresee that democracy might finally reveal itself as hostile to all claims of spiritual authority and thus become a force for undermining the very possibility of genuine religion. (He also proposed the evolution of moral conscience as the greatest of all historical laws, without foreseeing how that conscience, on abortion and other matters, is being systematically repealed.)

If evil produces good, although such production is often hidden from human eyes, the ironic view of history that Christians must espouse shows also that good produces evil. To overlook this is not a defense of the orthodox doctrine of providence but the reverse—a heterodox denial of human sinfulness, which is able to pervert the most sublime truths into errors. As Maritain said, drawing on the parable of the wheat and the tares, as all historically minded Christians must, good and evil exist together in the world, and there is a constant double movement, both upward and downward.[15] The work of redemption proceeds only slowly, against the inertia of human affairs.

Catholicism provides a finally more satisfactory explanation of evil than does Calvinist determinism, precisely in its emphasis on human freedom. Most of the moral evil in history can be explained in those terms, in God's mysterious willingness to grant this freedom and permit its full exercise, even when it is used to thwart the divine plan. As Maritain said, God's eternal plan operates in such a way as to anticipate these human failings. Butterfield saw the action of God in history as like a composer masterfully revising his music to overcome the inadequacies of the orchestra that plays it.[16]

The relation of freedom to providence remains finally one of the most tenaciously impenetrable of all theological mysteries, and thus for the Christian there can be no final understanding of history in all its fullness.

Maritain asked whether Brutus was free not to assassinate Caesar, and the obvious answer is that indeed he was. But beyond that, in what sense did God will the death of Caesar at that time and under those particular circumstances? Caesar's death, like most like most events of human history, was the result of the freedom that God gave to man, not of some pre-ordained script that had to be played out.

Thus the believing historian must rely on the theologian and the preacher to remind people of the reality of divine providence, whose workings remain hidden. Not being above the historical process, the historian cannot claim to discern this through empirical investigation. In dialogue with his unbelieving colleagues, he has the advantage of knowing that all things human eventually end badly, but this is never the last word of the story. He is permanently inoculated against unrealistic expectations of progress and against the concomitant despair that follows each disappointment. In purely worldly terms, he has achieved a ripe wisdom that is partly given to him by his faith.

A particular category of uncertainty concerning the discernment of the workings of providence are alleged acts of direct divine intervention—Constantine's vision at the Milvian Bridge, for example, or the Blessed Virgin's messages at Lourdes and Fatima. Believers are of course free to reject these as pious fictions or delusions. Indeed the Church itself has throughout its history instinctively followed a policy of scholarly skepticism, placing the burden of proof on those who claim a miracle and warning the faithful against credulity.

Yet some miraculous events, above all Christ's resurrection from the dead, are undeniable truths of faith, and the believing historian must judge how to include them in his work. Maritain thought that the historian is obligated to take into account all relevant information, including the supernatural, and should not bracket such events or treat them as having a natural explanation.

The Jesuit theologian Martin Cyril D'Arcy pointed to the encounter of the disciples with Jesus on the road to Emmaus as an instance of this dilemma—secular history has no way of dealing with such an occurrence, except perhaps by dismissing it as mere fiction, which is itself a dogmatically naturalistic assumption closed even to the possibility of the supernatural.[17] D'Arcy's solution was to point out that history is not "noumenal," in the Kantian sense—what is known today is not the past as such but the past as it presents itself to the present mind. Hence in a way all historical events remain mysterious. He also pointed out the improbability, in purely human terms, that great men who recorded profound religious experiences, such as Paul on the road to Damascus, were simply the victims of delusion. This hardly seems an adequate explanation for all that followed from such events. Marc Bloch, the great medievalist who was a secular-minded Jew (he perished in a German prison camp), observed that the real question concerning the history of Christianity is why so many people fervently believed that Jesus rose from the dead, a belief of such power and duration as to be hardly explicable in purely reductionistic terms.[18]

Once again, however, the historian must separate his faith from his scholarship, for the simple reason that historical scholarship is an instrument completely unsuitable for discovering the supernatural. There is no historical argument that could convince skeptics that Jesus indeed rose from the dead and appeared to his disciples. The cliché question as to what Christians would think if his body were discovered buried in Palestine overlooks the fact that such a thing could never happen. Even if Jesus did not rise from the dead, history and archeology have no conclusive way of proving whether such remains were really those of Jesus.

Thus the Christian historian ought not to become involved in fruitless discussions about the reality of the supernatural in history but should simply build upon such beliefs as themselves historical events—the powerful conviction that the early Christians had that Jesus indeed had risen, and the immense consequences that belief had for the future history of the world.

However, Christianity is a historical religion, which is a cliché only in proportion to one's ignorance of other religions that are decidedly not historical. Emanating from Judaism, which was itself a historical religion, Christianity stakes its claim to truth on certain historical events, notably the claim that at a precise moment in history the Son of God did indeed come to earth. Thus Christians can never be indifferent to the reliability of historical claims.

But the thrust of modern biblical scholarship has been steadily to diminish the historical reliability of the Bible, and, even though there are some signs of reversal, it is a process that seems fated to play itself out (as in the Jesus Seminar) to the point where Scriptures are thought to provide no reliable basis for any kind of faith.

The discipline of history as such has relatively little to contribute to this discussion, which proceeds from related disciplines such as philosophy, archeology, and papyrology. But the whole subject is a vivid illustration of the point made by Butterfield and others—the greatest challenge to the credibility of faith comes not from the physical sciences but from the historical disciplines, which are able to discredit Christianity precisely because it is a faith based on historical claims.

The believing historian's role here is secondary but not unimportant. He can, for example, trace the pedigree of modern biblical scholarship itself, showing his own presuppositions, how it has deliberately adapted itself to a "culture of suspicion." Beginning with the liberal attitude of agonized self-criticism, biblical scholarship has by now advanced to the point where many of its practitioners have a vested interest in discrediting as much of the Bible as they can. Modern biblical scholarship is part of intellectual trends that have a history of their own and cannot be accepted merely on their own terms. Historians can in effect "demythologize" modern biblical scholarship's claims, instructing believers in the ways of modern scholarship. Phrases such as "scripture scholars tell us" are almost meaningless in view of the fact that there are very sharp contradictions among such scholars. Finally, the mainstream of modern biblical scholarship tends to take a far more suspicious view of Christian origins than most historians would take toward other aspects of ancient history. What is not open to the believer is the rejection of the "Jesus of history" and a flight to the "Christ of faith." To reject the "Jesus of History" precisely denies Christianity's historical character and is a thinly veiled attempt to turn it into a myth. Thus, however troubling the theories of biblical scholars may be, the believing historian must continue to dwell on the level of historical inquiry. The problem has relevance to the entire history of the Church, since for over a century there has been a parallel, less well-publicized, debate over the reliability of Church traditions (the calendar of saints, for example). Bloch points out that, parallel with the emergence of the modern scientific method, the method of modern historiography also emerged in the seventeenth century, and that Catholics (notably the Benedictine scholar Jean Mabillon) were among its pioneers. The historical method grows out of Christianity by a natural process, and Christians can never reject it.

It has long been recognized that not only is Christianity a historical religion, but it played a crucial role in the development of the understanding of history itself, replacing the cyclical theories common to the ancients with the "linear" view now taken for granted by almost everyone. The cyclical view was really a kind of despair, an expression of the sense that men were trapped in a process that they could not control and that would be endlessly repeated, albeit with variations.

Christianity, on the other hand, gave history a goal, an eschatology, toward which it relentlessly moves, so that repetition is more apparent than real. Thus for the first time the actual movement of history could have meaning. (To a lesser extent Judaism had done the same by pointing history toward the coming of the messiah.)

Linear time is the same both for believers and for modern historians because it is genuinely open to the future. Among the many ways in which history falls short of being a science is that it does not lead to prediction, at least not prediction of a high order of probability. The great theologian Hans Urs von Balthasar pointed out that the Incarnation is the one absolutely unique event in all of human history, and by taking that as his starting point the Christian historian must see history as completely open to God's free action, thus as beyond both human control and final human understanding.[19]

The historicity of Christianity also makes it a very concrete religion, in both respects the exact opposite of myth. As Dawson said, in understanding Christianity it is necessary to ask why great deeds, central to all of history, occurred among an obscure Near Eastern people, why an obscure peasant in that same part of the world was hailed as the world's savior. This specificity has sometimes been an embarrassment to Christians, as well as a stumbling block to non-believers, and the Gnostic temptation (alive again in modern times) has always been to fly to the realm of atemporal myth, which seeks to obliterate all specificity. The traditionalism of the Church stems in part from the fact that, while God is present in all of history, Christians are also specially bound to a particular line of history, rather than to others, and are called to be faithful to that line.

But if Christianity is by far the most historical of all religions, that should not obscure the fact that from another point of view it is problematical why Christians should respect history at all. The problem is obvious—Christianity points to the termination of history, which is precisely that, a termination. History will end. Christians are taught to live with the knowledge that "all this will pass away" and they will be gathered up into eternity. If one is a mere pilgrim in this life, how is it possible to regard what happens in this life as finally significant? It is a question, of course, with which Christians have wrestled since the beginning, and will continue to do so until the end of time, when it will become meaningless.

Belief in providence is once again crucial. History has meaning because Christians know that God chose to reveal himself through history and that his providence works through history. Thus, even though believers cannot understand exactly how this occurs, they cannot dismiss history as unimportant. As Danielou pointed out, divine revelation reveals little about the inner nature of God; it mainly reveals his actions in history.[20] The Incarnation itself validates history, as the eternal descends into the temporal, and men have no way of working out their salvation except in this life. If history were solely the story of the saints, it would already be infinitely valuable. But its value lies also in the story it tells of sinners and of the entire great drama of human life.

But if the cyclical view of history expressed the pagans' sense that they were at the mercy of the historical process, Christianity by no means offers the prospect of the reverse. One of the deepest insights available to the Christian is that he cannot hope to dominate history, and Butterfield judged (perhaps too simplistically) that history bestows its hardest rebuffs on those who arrogantly try. Christians "escape" from history not by mastering it but through faith in the benign Lord of History.

As Maritain observed, once this lordship was denied, it became necessary for secularists to seek for final meaning within history itself, thus giving rise to the various great "systems" of interpretation beginning with Hegel, of which Marxism was the most ambitious and influential. But the search for a supra-historical vantage point from which to see all of history is obviously futile. The end of history is beyond history, and history cannot reveal its own inner meaning.

The great pioneer historians of the nineteenth century self-consciously spoke of history as "science" and tailored their research to subjects that lent themselves to such precision. They were thus forced to ignore vast areas of history, and as those neglected fields (religion among them) more and more came to be recognized, it became less and less feasible to think of history as a science, and today practically no one does. Here human experience merely confirms the wisdom of faith, for history could be a science only if human beings were not free. But, as Balthasar said, history is that space in his universe where God has created freedom.[21] As Maritain said, there can be no "necessary" laws in history, only "general" laws that are mere approximations.[22]

For Balthasar, the search for a final "system" of history is an important manifestation of the reality of sin.[23] Christ, he pointed out, did not anticipate the Father's will but allowed it to unfold in time, and the desire to break out of the constraints of time is a fundamental expression of sinfulness. Christ renounced sovereignty over his own life, as humans must also do because they are historical beings. All things happen in the "fullness of time," which cannot be known until it has already occurred. (As D'Arcy pointed out already in 1957, the once fashionable theories of the Jesuit theologian Pierre Teilhard de Chardin were in principle beyond the possibility of historical evidence, although positing the end of history allegedly on the basis of such evidence.)[24]

Just as the Christian "linear" view of history is now universally accepted, so also the fallacy of great historical systems is now all but universally conceded. Historians are content to cultivate their particular gardens and to offer their produce for whatever finite value they may have, a task with which the Christian historian should be content, although this does not of course preclude him from acting in other capacities at other times.

The fact that history is problematical for Christians is also seen in the fact, as Danielou pointed out, that there can be no progress beyond Christ. If Christ were merely a historical figure, he would then bring history to an end. However, he is also an eternal being whose reality permeates time, giving profound meaning to history, but a meaning that is hidden from the eyes of the historian. To D'Arcy, therefore, history is actually a kind of continuous present, although it does not seem that way to human experience.

As Dawson observed, the Christian approach to history is also perplexing to the secular mind because it is not completely linear, as all history is now assumed to be, but focuses around a central date—the coming of Christ—from which time is reckoned both forward and backward.[25] (The present Western dating system, which is under some attack, is more than a pious commemoration of Christ's birth. It expresses the fundamental Christian view of history. For this reason it is almost bound to be repealed once cultural leaders have determined how to overcome the practical problem that would entail.)

Dawson also observed that secular-minded people do not accept a view of history that has a beginning and an end, a view that seems to depend on belief in an all-powerful God. Debates about the origins of the universe are now among the most significant in Western culture, but the historian as such has nothing to say on that subject. Similarly, by definition the historian cannot even guess when time will end, and the believer is enjoined by Christ to refrain from such speculation. Although the stretch of human history seems immensely long to the limited mind, in reality history has to be viewed, according to Dawson, as a "small" space surrounded by the infinity of eternity.[26] If the human race survives another million years, its view of history will change profoundly, as all the carefully delineated eras now part of the historical record will recede into a very remote past, to be disposed of by future historians in the twinkling of an eye.   ◆

Secularized Christendom and the Age of Revolution

Christopher Dawson's Regional Historical and Sociological Analysis of the Sixth Period of Christian Culture

Edward King

The history of the secularization of modern culture has yet to be written, and the reasons for this are easy enough to understand. For on the one hand the mind of the secularized majority has been so deeply affected by the process of secularization that it cannot view that process in an objective historical manner, while on the other the religious minority has been forced into an attitude of negative opposition which is no less unfavorable to dispassionate study. Nevertheless, it is emphatically a problem which requires an historical approach. The process of secularization was an historical movement no less than was the Reformation, a minority movement which was gradually transmitted to wider circles until it eventually won the key positions of social and intellectual influence through which it dominated European society.[1]

Introduction: The Need for a Cultural Approach to the Study of the Christian Past[2]

THE sixth period of Christian culture—"Secularized Christendom and the Age of Revolution"—is the period about which Christopher Dawson devoted the greater part of his writing career. This may come as a surprise to those who regard Dawson as primarily a medievalist, but if we examine closely his twenty-three published books as well as the bibliography of Claude Locas (1970) that Christina Scott, Dawson's daughter and biographer, included in her book, we shall see that this is the case. It begins with one of his earliest essays, "The Passing of Industrialism," written during the First World War, and it ends with his Harvard lectures on "The Dividing of Christendom" (1965).

It was during the Second World War that Christopher Dawson turned his attention to "Education and the Crisis of Christian Culture" and a little later to "The Study of Christian Culture As a Means of Education" in order to reverse the trend toward the total secularization of modern civilization. The secularization of education preceded and accompanied the secularization of modern culture, and the only way to reverse this process and to desecularize modern culture was to make people in the West aware of their religious roots. This would enable them to counteract the appeal of the modern messianic and apocalyptic secular ideologies and the pressure to conform to the hedonism and materialism of modern mass civilization.

The scientific validity of Christopher Dawson's classification of six periods of Christian culture would recommend itself, I think, to the orientalists, who would readily admit to the importance of Islam in the Middle East and Africa, of the Confucian tradition in China, of Hinduism in India, and of Buddhism in North, East, and Southeast Asia. But the classification of Western culture into ancient, medieval, and modern history, which had its roots in the culture of the Renaissance and was passed on to the Enlightenment and then to the modern world, had an obvious appeal to the secular idealists who dominated the history faculties in the universities of Europe and North America. Thus Dawson was under no illusions as to the difficulty of getting his campaign for the study of Christian culture off the ground and accepted in the world of the secular universities.

This cultural approach to the Christian past also highlighted the shortcomings of the rigid division between ecclesiastical and political history. Such a situation, as he says, destroyed the intelligible unity of culture and left the history of culture "suspended uneasily between political and ecclesiastical history with no firm basis of either of them."[3] The cultural approach united what the ecclesiastical and political historians divided and widened the historical picture of Christian culture by including the sciences of sociology, ethnology, psychology, and comparative religion. One has only to read the chapters on Christian culture and its consequent secularization in his book *Progress and Religion*[4] in order to see the difference of approach and appreciate the advantage of the cultural study of the Christian past and present.

One historian of Christianity who made an attempt to paint the whole cultural picture was Kenneth Scott Latourette, an American missionary to China and the Far East. Dawson reviewed the final book of his seven-volume *History of the Expansion of Christianity* (1936–44) in the lead article of the *Times Literary Supplement* (August 3, 1946), titled "The Spiritual Colonists."[5] He praised Latourette for his impartiality and fairness and his efforts in each major division to assess the impact of Christianity on its environment and of the environment on Christianity.

But Dawson was critical of Latourette's optimistic outlook on the expansion of the Protestant voluntary type of Christianity in the nineteenth and twentieth centuries; Latourette tended to underestimate the centralization of power in modern Western secularized culture and its tremendous implications for Christians in the twentieth century. Nevertheless, I think Catholic and Protestant historians would benefit from Latourette's chapters on Christianity and its cultural environment that conclude each of his major epochs, since without this cultural background their histories tend to be situated in a sociological vacuum. This is strikingly exemplified in the last volume of the series *The Christian Centuries*, with its title *The Church in a Secularized Society*,[6] where no attempt is made to define the fundamental nature of the secularized culture in each of the regions covered in the book. And the same is true to a great extent of all the recent histories of the Church or Christianity by Christian scholars, from Henri Daniel-Rops in the fifties to Roger Aubert and Hubert Jedin in the seventies.

The secular historians with their focus on political and economic history in their treatment of modern Europe and modern Western civilization would also benefit from Dawson's analysis of the relation between religion and culture since the Enlightenment, because it is impossible to ignore the spiritual element in modern culture in its secularized form. I think the editors of *The New Cambridge Modern History* realized that when they asked Peter Burke to edit the *Companion Volume* (1978) after the series had been completed. His two chapters on "The Concepts of

Continuity and Change in History" and "Religion and Secularization" (1 and 9) necessitate a cultural analysis.

Apparently the sociologists of religion, judging from W. S. F. Pickering's review of Peter Glassner's book, *The Sociology of Secularization: A Critique of a Concept*,[7] could also benefit from Christopher Dawson's historical approach to the secularization of modern culture. He writes:

> Are we ever going to have a satisfactory approach to, and explanation of secularization? Most people are convinced that modern society is in some way secular. Extensive disagreement arises over the exact location of the secular and the reasons for its emergence. Such issues are the perennial problems of sociologists of religion. Books on the subject are legion, yet none has been acknowledged as a definitive answer—-none raised to the status of a classic. Permeating a great deal of infighting, there is the weakness that the sociology of religion in general, and secularization in particular, lacks an adequate theory. Thus, anyone who attempts to enter the arena—one might say jungle—must realize its great complexity and be prepared to approach it with humility, if not awe. Many minds have gotten lost in the undergrowth.

In reading this review, I was reminded of F. W. Maitland's comment on anthropology quoted by Dawson in his book *Progress and Religion*,[8] (50), where he says that "by and by anthropology will have the choice between being history and being nothing." Perhaps the same could be said about sociology at the present time.

Dawson's Regional Historical Approach to Secularized Christendom and the Age of Revolution

Europe as a Whole[9]

The present crisis of European culture . . . is due not to any decline in physical or social vitality, but to the internal division of Europe by an intensive process of revolutionary criticism which affected every aspect of Western culture. This process did not consciously aim at the destruction of European unity. At each successive stage it was inspired by a belief in social progress and the hope of a new European order. . . . But the revolutionary ideal of a new European order was frustrated by the conflicting aims of the different revolutionary movements—liberal, socialist, and nationalist—so that revolutionary movement became destructive of European unity and hostile to European culture. In the bitter intensive struggle of parties and ideologies the deeper spiritual foundations of Western culture were forgotten or rejected until the movement which had begun with the worship of liberty and the declaration of the Rights of Man ended in the concentration camps of the totalitarian state and the mass suicide of total war.[10]

During his writing career Christopher Dawson often turned his attention to the Europe characterized by a secularized Christendom and the Age of Revolution, the period covering the eighteenth, nineteenth, and twentieth centuries. Perhaps the best short synthetic account of this process is the chapter "The Revolt against Europe" in his 1952 *Understanding Europe,* which sums up succinctly what he had previously set out in greater detail.

He traces the movement's origin and development in the rationalist world of eighteenth-century France (209), its progress through the nationalist movement in nineteenth-century Germany (210–11), and its transplantation to Russia and its flowering in the nihilist movement (211–13), its spread to Central Europe as a revolutionary nationalist movement (214–15), and then its expression in the class conflict abetted by Socialism and Marxism as the Industrial Revolution completely transformed the life of the workers and the middle classes (216–18). Then four pages are devoted to Nietzsche (218–21), and the chapter concludes by situating the revolutionary movement in relation to the common spiritual elements that have made Europe what it was and the need for Europe to recover this tradition (222–24).

Why does Dawson highlight the importance of Nietzsche in this movement in the last half of the chapter? Primarily because of the truth and depth of his diagnosis of the nature and disease of European culture in *The Nature and History of European Nihilism.*

Although Nietzsche was a German of the Bismarckian era and was not unaffected by the exaggerations of contemporary German nationalism, he regarded himself first and foremost as a "good European" who was loyal to the great tradition of Western humanism as the source of all the higher spiritual values of European culture. At the same time he recognized that this humanist culture had exhausted its energy and that the spiritual values

that it had created were being dissolved in a mush of humanitarian sentiment and liberal idealism. Above all, the higher human types were being
absorbed and destroyed by the human herd that swarmed into the new
cities and that was being drilled into uniformity by the democratic and
bureaucratic state (218).

Now Dawson does not accept Nietzsche's attributing the main responsibility for this process of degeneration to the influence of Christianity. He
argues that Christian values and humanist values had both alike been deval-
uated. Only economic values remained, possessing no spiritual power and
providing no common cultural aim. "Science and technology had immea-
surably increased the knowledge and external power of Western man only to
leave him spiritually naked and empty before the abyss of Nihilism" (219).

He praises Nietzsche for realizing far more clearly than most of his
Christian contemporaries that the crisis of Western civilization was neither
political nor economic, but essentially spiritual—"a crisis in the soul of
Western man."

> On the other hand, his attempt to provide a solution to the problem by
> the gospel of Superman and the Will to Power is even more fallacious
> and irreligious than any of the solutions proposed by the socialists or the
> secular humanitarians and had a most disastrous influence on European,
> and particularly German, thought in the early twentieth century. For
> what is the Superman but a distorted shadow of the historic ideal cast on
> the abyss by the setting sun of humanist culture? And what is Nietzsche's
> Will to Power but the prevalent moral disease of modern culture in an
> exaggerated form? (219).

Dawson admits that there was much in nineteenth-century Christianity to excuse Nietzsche's mistaken views of Christian values and ideals. It
was a full retreat before the "rising tide of materialism and secularism."
Centuries of sectarian strife had profoundly weakened Christianity, and it
tended to drift into a cultural backwater. He sees in sectarian Christianity's
abdication of the Christian world mission a "profound misunderstanding"
of the meaning of Christianity, which from its beginning had announced
the coming of a new order in which mankind would be transformed by
the infusion of a higher spiritual principle.

Dawson ends his discussion of Nietzsche by noting "a resemblance which almost suggests an element of unconscious imitation" between his idea of the Superman and the transformation of culture, and the Christian idea of the New Man and the transformation of the present world order.

If this is so then the loss of the Christian faith and Christian moral values involved in the secularization of European culture is disastrous since as it proceeds it destroys all the common spiritual elements that have made Europe what it was and leaves only the conflicting forces of class and nationality and the social and scientific techniques that were the creation of the last phase of European culture (222).

The advance of scientific technology may have made it possible to create calculating machines and mechanical "brains," but there will never be a machine for the creation of moral values (223).

Germany and Central Europe[11]

"Consequently when Hegel transfers to the state by a *coup d'esprit* the rights and prerogatives of the spiritual community and arrays the grim skeleton of the police in the royal robe of Divinity, he is not only denying the Christian doctrine of supernatural order and a super-political society; he is not even doing justice to the social ideals of the Romantics, in which he once shared. The words which Hölderlin's Hyperion addresses to his friend Alabama before their parting are a prophetic criticism of the false path his friend was to follow, to the misfortune of Germany and of Europe."

"You grant the State too much power," he says. "For the gift of Love and the Spirit cannot be forced. Let it leave them untouched, or let men take its law and nail it to the pillory. By Heaven he knows not how he sins, who would make the State a moral schoolmaster. Whenever man has sought to make the State his Heaven, he has made it Hell. . . ."

> "O rain from heaven, O breath of the Spirit, Thou wilt restore to us the springtime of the peoples."
> "The State has no jurisdiction over thee. But if it does not hinder thee, thou wilt yet com'e, thou wilt come with thine almighty glory and raise us above mortality" (*Werke*, 456).

This eschatological vision of the descent of "the youngest, fairest daughter of time, the New Church," it is almost identical with the vision of the renewal of Christendom with which Novalis concluded his *Europa*, while at the same time in England William Blake was creating a similar apocalypse on a gigantic scale in the series of epics which culminated in *Jerusalem*. The descent from these cloudy summits of the romantic Sinai to the worship of the Secular State, that Golden Calf in the desert of materialism, is one of the strangest events in history of European thought, and the philosophy of Hegel remains as a mighty monument to and symbol of this spiritual journey into the wilderness.[12]

Dawson in each of the four decades of his writing career devoted an essay to German thinkers and the German tradition as part of secularized Christendom.

He claimed that the aim of Spengler's two volumes on *The Decline of the West* was a practical one—to plot out the descending curve of Western civilization and to make the present generation conscious of the crisis it is undergoing and the true task that lies before it. The final task of the German people is to take over the direction of the world from France and England through a practical, organizing, imperialistic type of Socialism, patterned on the type of Cecil Rhodes.

In the essays on Marx and Hegel we see how a secularized Jew and a secularized Lutheran became prophets of different secular absolutes to replace the lost vision of Christendom. Marx made absolute the "proletariat" in his apocalyptic judgment of the capitalist world, and Hegel identified the Prussian state with the movement of God in history.

However, it is in the 1952 chapter on "Germany and Central Europe" that Dawson gives a regional historical analysis of the German tradition. The focus is primarily on the nineteenth century and on the three Germanys that were capable of becoming the basis of a national German state—the Germany of the West and the South and the imperial states of Austria and Prussia, the latter "a colonial Baltic power which had elbowed its way into Germany and established an alien despotism on the ruins of the Reich" (69).

The fact that it was Prussian conservatism and not West German liberalism that eventually succeeded is attributed by Dawson to the superior quality of its leadership rather than to its inherent strength. In the intellectual sphere Prussia found its philosopher and teacher in Hegel, "the greatest of all West German converts to the Prussian idea" (75), while in the sphere of politics Prussia found a statesman of the first rank in Bismarck, whose "ruthless and revolutionary will to power" was at the service of the Prussian crown and state. But neither figure provided a final solution to the conflicting tendencies and tensions in Germany and Europe. Hegel's philosophy led either to the worship of the Prussian state or the ideal of social revolution, while Bismarck's *"Machiavellian statecraft"* made him a revolutionary and destroyer of the wider field of European and even Central European order.

A good illustration of this is the effect on Austria of the severance of its bond with Germany in 1866. Austria's international position made her the natural mediator between Germany and the rest of Europe. The Hapsburg monarchy had risen to greatness as the champion of a universal religious ideal and the patron of an international Catholic culture. But the self-assertion of German nationalism in the Second Reich after 1866 stimulated the forces of nationalism everywhere in Europe and found expression in the later nineteenth-century pan-German ideology, with its anti-Semitism, its anti-Catholicism, and its cult of the pure Nordic race.

The acceptance by Austria of these ideas was "an act of spiritual suicide" since it meant the denial and destruction of all the spiritual values on which Austrian culture had been built.

> Now all of this was to be cast aside, and the common heritage of baroque Austria and classical Vienna was torn to pieces between the rival fanaticisms of the Pan-Germans and the Pan-Slavs. Grillparzer, who remained loyal to the last to the old Austrian tradition, summed up the situation in 1848 in a prophetic sentence: "The path of modern culture leads from humanity through nationality to bestiality." (77–78)

The exclusion of Austria from the new German unity was ultimately disastrous for Germany itself. It meant the loss of those qualities of moderation and international responsibility and their replacement with the anxiety and uncertainty of the old Prussian tradition, which eventually drove the rest of Europe down the "fatal road" of competitive rearmament and the tragedy of the First World War.

The war destroyed the monarchies and empires of Prussia and Austria. The only course open for Germany was to return to the liberalism of West

Germany. Dawson views the appeal to the tradition of Weimar as a gesture of propaganda to cover the bankruptcy of the Second Reich. The leader of the new German democracy, the Socialist party, found its spiritual home in Berlin rather than Weimar, and two years after the war Spengler saw a deep underlying affinity between Socialism and the Prussian tradition. Dawson quotes Spengler, "Socialism spells Power" ("Macht, Macht und Weider Macht" 80).

The world needs a new Caesar, and the Prussian tradition alone provides the source of such a leader. Unfortunately, Germany found a new Cataline rather than a new Caesar.

Hitler was neither a Prussian nor a true Austrian.

> But he possessed a genius for utilizing all the destructive and negative elements in the different German traditions—Austrian, Pan-Germanic, Prussian militaristic and *Machtpolitik*, South Germanic political romanticism—each of which contributed its share to National Socialist ideology and the totalitarian party state. Thus Hitler succeeded at last in uniting the three Germanys and building a greater German Empire. But he did so at the expense of all that was best in both German and Austrian traditions. His victory led inevitably to the total war which has brought Germany, and Europe also, to a state of division and dissolution more complete than they have ever known, even after the Thirty Years War. (80)

Dawson however, does not end his chapter with Hitler. He goes back to the nineteenth century and holds Bismarck responsible for the catastrophe. Neither Metternich nor his Prussian rivals, nor the liberals, were prepared to sacrifice the cause of Europe and the unity of Central Europe to a one-sided solution imposed by violence:

> The fatal step was taken only when Bismarck decided to abandon the way of conciliation and to achieve national unity under Prussian leadership by the way of blood and iron. And it was the success of his Machiavellian statecraft and his ruthless use of military force which did more than anything else to change the current of public opinion in Germany and to popularize that worship of power and contempt for international morality, which have had such a demoralizing effect on the German mind during the last eighty years. (81)

Dawson underlines the irony of Bismarck's Protestantism in a secularized Christendom. Bismarck had no intention of destroying the moral character and authority of the German state, since he saw himself as "God's Soldier" and as loyal to the Lutheran ideal of a Christian state. But as his life-long opponent Constantin Frantz insisted, the contrast between his Lutheran piety within Germany and his organized piracy outside was bound in the long run to undermine the former.

Frantz believed that only a new system of federal organization offered a true solution to the problem of Germany and the problem of Europe, and this was the urgent political question at the time when Dawson wrote this chapter circa 1952. It is interesting to note that Dawson found it difficult to suppose that the existing division of Europe could be a permanent one, a remarkable comment given the revolutionary turn of events in Europe during the last decade.

Eastern Europe and Russia[13]

The history of Eastern Europe provides a wholesome corrective to the native confidence in material progress which was so characteristic of Western culture, alike in Europe and America, during recent generations. It shows us how painful and costly the work of civilization must be: how again and again the Christian peoples have seen their hard-won achievements destroyed in a moment so that they have had to start again from the beginning. Yet still the work went on. The ruined towns were rebuilt, the devastated fields were brought back into cultivation, and the tradition of Christian culture kept alive. All this forms a part of the common European achievement, since the efforts and sacrifices of the peoples of the East made possible the relative security of the peoples of the West that was the condition of their progress. Thus Eastern and Western Europe are not rival representatives of conflicting traditions of culture. They are members one of the other and owe each other a debt of mutual gratitude and understanding. Professor Halecki's book is a notable contribution to the payment of this debt.[14]

The tragic events in Eastern Europe after the Second World War and the ignorance of the British public concerning the history of this region resulted in Dawson's 1950 essay in *The Dublin Review*, "Christian Culture

in Eastern Europe,"[15] A great part of the essay focuses on the secularization of Christian culture in that area.

Down to the sixteenth century Eastern Europe shared in the common
cultural and religious life of Western Christendom. Then the new advance
of Islam severed the Christian nations of the Balkans in Southeastern
Europe from the rest of Christendom for five centuries, and the Hapsburg
Empire absorbed the other smaller kingdoms with the exception of Poland
and Lithuania. Dawson sees the Cossack revolt that swept over the Ukraine
in 1648 as the turning point in Eastern European history, since it actually
resulted in the ruin of both the Ukraine and Poland, to the benefit of
Moscow. It was Peter the Great in the early decades of the eighteenth century who launched not only Russia but the whole of Eastern Europe on the
path to secularization and absolute power through the international type of
court culture, as reflected in the palaces of Petersburg, Berlin, and Vienna.

The same community of type is to be seen in the military organization of these three absolutist states: Russia, Prussia, and Austria. Dawson
underlines Dr. Karl Mannheim's point that this military organization is
the first great institution for the artificial production of uniform mass
behavior. Thus it is one of the fundamental conditions of the modern
totalitarian state in Eastern Europe:

> The result of this achievement for Eastern Europe itself was nothing less
> than a profound change in spiritual values. The new army was the creator
> of the new state, and it took the place of the Church as the dynamic ele-
> ment in Eastern European society. Hitherto even in the West the rational-
> ist planning of the statesmen and officials had affected only the upper sur-
> face of society, and the life of the peasant and the local village community
> had continued to follow its traditional way of life. But men like Peter the
> Great and Frederick the Great took hold of the whole social system and
> made it the instrument of their ruthless political will and intelligence. (24)

This tradition of absolute power survived the downfall of the three
military empires during the First World War and was revived in a new
form under Lenin, Stalin, and Hitler. Dawson defines the totalitarian state
in Eastern Europe as "a monstrous hybrid born from the unnatural union
of Western revolutionary tradition and the Eastern tradition of the mili-

tary police state" (28–29). He sees the rise of this type of state as changing the whole pattern of political organization and the climate of culture in the world as a whole:

> Everywhere the threat of the totalitarian state and the prestige of the totalitarian ideal of mass planning have led to a great change of the balance of power as between the state and the individual, and to the narrowing or elimination of that margin of freedom, thanks to which the higher forms of culture have been able to grow and bear fruit. (30)

The conclusion of this article focuses on the Catholic tradition in Eastern Europe, using blunt language:

> One thing remains, however, the Christian kingdom of faith, the sphere of spiritual freedom—and so long as this remains intact there is still hope for the world. Now it is in this point that the immense importance of the Catholic tradition in Eastern Europe is to be seen. The sixty million—or whatever the number may be—of Catholics in Eastern Europe stand in the front line of the struggle which will decide the fate of humanity. (30)

He singles out the Catholics of the Uniate rite, who have always been the first to be attacked and the most bitterly persecuted. They have to face a new type of persecution, which is aimed with "diabolical cunning and persistence" at the very spirit of martyrdom itself. This new kind of Communist justice, which he calls "spiritual totalitarianism" culminates not in the martyr's witness and glorious death, but in a voluntary confession that deprives the martyr and his cause of moral prestige and is followed by a secret imprisonment or execution.

This threat to spiritual freedom by mass psychological pressure can be met not so much by new spiritual weapons as by sharpening the old ones, "which have been allowed to grow rusty during the long periods during which Christians have been unaccustomed to the prospect of martyrdom and to the problems of active persecution" (34).

Dawson, with his acute sense of history and geography, reminds the reader that this is not a new situation. Many times in history Eastern Christendom has been more exposed to attack than Western Christendom, and it has had to suffer for the Church as a whole. Going back in time to the Roman Empire, Eastern Europe was the region where the Church endured the greatest persecutions.

"It was the army of the Danube and its leaders, the Illyrian emperors, who were responsible for the most formidable attack on Christianity; it was the Eastern provinces that contributed the greatest number of martyrs; and it was at Sophia that the freedom of the Church was finally won by the Edict of Sardica in 311" (34–35).

The last paragraph ends on the note that this new danger might be only the beginning of a long struggle that will be fought out in the West as well as in the East. But at the present moment, it is the task of the Christians of the West to assert their solidarity with the faithful of Eastern Europe and not allow themselves to be misled or confused by propaganda that seeks to isolate Eastern Catholics and deprive them of their greatest strength and reward—their Christian witness.

Russia and Asia[16]

Consequently the triumph of Bolshevism was not a triumph of the popular will over Tsarist tyranny, or of revolutionary enthusiasm over conservative order. It was the victory of authority and discipline over democratic idealism and individualism. As we see clearly enough in the first volume of Trotsky's *History of the Russian Revolution*, it was the victory of a few men who knew what they wanted and allowed nothing to stand in their way over a vast majority that was driven to and fro by the uncertainty of the politicians and the passions of the mob. It was, above all, the victory of one man—Lenin—the most remarkable personality that the age produced.

. . . But Lenin's cynicism and hatred of "idealism" must not lead us to suppose that he undervalued ideas. He was above all a man of theory and he differed from the average Socialist leader, both among the Bolsheviks and outside the party, in his insistence on the philosophical absolutism of the Communist creed.

. . . Thus the Communist system, as planned and largely created by Lenin, was a kind of a theocracy, a spiritual order of the most rigid and exclusive type, rather than a political order. The state was not an end in itself, it was an instrument, or, as Lenin himself puts it, "simply the weapon with which the proletariat wages its class war—a special sort of bludgeon, nothing more."

Nothing could be more characteristic of Lenin's inhuman simplicity and directness than this sentence; for, unlike his Western admirers, Lenin was never afraid to call a bludgeon a bludgeon.[17]

Dawson's first article on Russia was probably prompted by his friend Edward Watkin, who had translated into English a study of Lenin and Bolshevism by a German sociologist, Waldemar Gurian, *Bolshevism, Theory and Practice*.[18] I have quoted a lengthy passage from the article in order to show how the movement of secularization in Russia at the beginning of the twentieth century illustrates Dawson's general thesis that it was a minority movement with its roots in the intelligentsia and proceeded from the absolute power that one section of it came to possess.

In the early years of the Second World War, Manya Harari asked Dawson to write an article on Russia for her new magazine, *The Changing World*. This gave him the opportunity to survey the course of Russian history, with most of the focus on the last three centuries—the period of the secularization of Russian culture. That article "What is Russia?" was later expanded to form chapter 6 in *Understanding Europe*, "Russia and Asia."

The introductory paragraph is worth quoting—it gives a vivid picture of Russia in place and time:

> Russia is not a country like the countries of Western Europe—a nation among the nations—it is a world apart which still remains a mystery to the average Westerner. There is no end to Russia—it is a land without frontiers, which stretches back endlessly in place and time. It is an open road into the heart of Asia. Along this road have come the great conquering peoples of the past—Huns and Avars, Khazas and Bulgars, Cumans and Mongols. They have founded their empires and passed away, but the Russian land remains.

Dawson distinguishes four periods in Russian history, which form four different worlds so to speak: those of Kievan Russia, Muscovy, Peter the Great, and Soviet Russia.

Although the movement of secularization commences with the days of Peter the Great, the actual form this movement took cannot be grasped without an understanding of Russian history. Dawson singles out in particular the period "of suffering and humiliation" under the "Tartar Yoke"—the Mongols and the world of Muscovy between the thirteenth and sixteenth centuries—as a time that had a profound impact on Russian consciousness, character, and destiny.

> It forged the Russian people into a solid mass with immense powers of endurance and resistance, but completely devoid of the personal humanist culture which had been growing in the West during the later Middle Ages. . . . The new Russia was a theocratic autocracy which regarded itself as the Third Rome, the successor of the Byzantine Empire, but which actually took the place of its old suzerain, the Tartar Empire of the Volga. (106)

That epoch was followed by the age of imperial expansion by the Muscovite State, a development accompanied by the progressive decline of the free elements in Russian society—the enslavement of the peasants by the landowners, the absorption of the nobles in the official class, and the complete subordination of the officials to the autocratic power of the Tsar. Peter the Great inherited this tradition. As we have seen, Dawson credits him with changing the course of Russian history and views his work as leaving an indelible impression on Russian culture. Indeed, Dawson sees him as

> one of the greatest rulers that the world has seen. Without sparing himself or anyone else, he drove his people relentlessly along the hard road to civilization. By sheer will-power and by thirty years of unremitting labour he triumphed over the dead weight of tradition, the inertia of the national character, the resistance of the aristocracy, the peasantry and the Church and the hostility of foreign powers, so that before he died the Russian state and society had been transformed from top to bottom. (109)

On the other hand, the very greatness of his achievement contained an element of weakness since it owed everything to the "autocratic will of a superman" and had no organic relation to the older tradition of Russian culture. This explains the divided state of national consciousness that characterized the whole period from Peter the Great to Nicholas II.

Dawson traces this consciousness among the educated classes in nineteenth-century Russia, among the Slavophiles, the Westernizers, and the

Nihilists. He sees the turning point in the history of modern Russia in the assassination of the Tsar Liberator (Tsar Alexander II) in 1881—the Tsar who had actually carried out the abolition of serfdom. This act of violence destroyed the hope of social reconciliation and peaceful reform, while the Marxists inherited the whole tradition of the revolutionary movement.

Although Marxism was a Western secular ideology, it was not without elements that had a special appeal to the Russian mind: the authoritarian element reflected in its dogmatic orthodoxy and party discipline; the historical fatalism leading to the apotheosis of the Communist state; the messianic spirit in relation to the liberating role of the proletariat, who are destined to create a new order of social justice:

> It was the first of these elements that proved the most decisive in the personality and work of Lenin, through which the fusion between Marxian Communism and Russian revolutionary tradition was finally achieved. Lenin was a born organizer with an intense will to power. It was he who forged the iron party discipline of the Bolshevik party and who transformed the Marxian theory of the dictatorship of the proletariat into the practical autocracy of a minority party based on revolutionary violence. (112)

Dawson points out that totalitarianism has a significance for Russia that is different from the West in that it has its roots in the Russian past and the Russian soul. This is especially evident in the Russian experience of slavery, which runs through every period of Russian history, from the Kievan period, the Mongol years, and to the third period, which was dominated by the institution of serfdom. He offers a wonderful quotation from one of Gorki's stories to show that a people that has endured such things cannot regard the State and the rights of man with the eyes of Western man (114–15).

Dawson views Stalin as a worthy successor to Lenin, who maintained the revolutionary dictatorship of the Communist party as a single organization of absolute power. He gives a dramatic example of this in the era of the middle thirties—the period that created the Constitution of 1936 declaring peace between the classes of the new society—but also inaugurated the time of terrorism and repression reflected in a series of wholesale purges.

The old party leaders, like Bukharin, Radek Zinoniev, were destroyed almost to a man, and after them in quick succession went the Communist exiles from Western Europe, the leaders of the constituent republics and the heads of the army and the G.P.U. No one was too influential or too unimportant to escape, and the fact that the vast majority of the accused admitted their guilt and accepted their condemnation with abject submissiveness gave a sinister impression of the irresistible power of the new autocracy. (118–19)

He ends the chapter on Russia with the question whether a secular ideology such as Communism is strong enough to create a lasting social unity between peoples of such diverse identity, culture, and traditions as the Slavs of Eastern Europe, the Turks of Central Asia, and the Chinese and other people of the Far East—a question that was answered two decades after Dawson's death in 1970.

England[19]

Yet throughout this period (1900–1950) the secularization of English culture has proceeded almost without a check, so that our position is no longer that of a Catholic minority in a Protestant society, but that of a religious minority in a secular or neo-pagan civilization. We have become so accustomed to this change that we are apt to forget its tremendous implications. During the last hundred years English Catholicism has developed under the protection of the Victorian compromise. We have accepted the Victorian principles of individual freedom, religious toleration, and the limited character of the State as elementary conditions of existence, which hardly needed to be defended. But, in proportion as civilization becomes secularized, all these principles and rights lose their moral validity. Secular civilization breeds secular ideologies, and these secular ideologies find their political expression in totalitarian States. . . . But it is obvious that English Catholicism cannot rely on the continuance of the conditions that prevailed during the first century of its restored existence. Sooner or later it must come up against the same forces that prevail in the rest of the world. . . . Today these familiar controversies are overshadowed by the world debate between Christianity and atheism, and we have to deal not with the validity of Anglican orders but with the existence of the human soul and the ultimate foundations of the moral order.

This is a tremendous task, since the gulf which separates the world of Newman's *Loss And Gain* or that of Mrs. Wilfrid Ward's novels from the world of George Orwell's *1984* or Koeslter's *Darkness At Noon* is not one that can be measured in terms of years or generations.[20]

Dawson often pointed out that the movement of secularization in England and America followed a different pattern from the one in Europe and elsewhere, with their violent revolutions and civil wars. He devoted a number of essays to different aspects of this movement: the revolutionary social and economic effects of industrialism; the Oxford Movement as an attempt to resist the secularization of the Anglican tradition; the totalitarian nature of the sociological changes taking place in England; the humanitarian tradition in Victorian England as the result of cooperation between Christians and secular idealists; and finally, the situation of English Catholicism in the twentieth century in relation to the vanishing protection afforded by the Victorian compromise.

The one essay that gives the best general picture of the course of English history and the secularization of English culture is "The World Crisis and the English Tradition," published in 1933. The crisis that arose in the modern world during the postwar period, he argues, cannot be solved by some simple remedy that can be applied to every society indifferently. Each people has to find the individual solution that is in conformity with its own sociological and historical structure.

Dawson sees the three centuries that followed the Renaissance and Reformation as the period during which English national culture acquired its characteristic form. The duality of culture on the Continent between the traditions of the court and the city on the one hand and the peasant tradition on the other were absent in England, where society and culture were single and homogeneous. It was essentially rural and centered on the family in the country houses or in the homes of the merchants.

> But with the close of the Georgian period a profound change begins to pass over English society. England ceases to be an agrarian State, and the new industry, which has been developing for more than half a century, becomes the dominant element in the life of the nation. The centre of gravity shifts from the village and the country house to the industrial town, the mine and the factory.

. . . With the twentieth century we see the coming of a new urban civilization, which has no contact with the English tradition. The old ideals have grown discredited, and the Englishman no longer disdains to dwell in flats. And with the flat comes a corresponding new anti-domestic ethos; divorce, birth control, the turning to outer society for all vital needs. (253–54)

This new urban-industrial civilization has a secular philosophy that inspires it, and that, as he says, invariably sacrifices sociology to economics and that even in economics prefers "immediate profit to ultimate advantage" (258). It sees the true foundations of society in commerce and industrial production and idealizes the consequent "standard of life," which results from the spread of urban and bureaucratic centralization and the expenditure of money on the so-called social services.

If England is to be saved from the destructive effects of this movement it must abandon the "economic fatalism" that has dominated English thought for the last hundred years and free itself from the "decaying remains" of nineteenth-century philosophy. It must base its national policy on sound sociological principles and recognize that the true foundations of society are to be found in the family and the land. Science and technology can be used in the service of rural life as well as of urban industry by restoring the life of the English countryside. But this is not an easy task since rural society is being deprived of social leadership.

The old landowning class filled so large a place in rural society that its disappearance leaves an immense gap in the social and cultural life of the countryside, and nothing is being done to fill it, owing to the concentration of all vital forces of the nation in the great cities. Here again there is a pressing need for the restoration of social equilibrium by a measure of cultural decentralization and by a more even distribution of the noneconomic resources of the nation between the city and the countryside. And all these changes are not merely desirable, they are absolutely necessary if England is to survive. (259–60)

Dawson again underlines the immense difficulty of this task in the concluding paragraph. What he calls a "movement of social regeneration" requires a vigorous moral effort and a consciousness of our responsibility, together with the need to review our whole scheme of social values. The "work of social restoration" must be preceded and accompanied by the rebuilding of England's intellectual and spiritual traditions—a revolutionary note on which to end the essay.

This secular philosophy of liberal capitalism and the movement toward urban and bureaucratic centralization formed part of a wider tendency toward the total secularization of English culture that Dawson underlines in his other writings on England and Western civilization in the thirties and after. From the sociological point of view, England was moving in the direction of the totalitarian state, with a different set of ethical and social ideals from those of the Fascists and Communists. He pointed out to the Christian Socialists in England that it was easy to denounce the un-Christian behavior of the Nazis because Englishmen have no temptation to behave as they do. In a passage often quoted by reviewers of *Religion and the Modern State*, he wrote:

> Nobody supposes that the Y.M.C.A. or Toc H are likely to start hunting down pacifists or trying to beat up Lord Melchett or Mr. Lansbury. Our temptations are more subtle but no less real. It may be harder to resist a Totalitarian State which relies on free milk and birth-control clinics than one which relies on castor oil and concentration camps. The latter offends all our humanitarian instincts and traditions, the former appeals to those very instincts and allies itself with the movement for social reform which is so intimately connected with modern English religion.[21] (108)

America[22]

Unfortunately the trend in this direction (a totalitarian technocratic civilization) comes not only from the Fascists and the Communists who have inherited the traditions of the autocratic police state and are going into it with their eyes open. It also comes from the mass civilization of the Western democracies which are going into it with their eyes shut. As Professor Karl Manheim pointed out years ago in "Man and Society" there is a growing similarity between the liberal democracies and the totalitarian states. And this is not only due to the reason he gives that the old liberal state has become a social services state which is committed to economic and social planning. It is due even more to the mechanization of social and economic life which has developed furthest in the United States where private capitalism and free enterprise still maintain themselves. For in the U.S.A. no less than in the U.S.S.R. we are conscious of the victory of the mass over the individual. Moreover we see in America how material prosperity and technical efficiency produce social conformity, so that without any intervention on the part of the state, men of their own accord tend to think the same and look the same and behave in the same way. None of this is peculiar to the United States. It is only that in America the standard of material prosperity is higher and the counter-balancing forces of authority and tradition are weaker. And consequently the United States has been the pioneer of a popular hedonistic mass civilization which is the chief alternative to the totalitarian ascetic mass civilization of Communism.[23]

In the twenties and the thirties Dawson studied the culture of America in the seventeenth, eighteenth, and twentieth centuries, but it was not until the fifties that he covered the four periods of American history that he viewed as four separate cultures, "four Americas and four American peoples." This conception of American history he develops with exceptional clarity in two essays: "Europe Overseas: The New World of America" (1952) and the "Development of the American Educational Tradition" (1955/61).

The second period of American history, 1774–1861, the period from the Revolution to the Civil War, saw the secular ideology of the *Rights of Man* become the basis on which various colonial cultures were united. In the "Europe Overseas" chapter, Dawson quotes a marvelous passage from Thomas Paine's pamphlet *Common Sense* (1776) to show how the legal and the constitutional issues were impatiently swept aside and replaced by a "flaming rhetoric" for the liberation of mankind and the creation of a new world.

> "O ye that love mankind," he writes, "stand forth; every spot of the old world is overcome with oppression. Freedom has been hunted round the globe. Asia, Africa have long expelled her. Europe regards her like a stranger and England has given her warning to depart. O! receive the fugitive and prepare in time an asylum for mankind. . . . We have it in our power to begin the world over again. A similar situation to the present hath not happened since the days of Noah until now. The birthday of a new world is at hand, and a race of men perhaps as numerous as all

Europe contains are to receive their portion of freedom from the event of a few months. The Reflection is awful—and in this point how tri-fling, how ridiculous do the little paltry cavillings of a few weak or inter-ested men appear, when weighed against the business of a world." (167)

Nevertheless, this second period of American culture did not lead to the secularization of culture in a way comparable with that Europe. Daw-son views the third age, from 1861 to 1921, as the decisive period in which the secularizing forces in American culture assume a predominant role both in the sociological and intellectual spheres. The leadership of America passed from the statesman-like Lincoln to the men of business—the great financiers and captains of industry such as Gould, Vanderbilt, Rockefeller, Carnegie, Armour, Cooke, and Pierpont Morgan.

These were the men who reaped the fruits of the Civil War and directed the vast movement of material expansion which took place during the last three decades of the nineteenth century. These men wielded a power which was undreamed of by the founders of the Constitution. They were economic imperialists who created new empires of gold and steel and oil. But they were also representative Americans who did more to determine the evolution of modern American civilization than either the thinkers or the politicians. (172–73)

The social inequality between this aristocracy of financial and industrial magnates and the proletariat of wage earners drawn from the over-popu-lated areas of southern and eastern Europe increased social tensions and class conflicts, which often expressed themselves with "extraordinary vio-lence and bitterness," and Dawson cites the Homestead Strike at Pitts-burgh in 1892 and the Pullman Strike at Chicago in 1894 as examples.

For the writers and thinkers who represented the old social traditions and the old spiritual ideals it was an age of disillusionment. Dawson men-tions Henry Adams and Mark Twain, but it is Herman Melville from whom he quotes to illustrate this change of attitude. In his early period Melville's faith in the American ideal was definitely a messianic one.

We Americans are the peculiar chosen people—the Israel of our time; we bear the ark of the liberties of the world. . . . [T]he rest of the nations must soon be in our rear. We are the pioneers of the world, the advance guard sent on through the wilderness of untried things to break a new path in the New World that is ours.[24]

A quarter of a century later, this optimism had disappeared and his messianic hope is replaced with apocalyptic despair.

> . . . 'Twill come, 'twill come!
> One demagogue may trouble much:
> How if a hundred thousand such?
> And universal suffrage lent
> To back them with brute element
> Overwhelming? What can bind these sea
> Of rival sharp communities
> Unchristianized? Yes, but 'twill come!
>
> Indeed these germs one may now view:
> Myriads playing pigmy parts,—
> Debased into equality:
> In glut of all material arts
> A civic barbarism maybe:
> Dead level of rank commonplace:
> An Anglo-Saxon China, see
> May on your vast plains shame that race
> In the Dark Ages of Democracy.[25]

But this is only one side of the picture. In two chapters of *The Crisis of Western Education,* "The Development of the American Educational Tradition" and "Education and the State," Dawson shows how the school and college took the place of the Church as the cultural center of American life and thus became a potent influence in the unification of American culture at a time when territorial expansion and foreign immigration made for disintegration. He singles out Lester Ward (1841–1913) and John Dewey (1859–1952) as apostles of the new faith in science and democracy in the world of education. To the latter, education was a humanitarian religion, "the pastoral ministry of the democratic community."

"Now Dewey, in spite of his secularism, had a conception of education which was almost purely religious. . . . It is inspired by a faith in democracy and a democratic 'mystique' which is religious rather than political in spirit. Words like 'community,' 'progress,' 'life,' and 'youth,' but above all 'democracy' itself, have acquired a kind of numinous character which gives them an emotional or evocative power and puts them above rational criticism."[26]

In the two following sentences we get a rare example of Dawson's humor.

> But when it comes to the question of the real significance and content of education we cannot help asking what these sacred abstractions really amount to. Do not the most primitive and barbarous peoples known to us achieve these ends of social participation and communal experience by their initiation ceremonies and tribal dances more than any modern educationalist with his elaborate programs for the integration of the school with life and the sharing of common experience? (104–5)

In the fourth age of American culture, from 1921 to 1952, Dawson draws the parallel between Europe and America and argues that since 1945 Western civilization on both continents is faced with the same problem of how to reconcile the old spiritual values with the new techniques of mass power and mass civilization.[27] He gives a long quote from de Tocqueville's *Democracy in America* [28] to show that it was in America that de Tocqueville discovered the totalitarian tendency inherent in mass civilization and the new dangers to human freedom that lay hidden in democratic institutions. On the other hand Dawson notes that de Tocqueville showed how the United States was protected by a series of factors that mitigated the tyranny of the majority, and he outlines the four major ones.

Nevertheless, a series of changes have made America of the fourth period a different social organism from that which de Tocqueville knew. Dawson twice makes the point that America cannot continue to live on the traditions of a vanished social order. Indeed this order is threatened by the techniques of modern mass civilization, which are bound to exert a growing influence on the world of politics unless they are controlled by some positive spiritual force and guided by some positive rational principles.

> In the past American society derived this force from the religious idealism of sectarian Protestantism, and its principles from the eighteenth-century

ideology of Natural Rights and rational Enlightenment. But today both
these forces have lost their power. American religion has lost its supernatural faith and American philosophy has lost its rational certitude.
What survives is a vague moral idealism and a vague rational optimism,
neither of which is strong enough to stand against the inhuman and
irrational forces of destruction that have been let loose on the modern
world. (181–82)

In the concluding paragraph Dawson returns to the theme of the crisis facing Western civilization. It cannot be saved either by Europe or by
America. It demands a common effort, which must involve a deeper
process of cooperation based on common spiritual principles.

It has been the strength of the American tradition that it was consciously
founded on these principles as represented by the eighteenth-century ideology of Natural Law and human rights. The great problem today is how
these principles can be re-established on foundations which are both spiritually deeper and sociologically more realistic than the rational construc-
tions of eighteenth-century philosophy. (182–83)

Dawson's Sociological Approach in the Essays
Dealing with the Twentieth Century

Selfish Civilization[29]

But this philosophy has proved incapable of providing an enduring basis
for culture, And today its ideals are being swallowed up by the subver-
sive forces which it has itself liberated. The idealism of the great liberal
thinkers ended in the materialism of the acquisitive capitalist society
against which the conscience of the modern world is in revolt. What we
are suffering from is the morbid growth of a selfish civilization which
has no end beyond itself—a monstrous cancer that destroys the face of
nature and eats into the heart of humanity. As in the days of ancient
Rome, but on a far larger scale, men have made themselves the masters
of this world and find themselves left with nothing but their own sterile
lusts. For this "leisure civilization" in which the people sit down to eat
and drink and rise up to play is the dark world which has turned its face
from God and from which God's face is hidden. It is terrible not only on
account of its emptiness but 'because there is a positive power of evil

waiting to fill the void, like the unclean spirit in the parable that came out of the waste places into the empty soul.

. . . It is the horror of this empty and sterile world far more than any economic hardship or political injustice that is driving men to revolutionary action.

. . . The only true solution must be a religious one which will restore man's spiritual freedom and liberate him from the world of darkness and the kingdom of death.[30]

These essays can be grouped for the sake of brevity under at least six headings using metaphors coined by Christopher Dawson. They repeat some of the main themes that I have highlighted in the regional historical essays, and they point to the need for the conversion of modern secular civilizations, if it is not to destroy itself.

1. "The New Leviathan": the centralization of power as the central socio-logical reality of the technological order in modern civilization.

2. "The Age of Frankenstein": the technological order and the will to power as the spiritual disease affecting all types of secular culture in the modern world.

3. "The Age of the Cinema": the pressure of modern hedonistic mass civ-ilization and and the destruction of the human personality.

4. "The Age of the Hot House Culture and the World of Make Believe": the artificial nature of modern culture and the creation of a sub-religious type of humanity—"the sub-religious is in a certain sense the sub-human."

5. "The Age of Total Secularization": as reflected in the vast development of material resources and luxury, and the vast development of power.

6. "The Age of Universal Education": as a powerful element leading to the total secularization of modern culture and the extension of State control in all areas of life.

Social Apocalypticism[31]

The transitory nature of what Dawson termed the "liberal humanitarian culture" is a point so important that I think it is worthwhile highlighting it in this section. This culture was especially strong in English-speaking lands, indeed taken for granted, like the air one breathes, but Dawson was aware of its failure to prevent the growing secularization of culture and its incapability to resist the tremendous appeal of the various types of what he termed "social apocalypticism."

He referred to this phenomenon throughout the four decades of his writing career. One of its most striking expressions is in the book review he wrote for the October 1945 issue of *Blackfriars*, dealing with Arthur Koestler's book *The Yogi and the Commissar*, in which he speaks about "the spiritual tragedy of modern man" as reflected in the experiences of the revolutionary intelligentsia in the thirties and forties. The latter created the Marxian ideology, which in turn produced the Communist state.

> But something has gone wrong in the process. The intellectuals believed and taught that the Dictatorship of the Proletariat would be followed by the "withering away" of the State. In fact, however, what has happened has been the development of a State power more absolute than any absolutism of the past, and it has been the intelligentsia that has "withered away." All Koestler's books have been a running commentary on this process by one who has personally witnessed and shared the slow crucifixion of the revolutionary intelligentsia in the concentration camps of Europe, and, as he shows in his present book, the process has not ended with the defeat of Fascism. On the contrary, it has only meant the swallowing up of one Leviathan by another, and the extermination of minorities who had maintained a precarious marginal existence between the two. (366)

Further on Dawson quotes a long passage from Koestler describing the present predicament of Western civilization—it has ceased to be aware of the values that it is in peril of losing, and foremost among these values are the humanitarian ones. Then he proceeds to argue that Koestler does not seem to realize how heavy is the responsibility of the intellectuals themselves for the situation he describes so well.

> For the truth is that if the totalitarian state has been constructed by men of action—soldiers and policemen and politicians and engineers—it would never have become so formidable a threat to man's spiritual freedom. It would have been at least an external threat like the despotisms of

the past. It was the revolutionary intelligentsia which invented the dictatorship of the proletariat, and it was romantic idealists like Nietzsche and
Sorel who invented the Fascist mythology of creative violence. (368)

From this Dawson concludes that the denial of God by the intelligentsia was the turning point in Western civilization, and from then on
the road has led directly to the concentration camps and slaughterhouses
of the totalitarian state in its German and Russian forms.

> For it is obvious that any atheistic socialism, whether of the Left or the
> Right can only think in terms of the whole and not of the individual, and
> that it will seem as reasonable and just for it to liquidate a class or exter-
> minate a few million of social or racial undesirables as it is for a surgeon
> to conduct a major operation for the health of the organism as a whole.
> The revolutionary realist has an unanswerable case against the revolution-
> ary idealist when he accuses the latter of willing the end and refusing the
> means on sentimental grounds, and it is as difficult for a Christian to
> judge between them as it was for Alice to make up her mind between the
> attitude of the Walrus and that of the Carpenter toward the oysters. (369)

It is at this point that Dawson discusses the humanitarian tradition.
The humanitarianism of the modern intelligentsia cannot be written off as
a mere matter of sentiment. It was based on deep and sincere convictions,
akin to the nature of a religious faith, and there are few movements in history that have had so great an effect on human life.

> Nevertheless, it belongs to the age of transition between Christian and
> secular culture, and its chief successes were the result of a working coali-
> tion with the forces of organized religion such as we see in the case of
> the abolition of slavery or the factory acts or the movements against the
> exploitation of uncivilized people. Where humanitarianism is left to its
> own resources in a purely secular environment it tends to wither away
> like political idealism. (369)

Twenty-three years later, Great Britain, the home of liberal democracy
and parliamentary institutions, led the Western world in another one those
"epidemics of ideological insanity" in which whole populations are destroyed
"for the sake of some irrational slogan."[32] The irrational slogans of the birth

controllers and the population planners created the paranoia underlining the "population explosion" and resulted in the "silent Holocaust" on the unborn.

One is tempted to draw the parallel between the dictatorship of the proletariat in the thought of Lenin and the dictatorship of the birth controllers in the thought of the neo-Malthusians during the same period of the early twentieth century. The neo-Malthusians believed that war, poverty, crime, and unemployment would also "wither away" once the good news about contraception, sterilization, and abortion was forced upon those ethnic groups who were breeding too quickly. But something has gone wrong with this utopian vision, and it is the weak and the defenseless who are withering away at the expense of the strong and the powerful.

Spiritual Vacuum in Modernized Culture[33]

The last and perhaps the most important theme in Christopher Dawson's sociological analysis of the twentieth century is one that actually covers the whole period of Secularized Christendom and the Age of Revolution. This is the concept of the spiritual vacuum in modernized culture and the consequent need of and search for a holy community to fill the vacuum.

He devoted a number of essays to the religion of Jean Jacques Rousseau and the Jacobins' version of the holy community as the solution to the spiritual vacuum in the aristocratic society of eighteenth-century Europe. Then there are the studies of America to which I have already referred and of the Revolution, with Thomas Paine as a kind of American Rousseau in the aristocratic society of eighteenth-century America, and later John Dewey as the prophet of the religion of democracy in the third and fourth periods of American culture.

Next there are the studies of Marx and Lenin as prophets of the messianic role of the proletariat as a holy community in nineteenth-century Europe and twentieth-century Russia. Finally there are essays of the thirties, especially those in *Religion and the Modern State* (1935) and *Beyond Politics* (1939), in which he restates the position so eloquently expressed in the concluding section of the 1925 essay "Religion and the Life of Civilization," with the wonderful quotes from Francis Adams, D. H. Lawrence, and Albert Einstein on the spiritual vacuum in modern secular civilization, "To wreck the great guilty temple, and give us rest."

The average Englishman and American who accepted unquestioningly the modern relation of religion and culture, with the former confined to one hour on Sunday and the rest of the week devoted to the making of money, must have been surprised by Dawson's claim that the bourgeois culture of the modern capitalist state fails to satisfy the deepest need of the human spirit, "so that the hungry and dissatisfied turn for relief to the dry husks of Communism."[34]

But Dawson's fundamental thesis was that human nature needs a holy community, and if this need expressed itself in the past, it would continue to do so in the present and future. He saw the source of the spiritual attraction of the movements of Socialism and nationalism in:

> the revolutionary appeal to an ideal community based on the brotherhood of blood or the brotherhood of the workers against the external legal compulsions which determined the relations of governors and governed, as capitalists and wage earners.[35]

The significance of the Great War of 1914–18, which destroyed the three great continental empires, was:

> To set loose the impulse to community which had been confined in the strait-waistcoat of bureaucracy. The leading characteristic of all the new regimes and political movements that have arisen since 1917 has been the tendency to merge the State in the community and to assert the supremacy of the common will over every legal and constitutional limitation. (67)

From this Dawson concludes that the essence of totalitarianism is to be found not in dictatorship, but in the mass consciousness and mass organization: "the real conflict is not that between democracy and dictatorship, but between individualism and communitarianism" (68–69).

But while Dawson realized that from the sociological angle the secularized culture of the modern world needed some type of spiritual community to satisfy its deepest spiritual needs, he was skeptical of the claims of the various forms of social idealism to provide this remedy, since they ultimately were secular religions that denied the transcendent order and the reality of original sin. There is a passage from one of his less familiar essays,

"The Catholic Attitude to War," in which he underlines the tremendous importance of these doctrines:

> But any peace propaganda which shuts the eyes to realities is worthless and may even increase the danger which it sets out to combat. It has been the fault of both pacifism and liberalism in the past that they have ignored the immense burden of inherited evil under which society and civilization labour and have planned an imaginary world for an impossible humanity. We must recognize that we are living in an imperfect world in which human and superhuman forces of evil are at work and so long as those forces affect the political behavior of mankind there can be no hope of abiding peace.[36]

Behind every civilization there is a vision, Dawson wrote in the twenties, and this leads to the question of the truth about reality, as the above quotation points out. Since the sixties a wave of social idealism has swept over the Catholic world as it did over the Protestant world in the earlier decades of this century, and many Catholics are ignoring the "superhuman forces of evil" at work in the world and are trying to build "an imaginary world for an impossible humanity."

Perhaps the beginning of wisdom might be for them to read the last six chapters of *Religion and the Modern State* and meditate upon the truths contained therein:

> Only it is necessary that Christians should recognize this frontier: that they should remember that it is not the business of the Church to do the same thing as the State—to build a Kingdom like the other kingdoms of men, only better; nor to create a reign of earthly peace and justice. The Church exists to be the light of the world, and if it fulfils its function, the world is transformed in spite of all the obstacles that human powers place in its way. A secularist culture can only exist, so to speak, in the dark. It is a prison in which the human spirit confines itself when it is shut out of the wider world of reality. But as soon as the light comes, all the elaborate mechanism that has been constructed for living in the dark becomes useless. The recovery of spiritual vision gives man back his spiritual freedom. And hence the freedom of the Church is in the faith of the Church and the freedom of man is in the knowledge of God.[37] ◆

Bibliographical Notes

There is no study, as far as I am aware, of Christopher Dawson's writings on the sixth period of Christian culture. Probably the best guide is the collection of chapters dealing with the books he wrote on this period in Christina Scott's biography of her father, *An Historian and His World: A Life of Christopher Dawson, 1889–1970* (London: Sheed & Ward, 1984; reprinted in 1991).

The recent book of Paul Costello, *World Historians and Their Goals* (DeKalb: Northern Illinois University Press, 1993) devotes a full chapter to Dawson, "Christopher Dawson: The Tension between History and Its End," 126–53, but as the title indicates, the main focus is on his view of world history, and the pages toward the end which discuss Dawson on the period of the Enlightenment and after, repeat the usual secular absolutes and judge Dawson from that angle.

Probably the best material on the sixth period of Christian culture are the long review articles of his books touching on this period and some studies of his work since his death in 1970 that focus on this period to a great extent:

1. Rachel Taylor's review of *Progress and Religion in Sociological Review* 22 (1930): 42–65.

2. H. B. Parke's general study "Christopher Dawson," *Scrutiny*, vol. 5, no. 4 (Cambridge) (March 1937): 365–75. His rationalism and naturalism make him unsympathetic to Dawson's Catholic absolutes.

3. Mason Wade's review of *Religion and the Modern State in American Review*, vol. 6, no. 5 (January 1936): 347–57.

4. Philip Temple's general essay "Christopher Dawson, Philosopher of History," *Catholic Library World* (March 1942): 1–8.

5. Ross Hoffman's "The Task of Restoring Christendom," *Thought*, vol. 17 (March 1943): 12–24. A discussion of *The Judgment of Nations* (1942).

6. V. A. Demant's analysis and discussion of *Beyond Politics* (1939), "The Importance of Christopher Dawson," *Nineteenth Century and After*, vol. 129, no. 767 (January 1941): 66–75.

7. H. N. Fieldhouse's address "Liberalism in Crisis," *The Canadian Historical Association, Historical Papers* (Toronto: University of Toronto Press, 1944), 98–109. Discusses *Beyond Politics* together with other conservative examinations of liberalism.

8. W. P. Davey's review of *The Judgement of the Nations, Thomist,* vol. 6 (January 1945): 136–46.

9. Harold Knight's review of *Understanding Europe* (1952) in *Hibbert Journal* 50 (October 1951–July 1952): 419–21.

10. John J. Mulloy, "Cleaning the Great Guilty Temple," *Triumph,* vol. 4, no. 12 (December 1969): 22–26.

11. E. E. Y. Hales, "The Dawson Legacy," *Tablet* (April 1, 1972): 299–300.

12. Leo R. Ward, "Dawson on Education in Christian Culture," *Modern Age,* vol. 17, no. 4 (Fall 1973): 399–407.

13. J. R. Bliese, "Christopher Dawson: His Interpretation of History," *Modern Age,* vol. 23, no. 3 (Summer 1979): 259–65.

14. Russell Hittinger, "The Two Cities in the Modern World: A Dawsonian Assessment," *Modern Age,* vol. 28, no. 1 (Spring/Summer 1984): 193–202.

15. John J. Mulloy, "Christianity, Capitalism, Marxism," in P. J. Cataldo, ed., *The Dynamic Character of Christian Culture* (Lanham, MD: University Press of America, 1984), 159–78. Mulloy analyzes them in the thought of Dawson.

16. Fernando Cervantes, "A Vision to Regain? Reconsidering Christopher Dawson, (1889–1970)," *New Blackfriars,* vol. 20, no. 831 (October 1989): 437–49. Published to commemorate the centenary of Dawson's birth.

17. John J. Mulloy, "J. C. Murray and Christopher Dawson: The Pluralist Society or Jerusalem and Babylon?" in Donald J. D'Elia and Stephen M. Krason, eds., *We Hold These Truths and More: Further Catholic Reflections on the American Proposition* (Steubenville, OH: Franciscan University Press, 1993), 46–61.

18. Christina Scott, "The Vision and Legacy of Christopher Dawson," *Downside Review,* vol. 114, no. 397 (October 1996): 283–93.

PART

III

The Catholic Historical
Complexion: Two
Specific Areas of Study

Galahad Naif: The Experience of a Student Wrestling with the Enlightenment

Carl B. Schmitt, Jr.

ONE of the first history courses I took in college was French medieval history in my sophomore year. In the opening lecture the professor was eager to explain that we could not approach the subject with a twentieth-century outlook. We had to come to grips with "the medieval worldview." He told us that we should not be afraid to get into how the Catholic Church looked upon man and his world.

What the professor had to say was mildly surprising. I had come to Harvard knowing that it was a bastion of a secularized view of things and that it stood watch in the vanguard of what its proponents like to call "the Enlightenment Project"—that open-ended struggle to build the city of man without God. I was even more surprised when Professor Charles Taylor went on to say that reaching for a particular Catholic doctrine to understand this or that aspect of medieval culture might not be enough. Those doctrines, he explained, were understood not as so many independent propositions; they rather came together as an expression of faith. "Keep in mind," he added, "that one of those doctrines—a key one—says that faith is a gift, a gift of God."

For a young Catholic who wanted to live his faith while profiting from a Harvard education, this was encouraging. When I went off to college, my father's parting words had been "Remember, my boy, you are not going to Harvard to get wisdom. You are there to get a training. Wisdom comes from the faith and from your family."

Those words meant something to me, because from my family upbringing I had constantly drunk in the notion that "the world"—as distinct from our family—was a thoroughly cockeyed place. I don't think I had heard of the Enlightenment, let alone an "Enlightenment Project." Usually it was more simply called "the modern world," or more often just "the world." I was thoroughly imbued with the idea that it was not only antagonistic to the faith, but destroying itself in an exaggerated commitment to a "social outlook" to the exclusion and diminishment of "family" and "person"; it was given over to money and temporal security without any notion of Providence.

This "family wisdom" involved something more than a solid upbringing in the faith. Its governing constituents can be summarized in this triad of "family, society, and person," and each of these elements was laden with associated notions in what in retrospect I can only call a complete Christian anthropology. To reduce that wisdom to a simple contrast between a "Godless society" and what one might get from a good Catholic upbringing in the family would miss the richness of my father's thought. In seeing me go off to Harvard, he was not resigning himself pessimistically to some fearful unknown; "society" was not intrinsically evil, and "the world" has a good meaning as well as a bad one in Christian tradition. In his view, man properly lived in all three dimensions, or "planes," as he called them. Family dealt with *origins*—in human birth and Christian baptism. Society, the second, had to do with *means*—"life lived" in survival and service in a world beyond the family, and again in a way that is both temporal and eternal. Origins and means finally point to *ends*—to death, which is also the gateway to the fullness of the eternal in the divine. Death and embracing the eternal is *personal*, and only in Christ's death does one find the fullness of the human in conjunction with the divine. Christianity is basically personal, but all three planes are important. All three should go together in balance for one to be truly human and fully Christian.

This "family wisdom"—really my father's wisdom—had a rich and profoundly human and Catholic content that my father had constantly conveyed through his own life as an artist and as father of a large and poor family. We were ten children; as one of the younger ones I profited from hearing, seeing, and feeling this wisdom in action as it incessantly percolated through a rich family life. It had all sprung from my father's profoundly Catholic aesthetic philosophy, which at the same time was coherent with his own deep and simple piety. Only a few of us showed enough talent to dare follow him in an artistic vocation (I not among them), but we all shared in his Catholic vision of things.[1]

Because of this, I knew exactly what he meant with that fatherly reminder as I headed off to college—including even his using the word "training." This was a good that "society" had to offer, and one should not shrink from getting the best training. Yet anything "social" had to be kept in its proper place by the "familial" and the "personal." This family background made me feel almost a stranger in the new college world I was entering. Not exactly a stranger, because I knew exactly why I was there, but I carried a perspective on everything that was all but impossible to explain and difficult to share with fellow students. At the same time, I carried this family wisdom with something of a superiority complex, tempered by my awareness that I still had a way to go in fully absorbing that inheritance and appropriating my own.

I had some grasp that the "social" world I was entering dealt with only aspects of man, whereas "family" and "person" dealt with the whole man. Family and person took man in the concrete—family, on the "first plane" of simple and direct encounter with the truth and beauty of being; and person, on the "third plane" of each one's most intimate and profound depths, where dying and the fullness of Being and glory meet. Between these two dimensions of man's existence lay the "second plane," the *social*. Here the person was dealt with in one or another abstraction from the concrete person, which means rationality, logic, categories, and classes of things, whether in science, technology, industry, or the market. Social categories and money go hand in hand; at this "dualistic" level the person tends to be seen merely as an *individual* in one or another socially defined group or even in the "mass" (and where the individual is even reducible to a number), whether it is community, corporation, or trade union, or more immediately for me, as college student, freshman, preppy/non-preppy—or even "Catholic."

Even as I looked forward to this "training" I knew I had to be on guard, because in our times "the social" is so all-embracing. Seeing matters this way put me at a distance even from most of my fellow Catholics, for the Church itself was equally victimized in our age by this same exaggerated "social" perspective, and all were affected. It was a familiar notion to me that the Church in fact is suffering a kind of death, comparable to Christ's own death. As a youngster I heard more than once from my father that today we in the Church "live in Holy Saturday." But Christian optimism was ever present. "You children," he would add, "will see the Resurrection."[2] I had in mind to major in political science and then go to law school, and with that *training* I would try to serve Christ and the Church in some small way.

For all that, in my freshman year I suffered the shock of discovering just how much this training was bound up with the Enlightenment Project, and yes, it was a time of tears. My first reaction was simply to get out of there; within only a few months I was ready to quit Harvard. It did not take too much, however, on the part of my father, but largely the wise words of an understanding older brother, to convince me that such a step would be a cop-out. Calm down; it was the Lord's own *"Quo vadis?"* that sent Peter back into the heart of Babylon. Yes, be prudent about the dangers, but the whole point of the faith is that it conquers all. "No matter what intelligent men throw at you, my boy, remember this: anything that is *really* intelligent is vindicated in Christ." Several months later I asked my father, "But how do you get wisdom?" The answer was immediate and succinct: "On your knees."

I was fully aware that as I wrestled with this "second-plane" world of *means*, I indeed had some way to go in approaching the fuller wisdom stemming from my origins and so to enter into the *personal* plane that would focus on it all in *ends*. It was no little help that I immediately befriended a Catholic upperclassman with a strong faith, at least once I invited him to visit my family—especially to meet and hear my father. And so it would be with many other friends in the course of my undergraduate years with whom I hoped to share in some small way the "family wisdom."

I took the occasion of those vacation-time visits to elicit from my father as much talk as I could, often extending into the late hours. One time he would be elaborating on how hierarchy and aristocracy are intrinsic to man in his familial origins, and how out of this there develops the distinct social dimension, which includes the notion of equality, which tends to egalitarianism and terminates in mass man. The two are held together in proper balance through the personal dimension of man. Another time the talk would be on the way social man limits intelligence to abstract reasoning—logic is *dualistic*, "second plane" thinking, an important and useful *means*, but one that knows nothing of *familial* intelligence that apprehends reality directly, nor of the higher personal intelligence that lies open to reality in *vision*, all of which the artist—and the saint—are especially gifted with. "You have to be suspicious of dichotomies and learn to think *trinally*," he would say. "When they ask you what comes first, the chicken or the egg, they are trying to lock you into a 'dualism'; your answer should be 'Tell me about the rooster.' "

I am not sure how all of this struck my friends.[3] For the most part the family wisdom remained my own private mainstay and wrestling with the Enlightenment in terms of that wisdom my private and even secret project. The introductory course in my chosen field of study was interesting and even exciting, covering as it did the political thought of the West from Plato and Aristotle to Mills and Marx. But even here, and more so in subsequent courses, basic ideas and their truth were not on the menu. I was hardly surprised that political science at Harvard was called Government. What we were studying of course was *ways* and *means*—how democratic government works—or might better work. I also began to sense that the danger to one's faith in this intellectual world lay not so much in any particular argument of the Enlightenment Project against it, but more simply in a tacit but overwhelming assumption about what was to be excluded from acceptable discourse.

A turning point for me came in the fall of my sophomore year, with Professor Sam Beer's course, "Modern Parliamentary Governments." Beer constantly insisted that to get at the peculiarities of the French, British, American, and other approaches in government you really had to understand the historical context and traditions involved in each. What hit me was that if you really look at parliaments historically, you are driven back well behind the nineteenth or eighteenth centuries to their origins in the Middle Ages, and this is true of a whole host of related institutions, such as representation and taxation by consent, not to mention the limitations on government and the rule of law.

Now if this is true of parliaments and governments, in what other aspects of our culture might it not be so? The rise of the middle class? It seemed to me that the bourgeoisie has been "rising" in every generation since the eleventh century, and with it commerce and its various instruments, from the corporation to credit and double-entry bookkeeping, not to mention manufacture. The Scientific Revolution of the seventeenth century was certainly a revolution, but had it no antecedents? Sam Beer's course opened to me that by studying history, and specifically medieval history, I might get a more complete perspective on the Enlightenment Project than majoring in government could provide.

The clincher for my decision to switch to history came from the family wisdom. That triad of family origins, social means, personal ends, involves a time sequence; while each marks out a distinct phase in human life to full maturity, all three dimensions are involved at every stage and with a balance between them peculiar to that stage.[4] The precariousness of this balance is ever evident in the actual vicissitudes of every life under the interplay of God's providence and human choices. This triple sequence, moreover, is writ large in mankind's own story: Just as Christ Himself went through all three phases—in His hidden life, His public life, and His passion and death—so His Mystical Body recapitulates this in its own history.

Christianity entered a Greco-Roman Empire by bringing the full personal (supernatural) dimension to a culture that registered a balance between the fundamental familial and concrete base of Rome and the superposition of Greek social abstract universalism. That balance was progressively undone as the crisis of the Empire began in the later third century, with the Roman familial base increasingly manifesting itself especially in the West, which had been less touched by the Hellenistic culture and where Christ was the simple God-man rather than the "Logos incarnate." The barbarian successor-kingdoms brought a new and progressive ascendancy of this concrete and familial aspect and marked the disappearance of social universalism. The "good phase" of relative balance yielded to a progressive imbalance—a "bad phase"—in which an exaggerated familial and hierarchic (and purely feudal) situation resulted in the loss and eventual exclusion of all sense of the social. This entire time then was characterized as "familial," moving through successive good and bad phases of roughly five hundred years each, and ending in the later ninth and tenth centuries in an exclusive familial dominance that finally spelled disaster for Europe and the Faith.

The eleventh century, in my father's historical view, marked the beginning of a new Christian social sense. As this grew in strength in the face of the entrenched family-feudal aspects, a balance was once again achieved, a "crossing balance," as it were, between the familial and the social.[5] The great culture of the High Middle Ages marked a new "good" phase of what turns out to be a second thousand-year period, this time defined as "social." For by the later thirteenth century this social aspect had become strong enough to start the same process of imbalance that had occurred in the second half of the first millennium, but this time with the familial aspects ever on the wane. The Reformation marked the mid-millennial break comparable to the end of the Roman Empire in the first millennium. The vertical and hierarchical notions of authority yielded increasingly to the horizontal and egalitarian, eventually leading to a comparable and ever more exaggerated imbalance of an exclusive "social" outlook, which has reached its destructive extreme in the later nineteenth and twentieth centuries.[6]

The opening to history that Professor Beer provided thus found a ready response on my part in terms of the family wisdom that was so closely connected with my father's aesthetic insights. Furthermore, history, like art, *begins in—and never leaves—*concrete reality. Thus also memory, which is integral to art, starts from and yet never loses contact with present existence. If the fullness of aesthetic vision implies a vision that is Christian—always being founded in the real—so also the human reality that history deals with makes sense only on the same terms. It began to strike me how ours is a historical faith—not only in its mode of revelation from the call of Abraham to its fullness in the very person of Christ, but also in its implications. Just as Christ lay at the heart of my father's aesthetic—conjoining human and divine reality in one concrete being—so He stands at the center of history and its meaning—and thus also of each individual as a concrete historical being. I knew I was not cut out to be an artist, but I saw new prospects in studying history. Instead of merely getting a training in college, I saw in history a way of somehow connecting my training more directly with that wisdom.

This new direction in my studies received a direct impulse when at some time point during my sophomore year a good friend introduced me to the writings of Christopher Dawson. But those remarks by Professor Taylor already mentioned constituted a first encouragement to my optimism. Protégé of C. H. Haskins and child of the Enlightenment that he was, Taylor was a careful and conscientious historian and one of the most intellectually humble men I have ever known. Undoubtedly I was fortunate in the number of truly admirable professors I encountered, and I began to grow in my appreciation for the honest, careful work I found in them—and many other outstanding qualities as well. Yet this talent and sometimes even brilliance was tightly bound up with their resistance to any intrusion of faith—even any sniff of it. In fact, rationalists that they were, they were resistant to any intrusion that did not "arise from the evidence"—and this is what I had to wrestle with.

In this I began to see how their empirical bent made them at base philosophical realists, for the most part without their realizing it, and this provided me with new encouragement. Historians are notably resistant to philosophizing. My mentors certainly played with various ideologies, but looking at the evidence from the past so often forced them to be cautious.[7] My respect for their respect for the tools of the historian's craft could only increase.[8]

At the same time, history is not a matter of reconstructing everything that has happened in the past. All of my mentors, in one way or another, were seeking to find some meaning in that mass of past events. Enlightenment history began with a rejection of the Christian faith as supplying that meaning, taking *reason* as its measure and taking *man* rather than believing man and the Church as history's central protagonist and the key to its meaning. But history belongs as much to men of faith and, in the perspective with which I was operating, even more to men of faith. The fact that my mentors misguidedly claimed it for themselves constituted the great gap that was challenging me as I took my first step along this way.

Interestingly enough the honesty with which my mentors pursued their craft also made them keenly aware that the successive meanings that they had produced since the eighteenth century were never quite satisfactory. The pursuit was still going on and seriously so: It was no paltry desire to be innovative or rebellious against earlier "orthodoxies." Indeed, they were being driven to see that the historian himself brings meaning of his own to his very work of inquiry, such that the search for meaning without faith had reached a new problematical stage. But as I saw it, proclaiming the futility of that project from a faith stance would be merely a defensive tactic. The family wisdom involved embracing all that was human; their search therefore had validity even if it plunged the inquirer toward the depths of doubt.[9] I had already learned that faith could not arise as a conclusion of reason, even as man is called to rejoice in all that is human; true hope reaches divine clarity in human hopelessness—and these honest men were still optimistic. It began to dawn on me, in short, that my mentors were wrestling with the same problem I was, even if blindly and from the bottom up, as it were—and not always so blindly as one might think. The interesting thing for me was that this was always related to their efforts to be very good historians.[10]

These perceptions about the "realism" of history and the "problematic" that Enlightenment historians themselves were engaged in (at least the best of them) were of course anchored by a consciousness of the gap between faith and unfaith that lay at the root of the difference between a Christian view of history and the Enlightenment approach. What was most on my mind as I plowed into my various courses was finding any of the ways that man's "social" dimension had begun to develop in the first centuries of our millennium and had then increasingly asserted itself to the exclusion of the familial and personal dimensions. I was filling in my father's scheme with the factual way some of those millennial "continuities" took shape and developed, with a special eye to the way in which during the creative period of the High Middle Ages the "social" aspects waxed as the "familial" aspects of the previous millennium waned. My goal, in short, was simply to explore my father's tripartite scheme of history worked out in the actual events of history. It was not a matter of testing the validity of that schema—and much less the notions behind it—but simply of working to articulate it more fully in historical terms. I wanted the history of the nonbelievers to demonstrate its validity and not have to appear merely as some curious schema sprouting from an artist's head.[11]

At the socioeconomic level, for instance, I was able to get into far more detail regarding the rise of towns and growth of a middle class and money economy, and how, from the eleventh century onward, a myriad of new social forms—commune, guild, corporation, and many more—assumed a new and ever greater importance compared to the hierarchical, feudal, and "familial" forms that had dominated in the earlier age.[12] Nor was it difficult to observe how in countless ways this new social emphasis continued its march through the later Middle Ages and the early modern period to achieve its dominance in modern times.[13] A similar pattern was to be found in the area of politics and governmental institutions, as the notion that the king was "over all" (with its egalitarian implications) increasingly won out (with the development of royal and common law, burgeoning bureaucracies, and the support of an ever-growing middle class) over the aristocratic elements, in a continuity that ran from the feudal monarchies of the twelfth and thirteenth centuries to the English and French revolutions and the formation of nation-states by the eighteenth and nineteenth centuries.[14]

The Church itself shared in this transition into the "social" age, beginning with the burgeoning papal administration and explosion in canon law that came out of the Reform movement of the eleventh and twelfth centuries; the growth of the schools, the rise of the great universities, and the training of clerics were also elements in this. The development from the isolated monastic houses of an earlier age into the great Europe-wide religious orders reflected the same transition into the new millennium. All of this contributed in no small measure to the flourishing of Christian culture that centered on the maturing life of cathedral and town and the energetic role played by the papacy and the clerical element in the Church vis-à-vis society at large.[15]

Indeed, this leadership by the Church's clerical element in guiding and shaping society was a dualistic image of the Church itself.[16] The very word "Church" would increasingly refer to its ecclesiastical part, especially as the development of the culture as a whole showed its vitality in new and diverse forms and modes of expression. In such a situation it was inevitable that the clerical/anti-clerical issue would likewise surface and grow. The clashes between Pope Boniface VIII and King Philip IV of France at the turn of the thirteenth century may have seemed a small incident compared to the extended and dramatic conflicts between papacy and empire in the time of Frederick II, but they were far more ominous, for they reflected a clerical-lay split within the body of the Church that was beginning to permeate the entire culture and would only increase in the era of the Avignonese papacy and Piers Plowman and beyond. This dualism, which had been so fruitful in the "good phase" of the millennium carried straight through the so-called decline of the Middle Ages into its "bad phase."[17] As part of the so-called millennial continuity extending right to our own day, it could only result in the Church's increasing separation and practical divorce from the broad developments in society at large.[18]

My mentors saw all of this as evidence of the failure of Catholicism. In their view the "medieval synthesis" was the model of the Church's relation to culture, and it could not help but break down in the face of the new forces that were on their way to creating the modern world. And this view was hardly exclusive to the history department; it permeated the attitudes and assumptions found in every field. The response among my fellow Catholics ranged from the healthiest down through degrees of hesitation and confusion. Some tolerated in themselves a defensive and vaguely hopeful schizophrenia as they persevered in a constricted personal piety; others simply abandoned their faith altogether.

I certainly identified with the stronger and did what I could to help the weaker, but all the while quietly convinced I was on a somewhat different course, which was not easy to share with others. I was working on how my father's schema could be transformed by the study of events into a historical narrative with explanatory power. The Enlightenment was mistaken in seeing the Christian Middle Ages as summing up *the* Christian view of God's purposes, with man as a cultured animal producing something admirable in its time but now passé. The divine purpose in history had to be seen, instead, as a working out historically in terms of man's free actions from the beginning. Pursuing this meant working in "their territory," in what I felt sure could result in a deeper and more effective Christian apologetic.

It was during my junior year that I was graced with a new light on this score. Taking a break from some intense study in Lamont Library, I picked St. Augustine's *City of God* from a nearby shelf and happened upon the following passage:

> Magnanimous and learned as he was, and with no thought but to save human nature as best he could, Cicero made his choice. He chose free

choice. To make certain, he denied foreknowledge. Thus, to make men free, he made them give up God.

A man of faith wants both. He professes both and with a devout faith he holds both firmly.[19]

The immediate question St. Augustine was addressing was how God knows in advance *(providere)* what men freely choose; he was affirming that the answer hangs on realizing that God in eternity is always present to every moment in time. It is not a matter of logic but a mystery. But ultimately the mystery involves holding to the divine omnipotence, in which God's power wholly encompasses man's freedom in his actual choices— and this *is embraced in faith as a free and devout act.*[20]

Here, it struck me, is the very heart of what I was wrestling with, and my mentors as well. In place of "Cicero" I read "all my professors." Yes, the Enlightenment Project wants to *start simply from man* and use *simply reason* to make men free. For this it is willing to make them give up God. In St. Augustine's Christian response I tasted the *reach* that human intelligence is capable of when unafraid of mystery and enlightened by faith: man's fullness in God's fullness. I found here a glimpse into what my father had said about real intelligence being vindicated in Christ.[21] With this I experienced a new confidence in my "private project." I vaguely sensed—but with the conviction of faith—that the gap between faith and the Enlightenment Project was to be crossed precisely in the arena of history; for it was here, in faith's view of man's freedom, that the notion of providence fully engaged the Enlightenment's notion of man making his own history.[22] In due time I decided to pursue St. Augustine's thought on this and do my senior thesis on his theology of history. Professor Taylor agreed to be my advisor.

It was really no surprise that I immediately ran into an obstacle in that bastion of the Enlightenment. I was told that I could not comply with the requirements for a senior paper in history by doing a theological study. But since my project precisely involved finding how to cross the barriers they felt compelled to put up, I was convinced that the obstacle should be overcome. When I indicated my readiness to inquire into the way that St. Augustine's theology suggested or invited a strictly human view of history—albeit based on his theology—the department gave its okay.

For my part, of course, I took St. Augustine's presentation of the Christian view of history as basic.[23] But what I pursued in my paper was not St. Augustine's overall schema nor even the divine interventions that brought about the history of salvation. It focused rather on how he saw the divine and human interplay at work in the kind of historical events Enlightenment history dealt with. In effect, human virtues—such as those exhibited by the Romans—had their positive effects, even if they produced only relative and temporal justice and felicity and proved ultimately useless for obtaining man's true end. Christian virtue rebounds to eternal felicity, but because it enhances human virtue, it can also produce greater temporal felicity than merely human virtue[24] and this can be read in the events of history, even if St. Augustine himself did not pursue this point.[25] I felt I had taken a first step along my way: His theology of history at least allowed for a way of looking at history the way the history I was trained in does. My thesis was accepted. I appreciated the irony that I had been forced by the very prejudices of the Enlightenment itself to get into St. Augustine's thought in a way that served my purpose better than I might have managed to do without such a pressure. I had already decided by then that I wanted to make history my career, although I was quite aware that my paper on Augustine was but a first, though promising, step in finding a way across the huge gap between the perspective of faith and the outlook of those committed to the Enlightenment Project.[26] I was therefore eager to pursue all of this more fully on my own, before embarking on graduate studies and the pressures of a Ph.D. program. I decided that spending a year in Europe would be the best way to go about this.

My one year in Europe in fact turned into two, all of which provided a blessed opportunity to visit museums and monuments, to travel in cities and through countrysides, to read randomly, attend classes given by leading lights as I chose, and generally to explore and ponder the European past.[27] It was an ideal situation, and a systematic plan of study was the reverse of what I wanted. My aim generally was to continue to come up with whatever tell-tale events of history—hopefully key ones—might further illustrate my father's historical schema. Ways in which the social aspects of European culture had created a new dynamic balance with the familialism of the previous age to produce the flourishing culture of the

High Middle Ages were of continued interest, but I especially wanted to look into the characteristics of the first millennium and its own peculiar historical dynamics. This would open the way to exploring how millennial transition from the familial age had actually come about; it would also be a help in going further with St. Augustine's thought and the distinctiveness of his approach.[28]

It intrigued me, for instance, that something like St. Francis's Ode to the Sun, so characteristic of the Christian culture of the thirteenth century, could not have been produced in the good phase of the first millennium. Celebrating created reality in this way would no doubt have caused confusion and even scandal in a time when Christianity had to counter the pagan divinization of nature; but something more than evangelization strategy and avoiding scandalous confusion was involved. After all, there had been no problem in adapting the Roman basilica or in finding a place for the imperial power in the Christian scheme of things. Yet one also had to take into account that the Holy Roman Empire of medieval times was very different from the Christian empire of Theodosius or Justinian, and that the basilica had been altogether transformed in becoming a Gothic cathedral. Getting further into the differences between the two millennia seemed critical.

In my efforts to clarify such questions, I gradually came up with two formations to characterize the distinctive ways in which Christianity dealt with its relation to man's culture at the outset of the second millennium. It evidently involved recognizing that the created order, precisely as created, had an intrinsic validity that could be appropriated and ordered to God—and indeed ought to be. That the created order was good and had *intrinsic validity* was of course Christian teaching from the beginning and therefore was operative in the first stage.[29] But in that age, distinguished by the *natural* and one might say *monistic* instinct to see all created reality—including one's own human operations—as properly bearing transcendent import and meaning, Christianity's main thrust had to be directed to affirming the radically supernatural character of the true God, who stood not only as the creator of temporal reality but as its true end, in relation to which everything temporal stood as a means and as nothing in itself.[30] From the eleventh century onward, however, paganism as such was no longer the issue, and the work of de-divinizing created reality was effectively complete.[31] That same basic doctrine brought a further implication and imposed a new demand: The created order's intrinsic validity could and should be appropriated through man's own abilities and powers for whatever it could yield in God's service. Hence my two formulations: The new millennium was distinguished by "a new Christian validation of the created order as such," and this opened up a new Christian impulse of "discovery, exploration and development of the created order."[32]

It was this that lay at the base of the "medieval synthesis" and its very dynamism in creating the flourishing culture of the High Middle Ages—a new and vibrant tension between a proliferation of new ways to enter into created reality coupled with the effort to keep it all oriented to God through the mediating agency of a multiplicity of newly devised social forms. Here lay the fundamental and creative Christian dualism of the age, whether in exploring the intricacies of logic in the context of the relation between reason and faith in the schools, or in ordering the new explosion in manufacturing and commerce in commune and guild, or even in establishing new ways to tame the fighting man to Christian service through a new sense of class and knightly code or in the papal "sun and moon" analogy for relating temporal to spiritual power. The list could be expanded, but I came upon a statement by Etienne Gilson to epitomize it all: "We are told that it is faith which constructed the cathedrals of the middle ages. Without doubt, but faith would have constructed nothing at all if there had not also been architects. . . . It is necessary to know geometry in order to construct a façade *which may be an act of love.*"[33]

What seemed clear from the way I had come to this view of the medieval synthesis was the implication that it did more than bear witness to the faith and its power to create a distinctive culture. The doctrine that underlay that achievement was present from the beginning, yet it only produced that historical effect in time and according to a human pattern of development. This meant that while the "faith and love" that produced the cathedrals was something that transcended history, that particular development itself was historical and subject to historical inquiry. This clearly invited looking into what, in *the historically traceable actions of men,* actually sparked the origins and powered the pervasive thrust of the new—and in effect revolutionary—social outlook at the end of the first age, when the familial outlook was so exclusive and dominant.

What I found, mainly in studying the great Reform movement launched in the eleventh century, exceeded my expectations. Tracing that very sequence of events brought to light in telling detail how the new and somewhat revolutionary social innovations were born; equally exciting was coming upon countless instances of how these innovations involved and illustrated that same process of "exploration, discovery, and development of a newly validated created order."[34] I felt increasingly ready to return to graduate school and get into a serious professional approach to the study of history.

At the same time, through all of this I found myself wrestling with how to explain at a *theological* level the fact that the unchanging doctrine of the Church—and specifically the teaching of goodness of creation— could assume such innovative form at a distinct moment in history. I already appreciated that St. Thomas Aquinas stood as the theologian par excellence of this new age.[35] Moreover, I sensed that at some point I would have to articulate how what I was wrestling with connected to Catholic teaching, particularly as set forth by St. Thomas. The closer I came to my goal, the more I felt pressed to wrestle with Aquinas's relation to St. Augustine—whom I had taken as *the* preeminent voice for a Christian view of history—even if St. Thomas's more analytical and systematic approach seemed distant from that of the historian.

Thus, with the end of my time in Europe approaching and the pressure to get on with a professional career upon me, I made a critical decision. It was time to move on toward earning a doctorate. But at this point, I felt that instead of going for a Ph.D. in history, I could best pursue the questions that still preoccupied me by entering the doctoral program in the University of Chicago's Committee of Social Thought.[36]

Very soon after arriving in Chicago, I came upon Gilson's powerful indication that the key to St. Thomas's thought lay in the notion of *being* and that the mainspring of his metaphysics was the biblical "I am Who am."[37] I was not confident about my getting deeply into his philosophy of being, but my instinctive reaction was that what St. Thomas had to be talking about at base is the *real Being* of God and the *real beings* of the created order—with all their accidents, operations, and interrelations, all seen in particular places and times—in short, being as the historian deals with it.[38] This suddenly opened up to me that St. Thomas stood as something more than the representative thinker of the medieval synthesis. With a metaphysics that set the full reality of the created order in proper relation to the truths of the faith, he provided the rationale underlying *the histori-cal formation* of that synthesis. This in turn meant that he supplied as well the Christian rationale for *all the subsequent* "discovery, exploration and development of the created order" and therefore all that underlay the Christian humanism and the science of the Renaissance itself—and even on through the Enlightenment's fastening on what man could do in the *saeculum*—which, as its "Project," has carried right into modern times.[39]

But there was more. This distinctive Thomistic light on history seemed to add a further dimension to the way Providence was seen in St. Augustine's theology of history. In St. Augustine, Providence governed both salvation history and temporal history, but while the former is obvi-ously presented as teleological, the latter is not. Temporal history simply provided the context and had no meaning in St. Augustine's apologetic in terms of the supra-temporal end of salvation history.[40] With a theology that was based on the fully validated created order, however, St. Thomas gave new significance and even urgency to Christian action in the tempo-ral order, with this having its beneficent or disastrous temporal effects according as human intention in those actions served or did not serve God's salvific purposes. For me, this meant that Providence had to be seen as involving more than God's *power over* created reality (including human freedom). It also operates with salvific intent *in conjunction with* human freedom, through His inspirations and grace—in a way that is *invitational*, as it were. The prototype for such action (as combining divine freedom with a fully human freedom) was of course that of Christ on the Cross in offering Himself as *man* in loving union with the Father's will. *Our* power to continue such action in history came as a direct and intended result of this through the Holy Spirit working through the Church, enabling the rest of us to perform human acts in union with Christ's action.[41]

I saw in this how Christ stood as Lord of History in a deeper way than I had previously thought, and I expressed it thus: "Christ on the Cross was present to and divinely validated all human acts." Every single human act came into His salvific intention on the Cross; for in taking all our sins he looked lovingly upon every single human action—embracing it to the extent that it embodied *any good whatsoever* that He Himself had created and therefore also *suffering* from it to the extent that it was not in conformity with the divine will. Christ's giving of Himself freed us from sin, but in the language of the historian He freed all of us from every single sin as embodied in all human actions.[42] This is what marked Christ's lordship over every human act and what history is all about. The Enlightenment was wrong in excluding God from history, but its insistence that history had to be universal and find its true meaning in man's search for freedom actually put it in touch with the divine story as being written in and through the lives of all.[43] Its very approach to history, moreover, appeared as the only way to get at, and tell, the real story.

All of this was exciting to me, and not least because of the connection it implied between St. Thomas and St. Augustine.[44] The most immediate practical conclusion I came to was that elucidating the Christian perspective on history could best be done by doing history and at this point not by further theologizing. I would now turn to doing history with the best of them, in their territory, with all the rigor that the best in the field would want and properly demand. My reason for being in Chicago had ended.[45] Before the year was out I decided to return to Harvard to get my Ph.D. in history.

Was my quest over? In a sense, yes. In another sense, the practical work of wrestling with the Enlightenment lay before me. As I embarked on graduate studies in history in Cambridge, I found myself in a situation akin to what Chesterton had said about trying to explain the faith: "There is about complete conviction a kind of huge helplessness. The belief is so big that it takes a long time to get it into action. And this hesitation chiefly arises, oddly enough, from an indifference about where one should begin. . . . I would begin it with a turnip or a taximeter cab."[46]

In my case, rather than hesitation, it was a matter of encountering every turnip and taxicab I could—anything that Enlightenment history could uncover and wanted to deal with. Every encounter opened up vistas in which the very meaning of the actual events of history I was studying connected with the overall Christian meaning—the only meaning that could tie it all together. Eventually, I thought, I would have to write something in which the entire human story itself would bespeak the divine theology simply in the telling—the glory and vindication of narrative history. At first this meant eventually writing "my book"; soon enough it seemed to me it would mean writing ten books—and maybe more.

It took another dose of realism to realize that all this would have to be the work of many minds. What was needed—what is needed—is careful, expert, and yes, specialized, inquiry in every field of history—far more than one man can manage by himself. The pronoun I had been using suddenly shifted: We Catholics need many dedicated historians willing to work and develop expertise in every field of history. But expertise without serious commitment to Christ and a vision of what His lordship in history really amounts to is not enough. Indeed, without a sense of all-embracing *human* teleology that His salvific purposes in history imply, without a living faith and solid doctrinal formation and the wisdom that comes from true piety, it would lead nowhere—or even to something worse. For Enlightenment history itself is simply the story of the Enlightenment Project. Wrestling with it is to engage the world in all its power, and trying to wrestle without head and heart in the right place is to court disaster—in one's work and witness if not in one's person.

Christopher Dawson long ago pointed out the positive implication that this has for every Christian and for the Church as a whole. Redeeming the Enlightenment approach to history implies redeeming the Enlightenment Project itself; the one marches with the other. If the Christian view of history tells us anything it tells us that every man is a player in the way he uses his freedom; the call to the Christian historian implies a call to every Christian, whatever our field of action in this world might be. Dawson put it this way:

> Every Christian mind is a seed of change so long as it is a living mind, not enervated by custom or ossified by prejudice. A Christian has only to be in order to change the world, for in that act of being there is contained all the mystery of supernatural life.[47] The promise contained in those words is also an invitation from the Lord of History Himself to those who can hear it—to put Christ "at the center of all earthly activities."[48]

"Regnare Christum volumnus" is a prayer pointing to an eternal kingdom that is beyond history—but that is already at work in history. Those who can pronounce it in a way that transforms their own lives play their proper role in the divine story.   ◆

Recovering a Legacy through History: The Catholic American Southwest and West

Patrick Foley

The Religious, Cultural, and Intellectual Heritage of Catholic Spain to the Americas

O N February 22, 1819, United States secretary of state John Quincy Adams and Spain's chargé d'affaires to America, Luís de Onís y Gonzalez, signed the international agreement that has come to survive through subsequent history as the Transcontinental Treaty. That pact recorded, among other stipulations, a concurrence between the two nations regarding their respective boundary claims from Louisiana to the Pacific Coast. Significant to our study here, that compact—also known as the Adams-Onís Treaty—acknowledged geographic and demographic circumstances that had historically been in the process of development since the middle decades of the sixteenth century. The covenant recognized formally that the vast territory lying south of the charter's line of demarcation had grown as part of New Spain and that Spain, from 1819 on, relinquished claim to any of the region north of the treaty line.

Running northward from the Gulf of Mexico along the Sabine River to the Red River and then veering due west to the one-hundredth meridian, the first leg of this Transcontinental Treaty Line defined the western extension of the American state of Louisiana as well as the southern perimeter of the area that would decades later become the state of Oklahoma. Cutting a path north once again along the meridian to the forty-second parallel, the boundary line then turned westward all the way to the Pacific Coast. Though the 1819 settlement made no specific mention of the point, that expansive land south of the boundary line, in having matured under the purview of Spanish colonization, had over the centuries assumed a deeply entrenched Roman Catholic identity that touched every phase of life: familial, religious, educational, social, political, artistic, and economic. Meanwhile, a population that, where religious, bragged of an overwhelming Protestant ethos, was in the process of forming the early stages of the nineteenth-century westward movement from America's eastern lands toward the West Coast, and in so doing opening up and settling the territories north of the Adams-Onís treaty line.

Soon, however, American imperialism under the concept "Manifest Destiny" inspired historical movements by the United States to violate the 1819 treaty. In 1821, Mexico had won its independence from Spain, and significant to our story, then possessed the grand area formerly known as northern New Spain. Twenty-five years later, in 1846, the United States invaded Mexico, bringing on the U.S.–Mexican War. With the end of that struggle in1848, and ratified by the United States via the Treaty of Guadalupe Hildago of that same year, from within the region designated in 1819 as belonging to Spain (and then later recognized as part of Mexico) and untouchable by the United States, America took land from Mexico in her northern territory. From that grand area United States would eventually carve out the states of Texas, New Mexico, Colorado, Utah, Nevada, Arizona, and California. All of this spacious acreage became Southwestern, or part of Western, United States.[1]

In teaching and writing about this domain, scholars have recorded that Roman Catholicism, as the faith historically for centuries had grown in Spain and then was transmitted across the seas to New Spain, eventually became cemented in the lives of the peoples of the Americas, Spanish as well as indigenous. Endemically, Roman Catholicism throughout the New World came to form the base for a religious, cultural, and intellectual synthesis that was to define the vision of human beings as people strove to work out their individual, familial, and societal destinies.[2] Such existed as the religious foundation from Western civilization that early on lay at the spiritual heart of the future American Southwest and West.

We need not to be reminded that the historiography of the English American colonies that ultimately matured as the first thirteen states of the new republic of the United States of America is saturated with studies that find in their narratives characterizations of Protestantism, of one denomination or another, as the formative religious cornerstones of those settlements—even in Catholic-founded Maryland. In today's scholarly world, where the religious substances of American history are often marginalized—in comparison to earlier histories—in favor of more up-to-date, often politically correct agenda-oriented approaches, the Protestant identity of the American *founding* continues to receive noticeable attention.

And so it should, given the historical truth of the presence of such a pronounced Protestant influence in the Anglo colonization of the Atlantic seaboard and inland of the North American continent. After all, coming to an appreciation for what developed as Puritan New England, Anglican Virginia, or for example the Holy Experiment of William Penn and his Quakers in Pennsylvania, is basic to any understanding of the Anglo Protestant roots of the American heritage. Such could be said also of the Dutch Reformed in New York or the Germanic pietistic sects (especially Mennonites, Dunkers, Schwenkfelders, and Moravians) of Pennsylvania.

However, the Roman Catholic legacy of New Spain—and later Mexico and other Latin American nations—proved to be no less essential to the foundations of those peoples and their societies that eventually grew into the American Southwest and West than those aforementioned Protestant roots of English colonial America. But—with the exception of excellent studies on various aspects of the Catholic history of the American Southwest and West that regularly are used in specialized areas of study by scholars—any such similar stress on the Catholic Hispanic character of the region has been much less visible in the writing about and teaching of American history at virtually all levels of education in the United States.

For example, our elementary school students all hear about the "first" Thanksgiving of the Pilgrims. But how many ever learn of the first *"Día de acción de gracias—dar gracias"* celebrated by the conquistador Francisco de Coronado and his entourage during their adventures through what became the American Southwest in 1540–42? Again, in the classrooms how often are students told of the *"Día de acción de gracias—dar gracias"* that Juan de Oñate's company offered in the spring of 1598 as it paused at El Paso del Norte on its way into the Kingdom of New Mexico? This situation, although improved somewhat in recent decades, continues today in spite of the historical reality that the Roman Catholic heritage began to be planted in the Americas through Spanish colonization more than a hundred years before English Protestants founded Jamestown, Virginia, in 1607.

The Catholic presence of the Southwest and West passed through what later became the nation of Mexico especially strengthened among the indigenous peoples—in fact countless peoples of Mexico—by the December 1531 apparitions at Tepeyac of La Virgen de Guadalupe, establishing a religious following that remains profound today, even among many Catholics who are not Hispanic. We need to understand that Catholic thinking, formed from a Christian unitary vision of existence— or being—had developed over a period of centuries. As one aspect of that tradition in Spain, the religious and civil vision of a Catholic world saw the interests of the ecclesiastical and the civil merged together when defining the course and goals of evangelization. Distinctions between matters ecclesial and governmental were well-defined and often intertwined. It was what sometimes was referred to as the *Unión del altar y del trono.* Conflicts between the altar and the throne did erupt, but with the Catholic unitary vision shared by both, the Church energetically supported the Crown and vice versa.

Regarding Texas in the northeast section of New Spain, the distinguished Spanish Borderlands and missions historian Félix D. Almaráz Jr. wrote:

> In the occupation and colonization of the province of Texas in the vast northeast corner of *Nueva España,* roughly bounded by the Red River, the Gulf of Mexico, and *Rio Nueces,* late in the 17th century the government deployed Franciscan missionaries and presidial soldiers into the wilderness to convert indigenous cultures. Viewed as a more humane and less expensive doctrine of royal policy, the process of conversion involved a tandem arrangement between representatives of the state and the church.[3]

That profound model of allegiance presumed a historic acceptance on the part of both the Church and the Crown that to Hispanicize meant to Catholicize. Such a religious-civil, and consequently societal and cultural, order emerged early in the Spanish Catholic colonization of New Spain.

From such an integral history New Spain witnessed the erection of its political foundation, municipal and administrative organization, juridical life, and economic structural formation.[4]

Much of that Roman Catholic essence in New Spain had come from a religious and intellectual base developed in Spain's great universities, especially Salamanca and Alcalá de Henares. In the Americas once Spanish colonization had begun, education emerged as a primary concern; and, as back in the mother country, the Church founded in cooperation with the Crown the colleges and universities. The earliest and best-known examples of this educational effort were the Colegio de San Tomás, established in 1533 on the island of Española, and Mexico City's Universidad de México, which opened its doors in 1553. Both institutions of higher education were under the care of the Dominicans. The latter university was founded on a charter that copied word-for-word that of Salamanca University in Spain.

The Hispanic colleges and universities, all operating through the auspices of the Church, were every bit as important to New Spain's historical development as were. for example, the English colonies' Harvard College, Yale, College of William and Mary, or any others. Yet, the Spanish Catholic schools rarely are mentioned today in textbooks or in the classrooms of America. In writing and teaching history, therefore, the historian would be compelled intellectually and spiritually (seeking the truth of history) to study thoroughly the relevance of this Roman Catholic endowment from Spain to the New World whose influence later expanded into those lands that were to become known as the American Southwest and West. Such truthfully is as significant to history as are the roles of the Puritans or other Protestant denominations and their development of colleges and universities in colonial America.

One major Catholic Spanish personage involved in Spanish colonialism, whom ethnocentric, anti-Catholic, and anti-Spanish writers regularly attack, is the conquistador Hernán Cortés, leader of Spanish conquest of Mexico, 1519–21, and Governor of Mexico from 1523 to 1526. However, notwithstanding his personal bad habits, throughout Mexico Cortés encouraged the burgeoning of a Catholic religious vision of colonization. A preeminent historian of the Catholic spiritual ascendancy in colonial Mexico, Robert Ricard, wrote of Cortés:

One cannot study the history of the evangelization of Mexico without giving emphasis to the religious preoccupations of the Conqueror Cortés. He was greedy, debauched, a politician without scruples, but he had his quixotic moments, for, despite his weaknesses, of which he later humbly repented, he had deep Christian convictions. He always carried on his person an image of the Virgin Mary, to whom he was strongly devoted; he prayed and heard Mass daily.[5]

In the area destined to mature ultimately as the American Southwest and West, that unitary Catholic Hispanic worldview grew as the ideal not only in the many Franciscan missions, but among populations of the presidios, municipalities, ranches, and tiny settlements known as *jacales* (a *jacal* is a small living structure supported by vertical wood poles covered with mud and roofed with timber and mud), in which herders and other rural Mexican people lived throughout the expansive area. With the essential presence of Catholicism, often in the form of popular religion—home altars, statues, and the like—a Catholic view of life flourished.

Gilbert Ralph Cruz, noted missions and Southwestern historian (his latest book, co-authored with James D. McBride, is titled *Arizona, Heartland of the Southwest: Handbook of History Research Materials*), recently explained that:

> To secure the northern frontier Borderlands, the Spanish imperial government implemented three colonial institutions—the mission, the presidio, and the town settlement. These institutions had distinct functions, but their larger goals were similar, namely, to implant on an enormous part of the North American continent Spanish linguistic, social, religious, and political values. Spanish town councils added distinct dimensions to the influence that New Spain once exerted over the American Southwest. By means of these *cabildos*, Spain introduced municipal law and order, patterns of local government, a rough democracy, and the concepts of justice based on law. Municipal governments were implanted in the Borderlands *ex mandato Regis Hispaniensis*. These civil governments assisted Spanish town settlers in conquering and subduing the land, and even in settling and Christianizing it for the king. Over the centuries, they preserved in New Mexico, Texas, and California the distinctive cultural, social, and language patterns characteristic of the present-day Southwest.[6]

From the Rio Grande of Texas and the shores of the Gulf of Mexico to the coast of California and the San Francisco Bay Area, Franciscan missions were established over a century and a quarter, from the latter seventeenth century through the late eighteenth century, with the missioning spirit to which historians Almaráz and Cruz alluded in their comments quoted earlier. In the present day, scholarly journals with a Catholic thrust often develop the stories of those missions. For example, *Catholic Southwest: A Journal of History and Culture,* situated in Austin, Texas, has published several articles on the missions, especially those of Texas and New Mexico. Another outstanding journal of this day, *Boletín,* the journal of the California Mission Studies Association, is headquartered at Santa Clara University in California. This educational institution, itself originally founded in 1777 as a Franciscan mission, is the only university in California affiliated with a mission. *Boletín* is dedicated to publishing about, among other areas of study, the Franciscan missions of California. Mention should be made also of one book, from among many, that details the lives of the missions, Stanley Young and Melba Levick's (with a foreword by Sally B. Woodbridge) beautifully illustrated 1988 tome, *The Missions of California.*

Dedicated missionaries brought Catholic teaching and the sacramental system to the indigenous peoples of the American Southwest and West. Great mission churches were erected. While most of the missions have been restored (often more than once) from their original construction and some of them moved from their initial site, they all remain as testimonies to the labors of missionaries—mostly Franciscans—to plant a Catholic presence among the peoples of the American Southwest and West. A few examples of the better-known among them would be Mission San Antonio de Valero (historically famous as the Alamo) and Mission San José y San Miguel de Aguayo—Queen of the Missions in Texas—both located in the San Antonio vicinity; San Xavier del Bac, originally a small unornamented mission erected by Fr. Eusebio Francisco Kino, SJ, in Tucson, Arizona, but now a majestic religious edifice; Mission San Diego de Alcalá, the first of California's missions, founded in 1769; Mission San Juan Capistrano, founded in 1776 and featuring an early California environment; Mission Carmel (San Carlos de Borromeo de Carmelo), the beautiful mission in the vicinity of Monterey, California, wherein Fr. Junípero

Serra, Father of the California Missions, is buried; and Mission Santa Clara de Asís, the beautiful mission already mentioned.

In addition to these, many other missions came into existence during the missions era. In Texas thirty-six missions—some historians argue possibly even thirty-eight—were erected, and in California there were constructed twenty-one in all. New Mexico, Colorado, and the land from which was later carved out the state of Arizona too saw additional missions established beyond those already highlighted. Southern New Mexico boasted of mission churches at several locales, including Las Cruces and Mesilla. Other Franciscan establishments were built northward. The first mission in Colorado was the one Fray Domingo de Anza founded in 1706, about fifty miles south of the present-day city of Pueblo.[7] As in Texas, for example, many of the missions of New Mexico, Colorado, and Arizona were not large grand ones, but rather small religious structures. With their simple but inspiring altars, shrines, reredos (retablos), sanctuaries, and well-cared-for gardens enhancing with their beauty and symbolism the spiritual environment of learning and work, those centers of missioning and evangelization existed as testimonies to that Christ-centered world vision inherited from Catholic Spain.[8]

As we have observed, Catholicism matured deeply entrenched in the Hispanic municipalities, with their parishes and other Church establishments usually at the center of family, cultural, social, political, legal, and economic life.[9] It can be asserted that no historian appreciated the depth of the Catholic base of the Hispanic population of that area more than the late Professor Herbert Eugene Bolton (first of the University of Texas at Austin and later of the University of California at Berkeley), originator of the historical term "Spanish Borderlands" and himself a Protestant. The late John J. Mulloy pointed out in a 1992 issue of *The Dawson Newsletter* that "Bolton did much to increase our understanding of the work of the Jesuit and Franciscan missionaries in laying the foundations for a rich and colorful civilization in California and the Southwest."[10]

Another Aspect of the Legacy: The Coming of Catholic European Immigrants in the 1800s

As the eighteenth century gave way to the nineteenth, various complex historical manifestations related to the nation's Catholic heritage came to maturity in the southwestern and western regions of America. Some aspects of these lessened the impact of the historic Catholic Hispanic presence, while others ultimately broadened the overall Catholic complexion of the land. Spain's secularization of the missions, commencing in the early 1770s and ending about 1830, juxtaposed with the independence of Mexico from Spain in 1821 and then the 1848 wrenching away from Mexico of the previously discussed expansive territory that eventually became the American Southwest and West, in ways worked to marginalize the Catholic Hispanic identity of the territory.

But from another perspective, Catholic immigration from Europe and America into the region had begun to become noticeable in those same decades, broadening noticeably the area's Catholic identity. Added to the historical-religious legacy that had found its roots in the Hispanic world were varied accounts of Catholics whose ethnic-religious backgrounds were Irish, Austrian, German, French, Wend (Germanic peoples), Czech, Polish, Italian, Belgian, or others. The seemingly countless European nationalities that in those years formed a significant substance of the universal Church were finding their places in the American Southwest and West.

As they would do in other parts of the United States, especially where Protestantism was prevalent, the Roman Catholic immigrants from Europe who ventured to the Southwest and West in the nineteenth century tended to cluster together in colonies or rural sites where their Catholic religious identity and nationality could more likely be preserved. The Irish, for example, no more could separate their religion from their being "Irish" than the Spaniards could from their being "Spanish."[11] Rachel Bluntzer Hébert, noted author of the Irish story in nineteenth-century Texas, in her book about the Irish Catholic colony of San Patricio titled *The Forgotten Colony, San Patricio de Hibernia,* offered her readers a moving account of the religious faith of a frontier Catholic family when she wrote of James McGloin, one of the co-founders of San Patricio in 1828. Relating how McGloin returned to his home in San Patricio one evening after a long and tiring trip, she described the scene thus:

> He opened the gate and strode toward the cabin, entered, and absent-mindedly barred the door. Bright flames leapt up the chimney and lit up a room that was neat and well arranged. The furniture was hand-made

and consisted of only the bare necessities. The roughly plastered walls were a background for a crucifix which hung above the bed and a holy water fountain near the front door. Two pictures flanked the chimney— one of the Virgin and another of Saint Patrick.[12]

James McGloin would go down in history as a dedicated Irish immigrant supporter of the Church in Texas.

A direct consequence of the Catholic immigrant influence was that the territories into which the migrant came witnessed the appearance of different cultures, with their customs and traditions associated with their European homelands: languages and dialects, literature, music, various manifestations of popular religiosity, and more.[13] Sometimes the manners of the immigrants expressing their identities seemed at variance with the host-nation Catholic Hispanics. But more obviously, such immediately erupted at odds with the incoming Protestant settlers. The latter was especially a reality for those Catholic immigrants settling in a Texas that by the mid-nineteenth-century would—from central Texas north—be identified with the Protestant Bible Belt.

As part of that immigrant migration came priests—secular and religious—sisters, brothers, and seminarians, and they influenced the establishment of diocesan-parish ecclesiastical structures. All of this historical-spiritual metamorphosis inspired the building of any number of national parish churches, the foundation of Catholic institutions, such as schools, academies, colleges, universities, hospitals, orphanages, and asylums. Significantly, a gradual but steady maturation in the immigrant communities of a Catholic vision of piety and public order came into being.

In Texas, for example, the year 1847 saw the erection of the Catholic Diocese of Galveston, the state's first such ecclesiastical structural establishment after Texas broke away from Mexico. The French vicar apostolic to Texas at the time, Vincentian Fr. Jean-Marie Odin, was named the new diocese's first ordinary.[14] Shortly thereafter, in 1850, French immigrant Fr. Jean Baptiste Lamy was named vicar apostolic of Santa Fe, New Mexico. Three years later he became bishop of Santa Fe, and in 1875 he was elevated to the posture of archbishop when Santa Fe was erected as a metropolitan see.[15] Citing just a couple of the several Catholic institutions of higher learning that were established early on during those decades: In 1852, Bishop Odin founded in San Antonio de Bexar a college that eventually became known as St. Mary's University, Texas's oldest such establishment. At about the same time, the previously alluded to Jesuit Santa Clara University was established as Santa Clara College in 1851.[16]

From St. Louis, Missouri, to the vicinities of Galveston, San Antonio, Houston, and Austin, Texas; Santa Fe, Albuquerque, and Las Cruces, New Mexico; Denver, Colorado; Tucson, Arizona; and then on to California came the Catholic immigrant and his Church. Matriculating with them in that immigrant era were priests and brothers of the Congregation of the Mission (Vincentians), Oblates of Mary Immaculate, Marianists, Jesuits, Conventual Franciscans, German Benedictines, German Carmelites, Polish Resurrectionists, Italian Franciscans, and others.[17]

There is no doubt but that almost countless Texas Catholic families—and sometimes Protestant clans also—benefited religiously, educationally, and culturally from the dedicated labors and prayers of the several religious orders of sisters who served in that spacious area bounded by the Sabine River, the Gulf of Mexico, the Rio Grande, and the Red River. Among those communities of nuns who ventured to the area were Ursulines, the first community of sisters in Texas, who came to Galveston from New Orleans at the behest of Bishop Jean-Marie Odin, C.M., soon to become ordinary of the new Diocese of Galveston, in January 1847. Following the Ursulines were Sisters of the Incarnate Word and Blessed Sacrament (from the Archdiocese of Lyon, France), Sisters of Providence, Sisters of Charity and the Incarnate Word, Sisters of St. Mary of Namur, Mercy Sisters from Ireland, Daughters of Charity, Dominicans, Sisters of Divine Providence, Servants of the Holy Ghost and Mary Immaculate, Benedictines, Franciscans, and later Sisters of Charity of Saint Joan Antida—who currently work in, among other areas, the Diocese of Amarillo.[18] Similar narratives of the missioning efforts of Catholic religious during the nineteenth century can be told and retold when recounting the histories of the other states of the American Southwest and West. Those religious and their successors' impact on life in the United States is well-documented.

Another chapter in the Roman Catholic history of the United States—one that the Hispanic-immigrant Church period engendered—treats the influence of Catholic social teaching on Catholic individuals as well as organizations such as labor unions. In his biography of the prominent Catholic historian the late Dr. Carlos Eduardo Castañeda, Almaráz carefully traced how Castañeda was formed in his civic thinking and action by the Church's social teachings.[19] The point is that, contrary to what often is seen today, for example, among some prominent Catholic personages in the United States—politicians, celebrities, and such—the Catholic vision of life that worked to earlier mold these individuals' and organizations' values came to the Americas as a significant aspect of the Catholic Hispanic or immigrant historical-religious base. This was particularly mirrored in the American Southwest and West.

There is so much more to the legacy of the Roman Catholic pilgrimage in the United States that is need of redress. It is with this in mind that we turn our attention to some difficulties that have proven obstacles in the path of a sincere attempt—in the name of seeking historical truth—to bring into the full epic of the growth of the American nation, especially in the Southwest and West, the presence of the Roman Catholics and their Church. Building from this, we offer some observations about how might be infused into the world of teaching and writing about American history the importance of Roman Catholicism, especially in the Southwest and West.

Setting Forth the Catholic Heritage

Our discussion to this point has shown that in those regions that over the centuries, following the arrival of the Spanish in the New World, grew into what eventually would become known as the American Southwest and West, not only was Roman Catholicism the first form of Christianity to appear, but it was that religious faith as it had blossomed historically in Catholic Spain as well as throughout other Catholic nations in Europe. Roman Catholicism gave a definite ethos to the region, its population and society, forming a distinct aspect of America's religious history.

Mirroring the thesis here is the argument that historians—especially secular ones or those scholars advocating views of history that downplay, ignore generally, or sometimes openly question the importance of the Catholicity of the early Southwest and West—have failed to grasp the depth and substance of that Catholic base. Such is not always the case, in that a number of historians—some Catholics, others not—have displayed a clear appreciation for the Catholic substructure of those lands. A good example of that is Professor Donald E. Chipman—a Catholic—who in his outstanding book, *Spanish Texas, 1519–1821* (1992), included relevant Catholic history in virtually every aspect of his tome. And that work is highly regarded by scholars and teachers throughout Texas. More typical though is the late Rupert N. Richardson's classic study, *Texas: The Lone Star State,* first published in 1943. That tome, used throughout Texas for decades in colleges and universities as a textbook, devoted only a few pages to the Catholic faith, with scant mention of the Hispanic era or the period of the Catholic immigrants. Chipman in his work intuitively reflected a Catholic historical perspective based upon serious research and a search for the full truth in the narrative of Texas history. Richardson seemed unconcerned that any such purview existed.[20]

Robert A. Calvert and Arnoldo De Leon, in their popular 1990 college/university textbook, *The History of Texas,* present a discussion of the interaction between the Church and the Crown, *La Unión del Altar y del Trono,* that suggests that the authors failed to fully appreciate the spiritual depth of the unitary vision of the Altar and the Crown in the colonizing of New Spain. Calvert and De Leon proclaim that:

> In the far North, Catholicism remained the sole religion, disseminated by missionaries from religious orders who labored for the crown and the church in the tradition of *patronato real* [my italics]. The king granted the padres financial support; in turn, the clergy protected the monarch's territories and provided spiritual care for the indigenous people, whom the king regarded as his subjects. In such an accord, the king held title to the land upon which the mission was built. Only the mission proper, composed of the buildings, cemetery, orchards, and vineyards, belonged to the Catholic Church. Therein the friars instructed the Indians, at first using the native tongue, then gradually Spanish, employing a rigid routine that encompassed daily mass, the recitation of prayer and the rosary, and instruction in the mysteries of the holy faith. Corporal punishment often was used to enforce this schedule. Once the neophytes had been deculturalized and converted into parishioners and taxpayers, the state-subsidized missionaries left for new ground and turned responsibilities for the preservation of the faith over to parish-supported priests (secular clergy).[21]

While there is a core of historical truth in Calvert and De Leon's obser-vations, nonetheless the two authors set the Catholic Spanish raison d'être for colonizing the indigenous peoples of the New World in the purview of "conquest" rather than "conversion." Moreover, later in their book the two Texas historians refer to Roman Catholicism as one of the many religious denominations in Texas.[22] The term "denomination" grew out of the histor-ical legacy of the sixteenth-century Protestant Reformation and is as such a reference to the many different "Protestant" denominations of churches that matured within the context of that historical-religious development. Such a word is not used by scholars in referring to Roman Catholicism. In employ-ing this appendance in regard to the Catholic Church, Calvert and De Leon reveal a lack of historical understanding.

On the national level, a similar scholarly attitude seems evident. Few college or university American history textbooks designed for survey courses offer creditable coverage of the Roman Catholic narrative. There are exceptions to this, such as Robert Divine et al., *America Past and Pre-sent.* It is not so much that Divine's book provides an extensive amount of historical material on the Roman Catholic heritage of the United States, but rather that what is presented is accurate and unbiased. Typical of Divine's comments are:

> The Spanish also brought Catholicism to the New World. The Domini-cans and Franciscans, the two largest religious orders, established Indian missions throughout New Spain. Some barefoot friars tried to protect the Native Americans from the worst forms of exploitation.[23]

Although the Divine book does compromise in the use of politically cor-rect terms and phraseology occasionally, it is one of few textbooks on the market that mentions the apparition of Our Lady of Guadalupe to St. Juan Diego in December 1531 and then goes on to explain the signifi-cance of that supernatural phenomenon to Catholic missioning through-out New Spain. Moreover, *America Past and Present* credits King Carlos I (Emperor Carlos V) with attempting "to bring greater 'love and modera-tion' to Spanish-Indian relations."[24] Finally, avoiding the black legend *(la leyenda negra)* approach—describing much about Catholic Spain in a neg-ative way—to narrating the Catholic Spanish colonization of Baja and

Alta California, Divine's tome traces that exploration and Catholic evangelization all the way to San Francisco Bay.[25]

This brief commentary on a few books that have been—or still are—available to historians and teachers of the history of the American Southwest and West suggests that there exist barriers needing to become overcome, as well as opportunities to be pursued, in setting forth the Roman Catholic heritage of that broad region of the United States. In most cases misrepresentations of the nature and substance of the American Southwest and West's Roman Catholic legacy surface within the context of certain Protestant attitudes, secularist purviews, or exaggerative regionalist ethos inherent in the personal background and/or professional and scholarly training of the author.

Understandably, it can be a struggle of conscience for serious Protestant scholars to avoid an almost subconscious marginalization of any need to master an in-depth knowledge of Roman Catholic history. Sometimes, however, they do make a valiant attempt at such. More frequently, the impact is that these historians treat Catholicism much the same as they might any Protestant denomination that is not one of their own primary concern. Secularists, on the other hand, push to the outer rim of their scholarly vision any importance attached to the religious tradition of peoples, seeing human society as a plane of life that excludes God.

Of significance, Texas seems most likely to attract the interest of people representing the third category we are studying, the exaggerative regionalist. To many Texans, and even some historians, the Lone Star State seems to be almost larger than life. I recall most vividly not long after my wife and I and our family moved to Texas, after having been born and raised in northern California and having lived for several years in Santa Fe, New Mexico, the appearance on automobiles and pickup trucks of a bumper sticker that said, "Welcome to Texas—Now Go Home." The main difficulty with this posture is that it often—usually—carried with it as part of the "exaggerated regionalist" perception of demography religious, racial, and other biases. Regarding historians and their work, the "exaggerated regionalists" regularly have been prone to gloss over the Hispanic Catholic and immigrant Church periods, focusing anticipatively on other areas of Texas history. Richardson's *Texas: The Lone Star State* was such an example.

The past two decades have witnessed the appearance on the academic scene of a radically different grouping of scholars—mainly Catholics—iconoclastic "revisionists" whose intellectual roots can be found in liberation theology and more recent ramifications of that school of thinking. While liberation theology has worn itself out and influences few serious scholars today, especially historians, it did produce ways of thinking historically that undermined the seeking of truth in history as a scholarly discipline developed over centuries. The main problem was that liberation theology and its related approaches to study were based upon the idea of cross-fertilizing the various scholarly disciplines of history, theology, sociology, psychology, political science, and others—and admixing popular religion themes with social activism based upon this approach. In this context, these clerics, professors, and writers aggressively pursued a hypothesis of history that proclaimed earlier approaches to historiography (which they often were unqualified to comment upon) out of date and irrelevant.

This "revisionist" approach to the study of Roman Catholicism, which has had a number of apologists in the American Southwest and West, is lamentably weak from a scholarly viewpoint.[26] In cross-fertilizing the disciplines without exhibiting careful concern for the identifying distinctions of each (What is a historian, a sociologist, a theologian, and so on?), and selectively citing their own and each other's published materials instead of carrying out extensive primary materials research in archives and other repositories while using a variety of highly respected secondary sources, these "revisionists" undercut one of the essential demands of historical scholarship: looking at the past in as much an unbiased fashion as possible while seeking historical truth. This same indictment must be made of those historians who in their writing and publishing, lecturing and teaching, and other intellectual efforts advocate other "agendas," such as radical feminism. Serious scholarly revisionism is certainly legitimate—in fact required—in the world of the historian and his or her work. But when such is based upon pre-conceived attitudinal platforms wherein supporting the "attitude" becomes the goal, then the so-called scholar has become a "revisionist."

Recovering the Catholic legacy of the American Southwest and West through history is but part of the broader perspective of seeing history within a Catholic vision of the substance of human civilization, being one that begins with God at its center. For historians the heart of the search for truth is found in studying the written record. Therefore, as John Gilmary Shea began advocating more than a century ago, thorough research among primary sources remains the essential base of historical writing and teaching.[27]

The region of the United States that has been the focus of our attention, the American Southwest and West, abounds in outstanding Catholic archives. Foremost among these repositories are the Catholic Archives of Texas located in the city of Austin; the Archives of the Archdiocese of Los Angeles; the Archives of the Archdiocese of San Francisco; the Archives of the Archdiocese of Santa Fe; the Archives of the Archdiocese of San Antonio; and the Archives of the Diocese of Tucson.[28] Throughout the ecclesiastical jurisdictions of this vast region are several, perhaps lesser-known but nonetheless important, depositories for Catholic sources and collections, a number of them being diocesan or university or college archives.

Turning to other mediums available to the historian for study: Scholarly journals or magazines can be excellent sources. As with the archives, there are several highly regarded Roman Catholic scholarly journals that can provide opportunities for both research and publishing. Among these *The Catholic Historical Review*, the journal of the American Catholic Historical Association, has been preeminent for over a century. Another journal, the *U.S. Catholic Historian*, is generally quite dependable. Of particular consequence to our area under analysis, in 1990 the Texas Catholic Historical Society began publishing an annual scholarly journal devoted to studying Catholic Texas, *The Journal of Texas Catholic History and Culture*. Broadening the society's vision in 1996, the journal's editorial board decided to expand its interest in and coverage of the Catholic heritage from northern Mexico through Texas to New Mexico, Arizona, and California. Thus, the editorial staff changed the name of its publication to *Catholic Southwest: A Journal of History and Culture*. Over the years this scholarly annual has won some thirty national awards for scholarship. In addition, the annual review of the Society of Catholic Social Scientists, *The Catholic Social Science Review*, began publishing in 1996 and has included in its volumes since then several articles on the Roman Catholic presence in the Southwest and West. Beyond these, the importance of

Boletín, the journal of the California Mission Studies Association, has already been mentioned.

Reference must be made to a few books that currently are playing a key role in telling the story of the Catholic faith and its pervasive growth in our land under study. Prominent in this grouping regarding the Catholic history of Texas are two volumes that Fr. James Talmadge Moore has authored as contributions to the Centennial Series of the Association of Former Students, Texas A&M University: *Through Fire and Flood: The Catholic Church in Frontier Texas, 1836–1900,* and *Acts of Faith: The Catholic Church in Texas, 1900–1950.* These thorough and well-written studies have received high praise. Félix D. Almaráz, Jr.'s outstanding 1999 biography of Carlos Eduardo Castañeda, *Knight without Armor: Carlos Eduardo Castañeda, 1896–1958,* is already being called a "classic." Of great interest to the teaching of the Catholic history of Texas is archivist of the Archives of the Diocese of Dallas Steve Landregan's thoroughly researched and beautifully illustrated 2003 narrative, *Catholic Texans: Our Family Album.* Many Texas Catholic scholars and archivists contributed to the appearance of this excellent textbook aimed at the general reader. The work is also published in Spanish as *Tejanos Católicos: Nuestro Álbum Familiar.*

Moving beyond Texas to the west, Professors Gilbert R. Cruz—former San Antonio Missions National Historical Parks historian and current adjunct professor at Arizona State University West—and James D.McBride—consulting editor for *Journal of Arizona History* and also adjunct professor at Arizona State University West, in 2004 co-authored a detailed and well-organized book on historical research, including much on Roman Catholic historical sources, titled *Arizona, Heartland of the Southwest: Handbook of History Research Materials.* Also in 2004, Msgr. Francis J. Weber, archivist of the Archives of the Archdiocese of Los Angeles, published another carefully researched and written, as well as beautifully illustrated, tome, this one celebrating the history of the cathedrals of that archdiocese, from St. Vibiana Cathedral to the new Cathedral of Our Lady of the Angels. The book is titled *Cathedral of Our Lady of the Angels.* Finally it must be mentioned that the many-years-long effort of the Academy of American Franciscan History and its "Publications of the Academy of American Franciscan History," in particular offering volumes on the labors of the Franciscans in this territory under discussion here, have added greatly to the materials available to historians of our expansive area.

Drawing from these many sources for research and study—and others as well—and inspired by the compelling need to search for historical truth throughout the intellectual and spiritual world, the Catholic historian must consciously offer not only the American nation, but the whole of human civilization as well, a penetrating Catholic vision of history, one certainly inspired by the writings of St. Augustine sixteen hundred years ago, but one also buttressed by the work of so many Catholic historians and other scholars throughout the centuries. Such can be accomplished not only through publishing Catholic books, monographs, and articles, but in contributing aspects of the Roman Catholic narrative to secular or other non-Catholic histories—textbooks, journals, and the like—as well. There should be, moreover, presentations on Catholic historical features and issues at both Catholic and non-Catholic history conferences, national, regional, and local. And, in conclusion, when other people—scholars or non-scholars—misrepresent or misconstrue the Catholic story in America in an inaccurate and perhaps prejudicial manner, their words should be open to review by Catholic historians. Nowhere can that be accomplished in a land where there exists a longer historically developed Catholic tradition than in the American Southwest and West.   ◆

Notes

Chapter 1 ◆ *Donald J. D'Elia,* **The Catholic As Historian: Witness in Every Age to Christ's Presence among Us** (pages 3–35)

1. St. Thomas Aquinas, *ST* II–II, 1, 2 ad 2, quoted in *Catechism of the Catholic Church* (Citta del Vaticano: Liberia Editrice Vatican, 1994), 46. Romano Guardini, *The End of the Modern World,* ed. and intro. Frederick D. Wilhelmsen (Chicago, IL: Henry Regnery Co., 1968). "The very doctrine of the Eucharist is the efficacious sign of this consecration and divinization. The deification of humanity is begun in Christ. It is in Christ that we are created anew. And it is in him that we become participators in the divine nature, *consortes divinae naturae.* Such is the key to Christianity," Claude Tresmontant, *Christian Metaphysics* (New York: Sheed & Ward, 1965), 112. Johannes Pinsk, *Toward the Centre of Christian Living: A Liturgical Approach* (New York: Herder and Herder, 1951), 42–44, 255–62.

2. Quoted by Fr. Bede Jarrett, OP, "Christendom," in *Social Theories of the Middle Ages, 1200–1500* (Westminster, MD: Newman Book Shop, 1942), 223–35. For a multivolume history of Christendom readers should consult the monumental work by that title of Warren H. Carroll.

3. Quoted by Moorhouse F. X. Miller, SJ, "Aquinas and the Missing Link in the Philosophy of History," in *The Catholic Philosophy of History*, ed. Peter Guilday, Papers of the American Catholic Historical Association 3 (New York: P. J. Kenedy and Sons, 1936; reprinted Freeport, NY: Books for Libraries, 1967), 90.

4. Eric Voegelin, *Political Religions,* intro. Barry Cooper, trans. T. J. DiNapoli and E. S. Easterly III, Toronto Studies in Theology 3 (Toronto: Edwin Mellen Press, 1986), xlii–xliv. For an excellent review of Dawson's *The Crisis of Western Education* (New York: Sheed & Ward, 1961), see Thomas P. Neill, *Social Justice Review* 54–55 (July 1961): 124–25. On the early caesarism of Alexander Hamilton, see Donald J. D'Elia, *The Spirits of '76: A Catholic Inquiry* (Front Royal, VA: Christendom Press, 1983), vi, 87–114.

5. Cf. Dawson, "The Christian View of History," *The Dynamics of World History,* ed. John J. Mulloy (New York: Sheed & Ward, 1957), 233–50; Christina Scott, *A Historian and His World: A Life of Christopher Dawson* (London: Sheed & Ward, 1984).

6. Antonin G. Sertillanges, trans. A. G. McDougall, *The Church* (London: Burns, Oates, and Washbourne, 1922), 48. M. C. D'Arcy, SJ, *The Sense of History: Secular and Sacred* (London: Faber and Faber, 1959), 250–51. For an excellent discussion of Belloc's "priceless sense of continuity" see Moorhouse F. X. Millar, SJ, *Unpopular Essays in the Philosophy of History* (New York: Fordham University Press, 1928), 5.

7. On the responsibility of the revolutionary intelligentsia, see Dawson's essay review of Arthur Koestler's *The Yogi and the Commissar, Blackfriars: A Monthly Review* 26, no. 307 (October 1945): 366–71.

8. Romano Guardini, *End of the Modern World*, Frederick D. Wilhemsen, ed. and Introduction (Chicago: Henry Regnery Co., 1968),52–59.

9. Quoted by Millar, 85–86. On Blondel see Johannes Hirschberger, *The History of Philosophy*, vol. 2 (Milwaukee: Bruce Publishing, 1959), 562–64. "The Mystical Body of Christ unites all ages into one company, " Frederick D. Wilhelmsen has written, "and I can talk to Augustine, not as to a memory, but as to a man. The Incarnation did not destroy time, but raised it to an altogether new dimension. The Catholic holds his youth against an aging universe, he begins his eternity while still a wayfarer within a world that passes," in *Born Catholic*, ed. Francis J. Sheed (New York: Sheed & Ward, 1954), 31–32, quoted by D'Arcy, 251.

10. Peter Wust, "Crisis in the West," in *Essays in Order*, ed. Christopher Dawson and J. F. Burns (New York: Macmillan, 1931), 141–42. On the threat posed by the "new totalitarian systems" to true, authentic individualism, see Dawson, "Christian Freedom," *Dublin Review* 422 (July 1942): 7 et passim.

11. Christopher Dawson and J. F. Burns, eds., "Christianity and the New Age," in *Essays in Order*, ed. Christopher Dawson and J. F. Burns (New York: Macmillan, 1931), 226. "In Jesus Christ we may 'come boldly before the throne of grace.' Our approach should be that of sons who know the Father's love; this is the quality of Christian prayer— a filial colloquy with the Father, for Christ's sake and in His name. The prayer of Abraham set us an example of this freedom: 'I have taken it upon me to speak to my Lord'; that is the liberty of the Saints at prayer," Jean Cardinal Danielou, SJ, *The Lord of History: Reflections on the Inner Meaning of History*, trans. Nigel Abercrombie (Cleveland: World Publishing, 1968), 347 et passim; Werner Stark, "John Henry Newman," in *Social Theory and Christian Thought: a Study of Some Points of Contact* (London: Routledge and Kegan Paul, 1958), 12, 109, 118, 125.

12. Jacques Maritain, "Confession of Faith," in *This Is My Philosophy*, ed. Whitt Burnett (New York: Harper and Bros., 1957), 255–57; Maritain, *Christianity and Democracy* (New York: Scribner's Sons, 1944), 21–38. For a discussion of Maritain's treatment of philosophy of history as a part of moral philosophy, see Joseph Koterski, "Religion and History in Maritain and Jaspers," *Dawson Newsletter* 3, no. 2 (Summer 1984): 11–14. "The personality of man, his authentic name is his own personal 'being for' the absolute Being," Michele Federico Sciacca "Individuality and Personality," in *The Human Person and the World of Values: A Tribute to Dietrich von Hilderbrand by His Friends in Philosophy*, ed. Balduin V. Schwarz (New York: Fordham University Press, 1960).

13. On Nietzsche and Kierkegaard, see James Collins, *The Existentialists: A Critical Study* (Chicago: Henry Regnery, 1952), 17–27. Commenting on what Gabriel Marcel called the "technique of degradation," *(Man against Mass Society)*, Alice Jourdain von Hildebrand has written, "Horrors we find throughout history, but those perpetrated in concentration camps assume a new and more subtle character; it is less a question of crushing a person's

body by refined means of torture, than an attempt to crush a person as person, to humiliate him to the very depth of his being, to let loose the beast in him, and make him acknowledge that this horrible caricature is his true self: 'thou art but that.' There is a diabolical logic that leads one from the hatred of God to the hatred of man's inalienable character as *imago Dei*, for example, as a person," "von Hildebrand and Marcel: A Parallel," in Schwarz, ed., *The Human Person and the World of Values: A Tribute to Dietrich von Hildebrand by His Friends in Philosophy* (New York: Fordham University Press, 1960), 24.

14. Eric Voegelin, *From Enlightenment to Revolution*, ed. John Hallowell (Durham: Duke University Press, 1975): 231, 70, 132. Anton C. Pegis wrote during World War II of the "complex calamity of our age that we should have to fight not only against the slavery of Nazism, but also against the disintegration of the West. Without a victory against such slavery, the future will sink into barbarities that only those who hate God can devise. With a victory, the West must still be saved from the dispersion that centuries of revolt against God and man have produced"; "Man and the Challenge of Irrationalism," in *Race, Nation, Person, Social Aspects of the Race Problem: A Symposium*, ed. G. Barry O'Toole (New York: Barnes and Noble, 1944), 90.

15. Etienne Gilson, "The Intelligence in the Vision of Christ the King," in *Christianity and Philosophy* (London: Sheed & Ward, 1939), 111–12. "Because human nature is not altogether corrupted by sin, namely, so as to be shorn of good of nature, even in the state of corrupted nature, it can, by virtue of its natural endowments, perform some particular good, such as to build buildings, plant vineyards, and the like, yet it cannot do all good natural to it, as to fall short in nothing. In the same way, a sick man can of himself make some movements, yet he cannot be perfectly moved with the movement of one in health, unless by the help of medicine he be cured," St. Thomas Aquinas, *ST* I–II, 109, 2. Quoted by Jacques Maritain, *On the Philosophy of History*, ed. Joseph W. Evans (New York: Charles Scribner's Sons, 1957), 143 et passim.

16. Werner Stark, 116. "Grace means the category of Christian existence and cannot be expressed more plainly than by the statement in the Epistle to the Galatians, 'I live, yet no longer I, but Christ lives in me' " (Gal. 2:20), Romano Guardini, *The World and the Person*, trans. Stella Lange (Chicago: Henry Regnery, 1965), 161–62.

17. *The True Life: Sociology of the Supernatural*, trans. Barbara B. Carter (Paterson, NJ: St. Anthony, 1943), 225. Cf. Romano Guardini, *The Lord* (Chicago: Henry Regnery, 1954) 509–13 et passim.

18. Don Sturzo, 225. "This conception of the Incarnation," in *The True Life* Christopher Dawson argued, emphasized the uniqueness of Christianity vis-à-vis modernist Gnostic doctrines such as Fascism that denied the "full humanity of the Logos made flesh," as the "bridge between God and man, this marriage of Heaven and earth, the channel through which the material world is spiritualized and brought back to unity, distinguishes Christianity from all other Oriental religions, and involves a completely new attitude to life," *Christianity and the New Age* (Manchester, NH: Sofia Institute Press, 1985), 225–26.

19. Henri de Lubac, "The New Man: The Marxist and Christian View," *Dublin Review* (Spring 1948): 17.

20. Preface to *Essays of a Biologist*, quoted in de Lubac, "The New Man: The Marxist and Christian View," *The Dublin Review* (Spring 1948): 9.

21. Hollowell, ed. Eric Voegelin, *From Enlightenment to Revolution*, (1975), 301–02.

22. Quoted in Gilmer W. Blackburn, *Education in the Third Reich: A Study of Race and History* (Albany: SUNY Press, 1985), 182. "Before I was baptized a Catholic, I was born

of a German mother," (Adolph Hitler, 1924), quoted in ibid., 153. On the importance of uniforms in the making of the "new man" of Fascism, especially in doing away with "class differences," see John H. E. Fried, "Fascist Militarization and Education for War," in International Council for Philosophy and Humanistic Studies, *The Third Reich* (New York: Howard Fertig, 1975), 746–48.

23. Eric Voegelin, perhaps alluding to Hitler's great interest in the occult, points out how this "idea of operating on the substance of man through the instrumentality of pragmatically planning" inevitably finds its "climax" in magic, Hallowell, *From Enlightenment to Revolution,* 302.

24. Quoted in Ger van Roon, *German Resistance to Hitler: Count von Moltke and the Kreisau Circle,* trans. Peter Ludlow (London: Van Norstrand Reinhold, 1971), 75, 77–81. "Evil therefore, is that which falls away from essence and tends to non-being. It tends to make that which is cease to be," St. Augustine, *De Moribus Ecclesiae Catholica,* 2, 2, 2. "Sin is nothing, and men become nothing when they sin," ibid. Hence the satanic logic of the Nazi death camps. "The loss of God," Fulton J. Sheen wrote just before the outbreak of World War II, "is the beginning of tyranny—an old historical truth," *Whence Came Wars* (New York: Sheed & Ward, 1940), 11. Cf. Jacques Maritain and Charles Journet on the nature of evil: Maritain, *St. Thomas and the Problem of Evil* (Milwaukee: Marquette University Press, 1942); Journet, *The Meaning of Evil,* trans. M. Barry (New York: P. J. Kenedy, 1963). Cf. Rev. Louis Bouyer, *Liturgical Piety* (Notre Dame, IN: University of Notre Dame Press, 1954), 95, et passim.

25. Delp, *Der Mensch,* ibid., *et passim.* cf. D. J. D'Elia, "Christ in Dachau: The Crisis of Modernity in Nazi Germany," lecture at Thomas More College, Merrimack, New Jersey, April 3, 1992. For this universalism, the "conviction that though the various expressions of truth unavoidably bear the mark of their local origins, truth itself, both in the speculative and in the practical order, is not true for a certain civilization, nor for a certain nation, but belongs to mankind as a whole," see Etienne Gilson's "Harvard Tercentenary Address," published as *Medieval Universalism and Its Present Value* (New York: Sheed & Ward, 1937).

26. Quoted in van Roon, *German Resistance to Hitler,* 80. "In all things," Fr. Delp wrote in his prison diary for November 22, 1944, "God wants to solemnize the encounter, and asks for and desires the adoring and loving response," *Dying We Live: The Final Messages and Records of the Resistance,* ed. Helmut Gollwitzer, Kathe Kuhn, and Reinhold Schneider, trans. Reinhard C. Kuhn (New York: Pantheon Books, 1956), 142.

27. Quoted in van Roon, *German Resistance to Hitler,* 79; December 31, 1944, Gollwitzer, ed., *Dying We Live,* 136; cf. Msgr. Eugene Kevane, *The Lord of History: Christocentrism and the Philosophy of History* (Boston: St. Paul Editions, 1980), 25–26 et passim. On Nazi mysticism and the German "Volk" as the "mystical body" of National Socialism, see, e.g., F. Gregoire, "The Use and Misuse of Philosophy and Philosophers," *The Third Reich,* 678–709.

28. Eric Voegelin, *The New Science of Politics: An Introduction* (Chicago: University of Chicago Press, 1952), 124.

29. Quoted in van Roon, 77. "I believe in God and in Life. And what we pray for in faith will be given to us . . . only in alliance with Him [is] it possible to live and to bear one's fate." (December 1944), in Gollwitzer, ed., *Dying We Live,* 143.

30. Gollwitzer, 144; Pinsk, *Toward the Centre of Christian Living,* 159–66.

31. Quoted in Gollwitzer, ed., *Dying We Live,* 148.

32. Quoted in D. J. D'Elia, "The Life and Thought of Titus Brandsma," *New Oxford Review* 53, no. 10 (December 1986): 12–14. "Seeking God, the Christian of the future

will scan the horizon in vain, nowhere in the new age will he find Him, but only in that love which conquers the world," Guardini, *The End of the Modern World,* 12.

33. Gollwitzer, ed., *Dying We Live,* (October 1944), 141; quoted in John M. Lenz, *Christ in Dachau, or Christ Victorious: Experiences in a Concentration Camp* (Vienna, 1960), 184, ten days before Fr. Delp's execution on February 2, 1945. Cf. Pinsk, *Toward the Centre of Christian Living,* 255 et passim.

34. Cf. Charles Journet, *What is Dogma?* trans. Mark Pontifex, vol. 4 of *The Twentieth Century Encyclopedia of Catholicism* (New York: Hawthorn Books, 1964). On this *pleroma* or fullness in Christ, see Bouyer, *Liturgical Piety,* 102–5. "The man therefore, who seeks life in its totality will of necessity discover the Church. For the individual Christian, no less than for Christ Himself, 'the Church is his *pleroma,*' his completion" (Eph. 1:23), Pinsk, *Toward the Centre of Christian Living,* 187–88.

35. Jean Cardinal Danielou, "The Conception of History in the Christian Tradition," *Journal of Religion* 30, no. 3 (July 1950): 171. "Progress in Christianity is not linear and horizontal, it is vertical. It aims at eternity, not the spinning out of time. The reason for the existence of time is that we should move out of it, soul by soul. When the number of souls foreseen by the Lord has been reached, time will come to an end, whatever the condition of humanity may be at that moment." A. D. Sertillanges, quoted in H. J. Marrou, *Time and Timeliness,* trans. V. Nevile (New York: Sheed & Ward, 1969), 33.

36. Bernard J. Cooke, SJ, "Christ's Eucharistic Action and History," *Wisdom In Depth: Essays In Honor of Henri Renard, SJ,* eds. Vincent Daues, SJ, and Maurice Holloway (Milwaukee: Bruce Publishing, 1966), 52.

37. Danielou, "The Conception of History in the Christian Tradition," 175.

38. Kevane, *The Lord of History,* 80–86.

39. Danielou, "The Conception of History in the Christian Tradition," 172–73.

40. Cf. Matthew M. DeBenedictus, *The Social Thought of Saint Bonaventure: A Study in Social Philosophy* (Westport, CT: Greenwood Press, 1972), 3, 18–22; St. Bonaventure, *The Soul's Journey into God,* in Ewart Cousins, ed. and trans., *Bonaventure: The Soul's Journey into God: The Tree of Life and the Life of St. Francis* (New York: Paulist Press, 1978), 60 et passim.

41. Pinsk, *Toward the Centre of Christian Living,* 177. Indispensable as background for this essay is John Lukacs, *Historical Consciousness, or the Remembered Past* (New York: Harper and Row, 1968). On Nazism and nihilism, the classic contemporary work is Herman Rauschning, *The Revolution of Nihilism: Warning to the West* (New York: Longmans, Green, 1939), 22–25.

42. Pinsk, *Toward the Centre of Christian Living,* 43. "Our life of Eucharistic prayer and adoration is, in fact, the beginning of that contemplation of God in Christ which will be our whole life when we enter into His glory. . . . When we grasp the meaning of this truth we will understand that although we may be praying alone in a small, dark, empty church, praying with difficulty, dry and distracted, we are in fact not only united by love to Christ in His Passion, not only prostrate in adoration before Christ in glory, but we are one body with those who are praying in different places and at different times." Thomas Merton, *The Living Bread* (New York: Farrar, Straus and Cudahy, 1956), 17.

43. Ludwig Ott, *Fundamentals of Catholic Dogma,* trans. Patrick Lynch, ed. J. C. Bastible (Rockford, IL: Tan Books, 1974) 140, 106, 371–78, "Gnosticism" in *Dictionary of Dogmatic Theology,* ed. Pietro Parente, Antonio Piolanti, and Salvatore Garofalo, trans. E. Doronzo (Milwaukee: Bruce Publishing, 1951), 111–12.

44. Pinsk, *Toward the Centre of Christian Living,* 187–88.

45. Journet, *On Evil,* 154, 224; Kevane, *The Lord of History,* 76–80; Danielou, "The Conception of History in the Christian Tradition," 174.

46. Patricia Treece, *A Man for Others: Maximilian Kolbe, Saint of Ausch witz, In the Words of Those Who Knew Him* (San Francisco: Harper and Row, 1982), 150, 156–57.

47. G. M. Garrone, "A Great Little Brother," *L'Osservatore Romano,* no. 21 (269), May 24, 1973, p. 8. Matthias J. Scheeben, *The Mysteries of Christianity,* trans. Cyril Vollert, SJ (St. Louis: B. Herder Book Company, 1946) is a standard work.

48. Jacques Maritain, *Christianity and Democracy,* trans. Doris C. Anson (London: Geoffrey Bles, Centenary Press, 1945), 10–11, 14. Cf. "Meditation on the Fourth Sunday of Advent, 1944," in *The Prison Meditations of Father Alfred Delp*, intro. Thomas Merton (New York: Herder and Herder, 1963), 52–53.

49. Maritain, *Christianity and Democracy,* 45–46.

50. Ibid., 36–37. On hope as a theological virtue, see of the Oratory, Louis Bouyer, ed., *Dictionary of Theology,* trans. Rev. Charles U. Quinn (New York: Desclée, 1965), 211–13.

51. "Meditation on the Third Sunday of Advent, 1944," in Delp, *Prison Meditations.*

52. "After the Verdict," in ibid., 186, 190.

53. Maritain, *On the Philosophy of History,* 160–61.

54. Maritain, *Man and the State* (Chicago: University of Chicago Press, nd.) 183, quoted by Maritain, *On the Philosophy of History,* 160 n. Cf. *Christianity and Democracy,* 37–38.

55. Maritain, *Reflections on America* (New York: Charles Scribner's Sons, 1958), 182–83.

56. Maritain, *Christianity and Democracy,* 39–40, 61; *On the Philosophy of History,* 58, 119–63. Cf. Rev. John Rager, "Catholic Sources and the Declaration of Independence," *Catholic Mind* 28, no. 13 (July 8, 1930): 253–68.

57. Maritain, *Reflections on America,* 72–73.

58. Ibid., 186–87.

59. Will Herberg, *Protestant, Catholic, Jew: An Essay in American Religious Sociology* (New York: Doubleday, 1960), 185 n.

60. Pinsk, *Toward the Centre of Christian Living,* 217. Dr. Peter V. Sampo, Dr. Glen Arbury, and the faculty of Thomas More College, "The Sense of Place in the Modern World," Summer Colloquium, July 8–10, 1994, Merrimack, New Hampshire. Cf. Leonard Swidler, "The Catholic Historian," in *The Christian Intellectual: Studies in the Relation of Catholicism to the Human Sciences*, ed. Samuel J. Hazo, prefatory note by John J. Wright (Pittsburgh: Duquesne University Press, 1963), 124–27.

61. Cf. Rt. Rev. Paul H. Furfey, *The Morality Gap* (New York: Macmillan, 1969), 72–73. Regis Martin, "Man without Grace Is Demonic Nothingness," in *We Hold These Truths and More: Further Catholic Reflections on the American Proposition*, ed. Donald J. D'Elia and Stephen M. Krason (Steubenville, OH: Franciscan University Press, 1993), 233.

62. Christopher Dawson, *America and the Secularization of Modern Culture* (Houston, TX: University of St. Thomas Press, 1960), 13. D. J. D'Elia, "We Hold These Truths and More: Further Reflections on the American Proposition," in *We Hold These Truths and More,* 62–76.

63. Quoted in Dawson, *Understanding Europe,* 181; Robert Riley, "The Truths They Held: The Christian and Natural Law Background to the American Constitution," in *We Hold These Truths and More,* 78–92.

64. Dawson, *America and the Secularization of Modern Culture,* 31.

65. Delp, xxvii, "The most pious prayer can become a blasphemy." Fr. Delp indicted all collaborators with militant atheism then and now, "if he who offers it tolerates or helps to further conditions which are fatal to mankind, which render him unacceptable to God, or weaken his spiritual, moral or religious sense."

66. "Stages in Mankind's Religious Experience," in Dawson, *The Dynamics of World History*, ed. John J. Mulloy (New York: Sheed & Ward, 1956), 179.

67. Francois Mauriac on Christ's "promise," *The Eucharist, the Mystery of Holy Thursday* (New York: Longman's, Green, 1944), 8. For the Eucharist as a pious fraud of the "Romish clergy," see, e.g., the essays on Thomas Jefferson, John Adams, and Benjamin Franklin in D. J. D'Elia, *The Spirits of '76: A Catholic Inquiry* (Front Royal, VA: Christendom Press, 1983), 16, 42, 137 et passim. An indispensable study of anti-Catholicism is that of Sister Mary Augustina Ray, B.V.M., *American Opinion of Roman Catholicism in the Eighteenth Century* (New York: Columbia University Press, 1936).

68. Charles Davis, *God's Grace in History* (New York: Sheed & Ward, 1966), 118. On the Christian "affirmation of created reality," in his theology of history in every age, see Josef Pieper, *The Edge of Time* (London: Faber and Faber, 1954), 137; Isaac Hecker, *Questions of the Soul* (New York: D. Appleton, 1855 Edition. (Reprinted New York: Arno Press, 1978).

69. Robert W. McElroy, *The Search for An American Public Theology: The Contribution of John Courtney Murray* (New York: Paulist Press, 1989), 146.

70. Robert Riley, *A Declaration of Independence* (Milwaukee: Bruce Publishing, 1941), 78–92, 121–31.

71. Frederick Wilhelmsen, *Citizen of Rome: Reflections from the Life of a Roman Catholic* (LaSalle, IL: Sherwood Sudgen, 1980), 285–86.

72. "The proper effect of the Eucharist is the transformation of man into God," quoted by Jill Haak Adels, ed., *The Wisdom of Saints: An Anthology* (New York: Oxford University Press, 1987), 82. Cf. Jacques Maritain, "The Conquest of Freedom," in *Freedom: Its Meaning*, ed. Ruth Nanda Anshen (New York: Harcourt, Brace, 1940), 631–49.

73. Wilhelmsen, *Born Catholics,* assembled by F. J. Sheed (New York: Sheed & Ward, 1954), 61 et passim. Cf. Christopher Dawson, *The Formation of Christendom* (New York: Sheed & Ward, 1967), esp. chap. 19, "The Catholic Idea of a Universal Spiritual Society." I would like to acknowledge the generous assistance given to me in understanding Dawson by the late John J. Mulloy as well as Edward V. King, the latter scholar having an essay in this volume.

74. Wilhelmsen, *Citizen of Rome*, 285–86. Dawson, *The Crisis of Western Education,* 160–65.

75. Dawson, *The Crisis of Western Education,* 185, 187. Cf. Jacques Maritain, *Three Reformers: Luther, Descartes, Rousseau* (New York: Thomas Y. Cromwell, 1970), passim.

76. John Cardinal Danielou, *Prayer As a Political Problem* (New York: Sheed & Ward, 1967), 51.

77. "The Conception of a Catholic University," in Walter M. Kotschnig and Elined Pry, *The University in a Changing World* (London: Oxford University Press, 1932).

78. Justus George Lawler, "The Mission of Catholic Scholarship," *Catholic World* 183 (July 1956), 34.

79. Thomas O'Brien Hanley, sj, "Charles Carroll of Carrollton: Founding Father (1736–1832)," in *Catholic Makers of America: Biographical Sketches of Catholic Statesmen and Political Thinkers in America's First Century, 1776–1876*, ed. Stephen Krason (Front Royal, VA: Christendom Press, 1993), 9, 16.

80. Christopher Dawson, "Arnold Toynbee and the Study of History," in Dawson, *The Dynamics of World History*, 400.

81. Quoted in D. J. D'Elia, "Charles Carroll of Carrollton: Catholic Revolutionary," *The Spirits of '76*, 67.

82. Mauriac Supra; Romano Guardini, *Meditations before Mass* (Westminster, MD: Newman Press, 1955), 140, 177.

83. Richard Purcell, "Charles Constantine Pise," in *The Dictionary of American Biography*, ed. Dumas Malone (New York: Charles Scribner's Sons, 1934), vol. 7, part 2, 634–35, quoted in D'Elia, *Spirits of '76*, 55.

84. D'Elia, *Spirits of '76*, 69–70.

85. Quoted in D'Elia, *The Spirits of '76*, 70. That Carroll had been taught by his Jesuit teachers here and in France to receive Holy Communion as often as possible, even daily, seems probable from St. Ignatius of Loyola's own teaching, e.g., to Teresa Rejadell, November 15, 1543, in *The Spiritual Exercises and Selected Works*, ed. George E. Ganss, SJ (New York: Paulist Press, 1991), 339–41.

86. Rev. Paul Hanly Furfey, *Fire on the Earth* (New York: Macmillan, 1936; reprinted New York: Arno Press, 1978), 56.

87. Christopher Dawson, *The Gods of Revolution: An Analysis of the French Revolution*, with an introduction by Arnold Toynbee and appreciation by James Oliver (New York: Minerva Press, 1975), chap. iii, 32–47. For the Jewish origins of this Christian interpretation, which is not Hellenic-Aristotelian in nature, see Dawson, "The Christian View of History," in Dawson, *The Dynamics of World History*, 234 et passim.

88. Quoted in D. J. D'Elia, *Benjamin Rush: Philosopher of the American Revolution* (Philadelphia: American Philosophical Society, 1974) (*Transactions*, new ser. Vol. 64, part 5), 85n, 85, 88.

89. Cf. Maritain, "True and False Political Emancipation," *Freedom: Its Meaning*, ed. Ruth N. Anselm, (New York: Harcourt, Brace, 1940), 637–44; and D. J. D'Elia, "The Real Bicentennial: Notes on the Continuous Quest for a Therapy of Order," *Faith and Reason* 13, no. 4 (1975): 353–62.

90. Quoted in D'Elia, *Benjamin Rush*, 97.

91. Ibid., 57, 67.

92. Ibid., 87, 89.

93. St. Thomas, *ST* III, quest. lxii, art. 6.

94. D'Elia, *The Spirits of '76*, 87–114.

95. Christopher Dawson, "Catholic Culture in America," in *Through Other Eyes: Some Impressions of American Catholicism by Foreign Visitors from 1777 to the Present*, ed. Dan Herr and Joel Wells (Westminster, MD: Newman Press, 1965), 229–41.

96. D'Elia, *The Spirits of '76*, 98, 99.

97. Ibid., 95–96.

98. Jacques Maritain, *Freedom in the Modern World*, trans. Richard O' Sullivan, K.C. (New York: Charles Scribner's Sons, 1936), 92.

99. Anshen, ed., *The Conquest of Freedom: Its Meaning*, 643, 44.

100. Quoted in D'Elia, *The Spirits of '76*, 107.

101. Ibid., 110.

102. Ibid., 111; quoted in Don C. Seitz, *Famous American Duels: With Some Account of the Causes That Led Up to Them and the Men Engaged* (Freeport, NY: Books for Libraries Press, 1966), 98.

103. Quoted in D'Elia, *The Spirits of '76,* 112.

104. Danielou, *Lord of History,* 94–95.

105. "The Nature and Destiny of Man," in *God and the Supernatural,* ed. Fr. Cuthbert Hess, OFM (London: Longmans, Green, and Co., 1920), quoted in Scott, *A Historian and His World,* 71.

106. Journet, *What is Dogma?* 92. On the Catholic historian as the "heir of a universal tradition" who can say with Orosius, "Everywhere is my country, everywhere my law and my religion . . . for it is as a Roman and a Christian that I address Christians and Romans," 80.

107. For the "sacramental mystery of Regeneration" and its "consummation in the mystery of the Resurrection," see Christopher Dawson on the "Future Life," in *Religion and World History: A Selection from the Works of Christopher Dawson,* ed. Oliver and Scott, (Garden City, NY: Doubleday, Image Books, 1975), 343.

Chapter 2 ♦ *Michael B. Ewbank,* **Faith's Past, Hope's Future, Charity's Present: The Enduring Role of the Catholic Historian** (pages 37–55)

1. Etienne Gilson, "Le moyen age comme 'saeculum modernum,'" in *Concetto storia, miti e immagini del Medio Evo,* ed. Vittore Branca (Firenze: Sansoni, 1973), 1–10.

2. "The forms which history has taken reflect the basic differences of methods." R. McKeon, *Freedom and History and Other Essays,* ed. Z. McKeon (Chicago: University of Chicago Press, 1990), 160–241. See especially 182–84.

3. J. Le Goff, *Histoire et Memoire* (Paris: Gallimard, 1988), 257.

4. J. Lukacs, *Historical Consciousness, or the Remembered Past* (New York: Harper and Row, 1968), 262.

5. H. Marrou, *The Meaning of History* (Baltimore: Helicon, 1966), 161, 236.

6. B. Muller-Thyme, "Of History As a Calculus Whose Term Is Science," *The Modern Schoolman* 19 (1942): 41–47, 73–76. For an inventory and explication of subsidiary sciences and disciplines that the historian utilizes, see *L'histoire et ses methodes,* ed. C. Samaran (Paris: Encyclopédie de la Pléiade, 1961), especially the essay by H. Marrou, "Comment comprendre le métier d'historien," 1467–1540.

7. J. Le Goff, "Mentalities: a History of Ambiguities," *Constructing the Past: Essays in Historical Methodology* (Cambridge: Cambridge University Press, 1985), 166–80, especially 170.

8. Most notably in Herbert Marshall McLuhan, *The Guttenburg Galaxy* (Toronto: University of Toronto Press, 1962); *Understanding Media* (New York: Penguin, 1964); *War and Peace in the Global Village* (New York: McGraw Hill, 1968).

9. A convenient overview of the central characteristics of prudence may be in St. Thomas's *Summa theologiae* 1.2, q. 49.

10. Cf. St. Thomas Aquinas, *Exposition of Aristotle's De memoria et reminiscentia,* lect. 4–7, 356–86; and in as well J. Coleman, *Ancient and Medieval Memories* (Cambridge: Cambridge University Press, 1992), 450–560.

11. T. G. Chifflot, *Approaches to a Theology of History* (New York: Desclée Co, 1965), 85.

12. L. Strauss, *The City of Man* (Chicago: University of Chicago, 1964), 3–4.

13. Eric Voegelin, *History of Political Ideas: The Middle Ages to Aquinas* (Columbia, MS: University of Missouri Press, 1997), 108.

14. T. Molnar, "Crisis," *Modern Age* 31 (1987): 215–21, esp. 220.

15. J. Lukacs, *The End of the Twentieth Century and the End of the Modern Age* (New York: Ticknor & Freids, 1993).

16. Ibid., 284.

17. J. Lukacs, *The End of the Twentieth Century and the End of the Modern Age* (New York: Ticknor and Fields, 1993), 1, 70, 284.

18. J. Lukacs, *The Passing of the Modern Age* (New York: Harper and Brothers, 1970), 190.

19. S. de Grazia, *Of Time, Work and Leisure* (New York: Doubleday Vintage, 1990), 349.

20. F. Juenger, *The Failure of Technology* (Hindsdale: Henry Regnery Co., 1949), 177.

21. A. Borst, *The Ordering of Time; From the Ancient Computus to the Modern Computer* (Chicago: University of Chicago, 1993), 130–31.

22. Juenger, *The Failure of Technology,* 128.

23. F. D. Wilhelmsen, and J. Bret, *The War in Man: Media and Machines* (Athens, GA: University of Georgia Press, 1970), 15, 117.

24. For an inventory of novel problems, approaches, and objects for the contemporary historian, consult J. Le Goff and P. Nora, eds., *Faire de l'histoire,* 3 vols. (Paris: Editions Gallimard, 1974). Cf. T. R. Potvin "*Non nova sed nove:* Diere des choses d'une maniere nouvelle sans dire pourtan des nouveatutes," *Science et Esprit* 53 (2001): 427–49.

25. *Traditions et Progrès: Le Commonitorium* (Paris: Desclée de Brouwer, 1978) esp. 328–29.

26. J. Anderson, "Language, Thought, and History" *The New Scholasticism* 50 (1976): 323–44, esp. 328–29.

27. J. Pieper, "Tradition: The Concept and Its Claims upon Us," *Modern Age* 36 (1994): 217–50, especially 225; "The Concept of Tradition," *Review of Politics* 20 (1958): 465–91.

28. T. Haecker, *Der Christ und die Geschichte* (Leipzig: Jakob Hegner, 1935), 94, 98.

29. St. Thomas, *In 3 Sentences,* 25, 2, 2, 1, ad 5.

30. Cf. H. Donneaud, "Histoire et Théologie Speculative: Une discussion entre Charles Journet et Marie-Michel Labourdette," in *Ordo Sapientiae et Amoris,* ed. C. J. Pinto de Oliveira (Fribourg: Editions Universitaires Fribourg, 1993), 399–423.

31. St. Thomas, *In Symbolum Apostolorum Exposito,* prologue, no. 860, art. 9, nos. 982, 984.

32. Ibid., nos. 973–75.

33. Etienne Gilson, *Les metamorphoses de la cite de Dieu* (Louvain, 1952), 284–85, 288.

34. F. Daquet, *Theologie Divin Chez Thomas d'Aquin: Finis Omnium Ecclesia* (Paris: Librairie J. Vrin, 2003).

35. Aquinas's reflections on 1 Cor. 15:42–45 may be found many places. See, for example, *In IV Sent.,* 49, 4, 5, 3; *Supra primam epistolam: ad corinthios lectura,* XV, lect. vi, nos. 979–84.

36. M. McLuhan and E. McLuhan, *Laws of Media: The New Science* (Toronto: University of Toronto Press, 1988), viii, 129–30.

37. Ibid., 227–38.

38. Ibid., 182–83.

39. Concerning details of these sense powers, consult J. Owens, *Cognition: An Epistemological Inquiry* (Houston, TX: Center for Thomistic Studies, 1999) 103–35.

40. *ST* II–II, 2, 5, 180.

41. Three objective noetic relations are presupposed even though contemporary fictional interpretations ambiguously and exhuberantly assume as "nearly complete" that

termed "terminal identity." Cf. Scott Bukatman, *Terminal Identity* (Durham: Duke University Press, 1993), 241–98, esp. 248.

42. This remark would assuredly be assented to only by those who understand the essential affinity of a sacramental order with man's constitution as an embodied intellectual being.

43. "The computer is not ethically neutral: it has unique features that encourage an amoral perspective," G. Simons, *Silicon Shock: The Menace of the Computer Invasion* (Oxford: Oxford University Press, 1985), 114.

44. M. Heidegger, *Wegmarken* (Frankfurt: Vittorio Klostraman, 1976), ii.

45. John Griffin and Yves Simon, *Jacques Maritain: Homage in Words and Pictures* (Albany: Magi Books, 1974), 54.

46. W. Ong, *Orality and Literacy: The Technologizing of the Word* (London: Routledge, 1982); W. Ong, *Interfaces of the Word: Studies in the Evolution of Consciousness and Culture* (Ithaca: Cornell University Press, 1977); W. Ong, *Rhetoric, Romance, and Technology: Studies in the Interaction of Expression and Culture* (Ithaca: Cornell University Press, 1971); W. Ong, *The Presence of the Word* (New Haven: Yale University Press, 1967).

47. R. Lannham, *The Electronic Word* (Chicago: University of Chicago, 1993), 130–31.

48. Ibid.

49. Concerning these matters, consult F. D. Wilhelmsen and J. Bret, *The War in Man: Media and Machines* (Athens, GA: University of Georgia Press, 1970); and F. D. Wilhelmsen and J. Bret, *Telepolitics: The Politics of Neuronic Man* (Montreal: Tundre Books, 1972).

50. "[W]e find the modernist view of culture as a linear sequence of phases being replaced by this postmodern idea of a synchronic polyphony of styles." R. Kearney, *The Wake of Imagination: Ideas of Creativity in Western Culture* (London: Hutchinson, 1988), 24, 392.

51. George Gilder, *Life after Television* (New York: W. W. Norton and Company, 1990), 32.

52. Ibid., 115.

53. *Decretum de oecumenismo*, 1.4.

54. Speaking of the emerging structures, Gilder asserts, "This is the age of the individual and family. . . . History has capsized every prophecy of triumphant bureaucracy." G. Gilder, *Microcosm* (New York: Free Press, 1990)368–69.

55. C. Dawson, *The Crisis of Western Education* (New York: Sheed & Ward, 1961), especially 205–46.

56. Cf. "End of the Constantinian Era," *Listening* 2 (1967): 173–83; "Consecrato Mundi," in *The Sacred and the Secular*, ed. M. Taylor (Englewood Cliffs, NJ: Prentice Hall, 1968), 123–35; and "Profanidad del mundo—Sacramentalidad del mundo," *Ciencia tomista* 101 (1974): 183–89.

57. For an introduction to the implications of certain of St. Thomas's principles concerning worship, consult L. G. Walsh, "Liturgy in the Theology of St. Thomas," *Thomist* 38 (1974): 557–83; C. M. Travers, *Valeur sociale de la liturgie* (Paris: Editions du Cerf, 1946).

58. In reflecting on the historical origins of an insular clericalism within the Western Church that depreciated the priesthood of the laity to a passive status and role, Congar noted that "[t]he Middle Ages founded our priesthood upon Aaron and thus anchored it to the cultural-ritualist priesthood of the Ancient Disposition. Thus it defined this same priesthood by the power to celebrate the Eucharist. Finally, the French school of the seventeenth-century (Berule, Condren, Olier), from which largely was derived the teaching given in seminaries and religious congregations, defined the priest as a religious and adorer of God. From all this there resulted a notion of the priesthood that is principally cultural. . . . It is not cultural if

one understands this term in the ritualistic meaning, within the line of a consecration to exist apart from the Ancient Alliance. But one can use the term cultural if one restores the New testament truth of cult. . . . This is the meaning of the Council." Y. Congar, "Religion et Institution," in *Theologie d'aujourd'hui et de demain* (Paris: Editions du Cerf, 1967), 81–97.

59. For the medieval origins of a tendency to confound aspects of the power of jurisdiction and sacramental power under the notion of "hierarchy," as well as to equate "spiritual" with the religious state and "carnal" with the laity, implying a depreciation of the spirituality of the latter—all developments opposed to those of the greatest theologians of the mendicant orders, especially St. Thomas Aquinas, consult Congar, "Aspects ecclesiologiques de la querelle entre mendicants et seculiers dans la seconde motie du xiii siecle et le debut du xiv," *Archives d'histoire doctrinale et litteeraire du moyen* 28 (1961): 35–151.

60. *Decretum de instrumentis communicationis socialis,* 2.23.

61. *De principiis generalibus ad sacram liturgiam instaurandam atque fovendam,* 2.34–35.

62. On the issue of contemporaries seeing the need to exercise some activities out of a need to preserve the past and peoples of other eras having experienced similar retrievals, and the modern method of discussion, analysis, and resolution that was fashioned in the twelfth and thirteenth centuries being a novel synthesis of ancient and medieval sources "for exploration of an issue and rhetorical persuasion," cf. G. Pare, A. Brunet, and P. Tremblay, *La renaissance du XII siecle* (Paris: Librairie J. Vrin, 1933), 267–74; R. McKeon, *Rhetoric: Essays in Invention and Discovery* (Woodbridge, CT, 1987), 150.

63. Wilhelmsen and Bret, *The War in Man,* 1–49.

64. "It is my contention that in the nature of electronic technology, and what it is doing to our society and the men who live in it, are seeds of hope for the development of an Incarnational politics, a Catholic politics, whose lineaments can be dimly glimpsed on the horizon today." F. D. Wilhelmsen, "The Hour Is Short, The Hour Is Now," in *Citizen of Rome: Reflections from the Life of a Roman Catholic* (LaSalle, IL: Sherwood, Sugden and Company, 1980), 174–83; "Reflections in his Liberty, made of understanding and love, is the demiurge of this return [of the material order]. . . . This traditional vision finds today an extraordinary resource within the realization of this mastery of man over the universe." M. D. Chenu, "Theologie du Travail," *L'Evangile dans le temps* (Paris: Heisenberg, 1964), 543–70.

65. J. de Ghellinck, *L'essror de la literature latine au XII siecele* (Brussels: Desclée de Brouwer, 1954), 313.

66. O. von Habsburg, *Charles V* (London: Weidenfeld and Nicolson, 1967), 215, quoting historian Kart Burckhardt on the life of Emperor Charles V.

Chapter 3 ◆ *Rocco Buttiglione,* **Nature, Culture, and History** (pages 57–70)

1. Cf. L. Giussani, *Tracce di esperienza cristiana* (Milan: Jaca Book, 1972).

2. Cf. K. Marx and F. Engels *The German Ideology* (Moscow: Progress Publishers, 1976), especially the chapter on Feuerbach, where they criticize the identity established by Feuerbach between existence and essence (which corresponds to the Hegelian identity between the real and the rational) and imply that there is no contradiction between existence and the destiny of man. Marx and Engels are here just a step away from recognizing original sin.

3. Cf. K. Marx, *The Jewish Question,* first English ed. (Mexico City: Ediciones Pioneras, 1950).

4. Karol Wojtyla, *The Acting Person* (Dordrect/Boston/London: Reidel, 1979), 76 ff.

5. Cf. L. Barlay, *Geist und Umweltbewusstsein* (Frankfurt a M./Berlin/Munchen: Diesterweg, 1982).

6. Cf. Agosto del Noce, *Il caratteri generali del pensiero politico contemporaneo* (Milan: Guiffré, 1972), 14 ff.

7. Let me refer on this point to my book *Il uomo e il lavoro* (Bologna: CSEO Bibl., 1982).

8. It is above all Alberto Ferre and more recently Juan Carlos Scannone who have in recent years made penetrating contributions to this theme.

9. Cf. Wojtyla, *The Acting Person,* 261 ff.

10. Antonio Gramsci, *Quaderni del carcere* (Turin: Editori Riuniti, 1975), 546–47.

11. Ibid.

12. It is above all Jacques Maritain who has stressed the responsibility of the layman in political action. This stress, however, has not for the most part been understood as a justification of the Christian Democratic parties, but it is not impossible to use his arguments in the defense of a subjectivity of the "movements." Cf. Maritain, *Integral Humanism.*

13. We can point out here a contradiction between the early Gramsci (the Gramsci of *Ordine Nuovo*) and the later Gramsci (author of *Quaderni del carcere*). In this latter work his sensitivity toward the cultural dimension is keen, even if he never succeeds in arguing adequately for its autonomy and centrality.

14. We connect here the term culture with the term *work* taken in the subjective sense. Cf. *Laborem exercens*, paragraph 6. Cf. L. Giussani, *Il senso religioso* (Milan: Jaca Book, 1986), 52 ff.

15. Cf. Joseph Ratzinger, "Liberta e liberazione," *Il Nuovo Areopago* 3 (1986): 16 ff.

16. For the theological background of these affirmations, see the proceedings of the convention *Movements in the Church in the Eighties*, ed. Massimo Commisasca and Maurizio Vitalli (Milan: Jaca Book, 1982).

17. The recognition of this truth is the positive side of the philosophy of Blondel. Cf. Blondel, *Action.*

18. This is the danger that one notices in Gustavo Gutierrez, *Teologia della Liberazione* (Brescia: Morcelliana, 1972), especially 93. Gutierrez identifies the category of a social movement, but he does not succeed in adequately connecting movement to Church, perhaps because of the lack in the 1970s of any theology of movements, which was only then getting underway.

19. This anthology constitutes in a sense a unity of legal naturalism and historicism, which follows when one thinks of nature as the *nature of a person who is free by his essence* and when one as well thinks of history as the history of the freedom of the person, who in actualizing himself is bound to his "destiny" or "vocation," or to his "nature."

20. The affirmation of the necessity of a historical anthropology in a sense close to the position that we have laid out is a theme frequently found in German philosophy in this century, from Theodore Adorno *(The Negative Dialectic)* to Hellmut Plessner. For an overview of these studies, see D. Kamper, *Geschichte und menschliche Natur* (Munich: Carl Hanser Verlag, 1973).

21. For a further development of these statements I refer to my book *Il Pensiero di Karol Wojtyla* (Milan: Jaca Book, 1982); English translation, K. Wojtyla, *The Thought of the Man Who Became Pope John Paul II* (Grand Rapids, MI/Cambridge, UK: W. B. Eerdmans Publishing Company, 1997).

Chapter 4 ◆ *Robert A. Herrera,* **Christianity and the Philosophy of History** (pages 71–80)

1. Lewis Mumford, *Technics and Human Development* (New York: Harcourt Brace, Jovanovich, 1967), 1–163.

2. *Poetics,* 1451b1–7.

3. *Enneads* III, 2.

4. Cited by Arthur Herman, *The Idea of Decline in Western History* (New York: Free Press, 1997), 78.

5. Josef Pieper, *The End of Times: A Meditation on the Philosophy of History,* trans. Michael Bullock (New York: Pantheon, 1954), 13 ff.

6. As Collingwood states: "Eschatology is always an intrusive element in history. The historian's business is to know the past, not to know the future. . . . [It is] . . . deliberately and repulsively wrong-headed." *Idea of History* (New York: Oxford University Press, 1956), 54, 56.

7. Frank E. Manuel, *Shapes of Philosophical History* (Stanford: Stanford University Press, 1965), 82.

8. T. E. Glasson, *Greek Influence on Jewish Eschatology* (London: Nonsuch, 1961), 48.

9. *On Generations and Corruption,* 336b28–33; 337al; 338al16–18; 338b8–9, et al.; *Metaphysics,* 1074b15–34 et al.

10. *Laws,* 624s; *Apology* 42a.

11. Including the "Little Apocalypse" of the Gospel (Mark 13; Matt. 24–25; Luke 21).

12. "In various cultures weeks of four, five, six, seven, eight, ten or fifteen days have been known to exist. . . .[T]he seven day week is probably of Israelite origin. . . .Even the sectarian calendaria of Job 6: 29–38, Enoch 72–75, and Qumran . . . left the seven day week intact." E. B. Schafer, "Week," in *The Interpreter's Dictionary of the Bible,* supp. vol. (Nashville: Abingdon Press, 1976), 946.

13. *Epistle of Barnabas,* 15:4–5.

14. Xavier Zubiri, *Naturaleza, Historia, Dios* (Madrid: Editoria Nacional, 1963), 229.

15. Whether Augustine's speculations belong to the philosophy or the theology of history is a moot question given the theological ground that pertains to the former.

16. *The Seven Books of History against the Pagans.* Refer to Karl Lowith, *Meaning in History* (Chicago: University of Chicago Press, 1949), n. 1.

17. The distinction between "Augustinians" (via Boethius) and "Augustinisants" (via Pseudo-Denis) is made by A. de Libera, "Augustin et denys au moyen age," in *Saint Augustin,* ed. P. Ransom (Paris: L'Age d'Homme, 1988), 282.

18. *The Libro de las Profecías of Christopher Columbus,* trans. and commentary Delno West and August Kling (Gainesville: University of Florida Press, 1920).

19. Cited by Isaiah Berlin, *Russian Thinkers,* ed. H. Hardy and A. Kelly (New York: Penguin, 1981), 22–23.

20. Manuel, *Shapes of Philosophical History,* 144 ff.

21. *Lectures on Divine Humility,* trans. Peter Zouboff, rev. and ed. Boris Jaki (Hudson, NY: Lindisfarne Press, n.d.), xiii–xiv, 1, 10.

22. Vladimir Soloviev, *War, Progress, and the End of History,* trans. Alexander Bakshy (London: University of London Press, 1915), 227 ff.

23. *Introduction to the Reading of Hegel,* trans. James H. Nicholas Jr. (New York: Basic Books, 1969), 43–44 ff.

24. Francis Fukuyama, *The End of History and the Last Man* (New York: Free Press, 1992), 46, 49–50, 66.

25. For an extensive treatment of the theme under consideration and pertinent bibliography, refer to my *Reasons for Our Rhymes: An Inquiry into the Philosophy of History* (Grand Rapids, MI: Eerdmans, 2001).

Chapter 5 ◆ *Glenn W. Olsen,* **Christian Philosophy, Christian History: Parallel Ideas** (pages 81–96)

1. For orientation see Etienne Gilson, *Christian Philosophy: An Introduction,* trans. Armand Maurer (Toronto: Pontifical Institute of Mediaeval Studies, 1993). This is a translation of a French work published in 1960 and gives Gilson's mature views. My summary of Gilson is particularly dependent on this book and its helpful "Translator's Introduction."

2. For instance, *The Christian Philosophy of Saint Augustine,* trans. L. E. M. Lynch (New York: Random House, 1960); in the original French, *Introduction a l'etude de Saint Augustin* (Paris: J. Vrin, 1929), and *The Christian Philosophy of St. Thomas Aquinas,* trans. L. K. Shook (New York: Random House, 1956); in the fifth edition of the original French, *Le Thomisme: Introduction a la phillosophiede saint Thomas d'Aquin* (Paris: J. Vrin, 1948).

3. Maurer, "Translator's Introduction," Gilson, *Christian Philosophy,* ix, x.

4. Norman Cantor, *Inventing the Middle Ages: The Lives, Works, and Ideas of the Great Medievalists of the Twentieth Century* (New York: W. Morrow, 1991), 328. I have had my say about the inadequacies of this book in "Inventing the Middle Ages," *Dawson Newsletter* 10 (Spring 1992): 4–10.

5. Maurer, "Translator's Introduction," Gilson, *Christian Philosophy,* 1, for the first quoted phrase. As Maurer points out, Gilson traces his own thinking on such matters in *The Philosopher and Theology,* trans. Cecile Gilson (New York: Random House, 1962).

6. *The Evolution of Medieval Thought,* ed. D. E. Luscombe and C. N. L. Brook, 2nd ed. (London: Longman, 1988), 83.

7. Josef Pieper, *Leisure, the Basis of Culture* (New York: Pantheon Books, 1952), is a powerful, brief account dwelling on the origins of Greek philosophy, of the intertwining, of how philosophy emerged from contemplation and was a form of "thoughtful religion."

8. Henri de Lubac, *The Mystery of the Supernatural,* trans. of revised version Rosemary Sheed (New York: Herder and Herder, 1967).

9. See for instance Stanley L. Jaki, *The Road of Science and the Ways to God* (Chicago: University of Chicago Press, 1980).

10. I have developed the idea of "Protestantism by other means" especially in two articles, "The Meaning of Christian Culture: An Historical View," in *Catholicism and Secularization in America: Essays on Nature, Grace, and Culture,* ed. David L. Schindler (Notre Dame, IN: Our Sunday Visitor, 1990), 98–130; and "John Rawls and the Flight from Authority: The Quest for Equality As an Exercise in Primitivism," *Interpretation: A Journal of Political Philosophy* 21 (1994): 419–36. I have drawn specific instances of how the larger historical context determines how moral questions are addressed in "1492 in the Judgment of the Nations" (The *Acta* of the Second Conference on European Culture, October 28–31, 1992, Pamplona, Spain around 1994), 175–81.

11. *The Unity of Philosophical Experience* (New York: C. Scribner's Sons, 1947).

12. Study this desacralization of the Greek world in "Cultural Dynamics: Secularization and Sacralization" in *Christianity and Western Civilization* (San Francisco: Ignatius Press, 1995), 97–122.

13. Erich Auerbach, *Mimesis: The Representation of Reality in Western Literature,* trans. Willard Trask (Garden City, NY: Doubleday, 1957), is the great study of how changing ideas of what is real and important have influenced "the representation of reality" in Western culture.

14. I have explored some aspects of Augustine's construction of a narrative around his spiritual development in "St. Augustine and the Problem of the Medieval Discovery of the Individual," *Word and Spirit: A Monastic Review* 9 (1987): 129–56.

15. I am thinking primarily of the analysis developed by Auerbach in *Mimesis*, chap. 4, and revised somewhat in his *Literary Language and Its Public in Late Latin Antiquity*, trans. Ralph Manheim (New York: Pantheon Books, 1965).

16. Glenn W. Olsen, "Bede as Historian: The Evidence from His Observations on the Life of the First Christian Community at Jerusalem," *Journal of Ecclesiastical History* 33 (1982): 519–30; and "From Bede to the Anglo-Saxon Presence in the Carolingian Empire," in *Angli e Sassoni al di qua e al di la del Mare*, vol. 1, Settimane di studio del Centro italiano di studio sull'alto medioevo 32 (Spoleto: Presso La Sede del Centro, 1986), 305–82.

17. Karl Lowith, *Meaning in History* (Chicago: University of Chicago Press, 1949).

18. Francis Fukuyama, *The End of History and the Last Man* (New York: Free Press, 1992).

19. Peter Novick, *The Noble Dream: The "Objectivity Question" and the American Historical Profession* (Cambridge: Cambridge University Press, 1988), is a good introduction to the quest for objectivity. I have tried to develop defensible ideas of objectivity and relativism in "Transcendental Truth and Cultural Relativism: An Historian's View," in *Historicism and Faith*, ed. Paul Williams (Scranton: Northeast Books, 1980), 49–61.

20. Two of the sharpest critics of such views have been Hans Urs von Balthasar, who forms a great alternative in the seven volumes of his *The Glory of the Lord: A Theological Aesthetics* (see beginning of vol. 1: *Seeing the Form*, trans. Erasmo Leiva-Merikakis (Edinburgh: T&T Clark, 1982), 23 ff.; and Joseph Cardinal Ratzinger, as in *Behold the Pierced One: An Approach to Spiritual Christology*, trans. Graham Harrison (San Francisco: Ignatius Press, 1986).

21. I have studied the influence of this idea in "From Bede to the Anglo-Saxon Presence" (above n. 16), and in "Twelfth-Century Humanism Reconsidered: The Case of St. Bernard," *Studi Medievali*, 3a Serie 31 (1990): 27–53.

22. *Julian of Norwich: Showings* (Long Text), trans. Edmund Colledge and James Walsh (New York: Paulist Press, 1978), chap. 27 (Thirteenth Revelation), 225.

23. Herbert Butterfield, *Christianity and History* (New York: Scribner, 1950).

24. See my "Marriage, Feminism, Theology, and the New Social History: Dyan Elliott's *Spiritual Marriage*," *Communio* 22 (1995): 343–56.

25. This is found through his writings, but see Hans Urs von Balthasar, *A Theology of History* (New York: Sheed & Ward, 1963), esp. 134–40.

26. Hans Urs von Balthasar, *Word and Revelation*, trans. A. V. Littledale (New York: Herder and Herder, 1964), 22, ff. I have written on the senses of Scripture in "Allegory, Typology and Symbol: The *sensus spiritalis*, Part 1: Definitions and Earliest History," *Communio* 4 (1977): 161–79, "Part II: Early Church through Origin," ibid., 257–84.

Chapter 6 ♦ *Warren H. Carroll,* **Banning the Supernatural: Why Historians Must Not Rule Out the Action of God In History** (pages 95–107)

1. G. K. Chesterton, *The Everlasting Man* (New York: Dodd, Mead, 1925), 334–35.

2. Prosper Gueranger, *Le sen chretien de l'histoire* (Paris: Bruxelles, 1976), 6–7.

3. *Jerusalem Bible,* ed. Alexander Jones (Garden City, New York: Doubleday, Darton, Longman, and Todd, 1966), Old Testament, 1125.

4. Bishop Papias of Hierapolis in Asia Minor, writing about A.D. 125 within living memory of the evangelists, who is quoted verbatim in the history of Eusebius of Caesarea, testifies that these gospels were written by the apostles whose name they bear. The Apostle John's own scribe bears personal witness to the authorship of John's Gospel (John 19:32–37). The Rylands papyrus shows John's Gospel to have been circulated as far away as Upper Egypt by about A.D. 130 Tresmontant's recent work on the Gospel of Matthew (Front Royal, VA: Christendom Press, 1996) provides the clearest evidence yet for its having been originally written in Hebrew or Aramaic.

5. Giuseppe Ricciotti, *The Life of Christ* (Milwaukee: Bruce Publishing Co., 1947), 157–61; M. J. Lagrange, *The Gospel of Jesus Christ* (Westminster, MD: Newman Bookship, 1938), I, 97–98; Jack Finegan, *Handbook of Biblical Chronology* (Princeton, NJ: Princeton University Press, 1964), 88–92, 260, 268; Eugen Ruckstuhl, *Chronology of the Last Days of Jesus* (New York, 1965), 6; Harold W. Hoehner, *Herod Antipas, a Contemporary of Jesus Christ* (Grand Rapids, MI: Hoehner, Eerdmans, 1972), 308–12.

6. Flavius Josephus, *The Jewish War,* trans. and ed. G. A. Williamson, rev. ed. (London: Dorset Press, 1970), 398–400. Williamson vigorously defends the authenticity of the Old Slavonic version of this book by Josephus.

7. A notable recent example is the violently hostile academic reaction to Rev. Jose O' Callahan's discovery of a fragment of the Gospel of Mark in the Dead Sea scrolls, probably dateable to about A.D. 50 and in any case before 68—much earlier than "higher critics" of the New Testament had believed that Gospel was written.

8. See especially Frances Giles, *Joan of Arc: the Legend and the Reality* (New York: Harper & Row, 1982), 23–28, and Victoria Sackville-West, *Saint Joan of Arc* (New York: The Literary Guild, 1938), 343–56. Sackville-West, a non-Catholic but also not a professional historian, in a fascinating passage admits that, as between "the scientific and the religious" explanations, "I have been painfully torn myself. There are moments when I am not at all sure that the religious line of approach may not, in the end, prove right" (Sackville-West, 345). Rare was the historian in 1938—and rarer the historian today—who would admit to entertaining such a thought; and even Sackville-West in the end did not accept it.

9. Mosén Diego de Valera, *Memorial de diversos hazanas, crónica de Enrique IV,* ed. Juan de Mata Carriazo (Alonso de Palencia's Crónica de Enrique IV (Madrid: Atlas, 1973); and Galíndez de Carvajal, "Crónica de Enrique IV," in Juan Torres Fontes, *Estudio sobre la "Crónica de Enrique IV"* (Murcia, Spain, 1946), 271–72. .

10. Philip S. Callahan, "The Tilma under Infra-Red Radiation," *Case Studies in Popular Devotion,* vol. 2: *Guadalupan Studies,* no. 3 (Washington: The Center of Guadalupan Studies, 1981), 9–15.

11. See the excellent summary of the manner in which reported miracles of healing at Lourdes are investigated, and some of the most striking cases, in Zsolt Aradi, *The Book of Miracles* (New York: Monarch Book, 1956), 216–34.

12. William Thomas Walsh, *Our Lady of Fatima* (New York: Doubleday, 1958), 81–82, 144–49; John M. Haffert, *Meet the Witnesses* (Asbury, NJ: 101 Foundation, 1961).

13. Robert Ricard, *The Spiritual Conquest of Mexico: An Essay on the Apostolate and the Evangelizing Methods of the Mendicant Orders in New Spain, 1523–1572* (Berkeley: University of California Press, 1966), 91.

14. Yusupov's account was translated into English and published by J. Cape in London in 1927 under the title of *Rasputin: His Malignant Influence and His Assassination*.

15. For example, Bernard Pares, *The Fall of the Russian Monarchy* (New York: J. Cape, 1939), 405–9; Harrison Salisbury, *Black Night, White Snow: Russia's Revolution, 1905–1917* (New York: Da Capo Press, 1978), 297–307; W. Bruce Lincoln, *Passage through Armageddon: The Russians in War and Revolution, 1914–1918* (New York: Simon and Schuster, 1986), 306–9; Richard Pipes, *The Russian Revolution* (New York: Knopf 1990), 263–66. I vividly remember first reading one of these accounts before my conversion to the Catholic faith, when I believed neither in miracles nor in the existence of the Devil, and wondering how any conscientious historian could report these events without at least making some attempt to explain them.

16. Pipes, *Russian Revolution,* 266.

17. John H. Dunlop, *The Rise of Russia and the Fall of the Soviet Empire* (Princeton, NJ: Princeton University Press, 1993), 227–45; David Remmick, *Lenin's Tomb: The Last Days of the Soviet Empire* (New York: Random House, 1993), 483.

18. Remmick, *Lenin's Tomb,* 483.

19. Gueranger, *Le sen chretien de l'histoire,* 27–28.

Chapter 7 ◆ *Thomas Molnar,* **Why Teach History?** (pages 109–16)

This chapter has no notes.

Chapter 8 ◆ *James Hitchcock,* **Things Hidden since the Beginning of the World** (pages 117–134)

1. Herbert Butterfield, *History of Human Relations* (New York: Macmillan Co., 1952), 149.

2. Ibid., 118–19.

3. Jacques Maritain, *On the Philosophy of History,* ed. Joseph W. Evans (New York: Charles Scribner's Sons, 1957), 15–16.

4. Christopher Dawson made this clear in his book *The Crisis of Western Education* (New York: Sheed & Ward, 1961).

5. Patrick H. Ahern, *The Catholic University of America, 1887–1896* (Washington: Catholic University of America Press, 1948).

6. Leopold Von Ranke, *The Theory and Practice of History,* ed. George G. Iggers, Konrad von Moltke, and Wilma A. Iggers (Indianapolis: Bobbs-Merrill Co., 1973), 53 (from "On Progress in History" [1854]).

7. Butterfield, *History of Human Relations,* 154.

8. Ibid., 135.

9. John Henry Cardinal Newman, *Apologia pro Vita Sua,* ed. David J. DeLaura (New York: W. W. Norton, 1968), 217–18.

10. R. G. Collingwood, *The Idea of History* (New York: Oxford University Press, 1956), 46.

11. Jean Cardinal Danielou, *The Lord of History* (Chicago: Regnery, 1958), 103.

12. James Joyce, *Ulysses* (New York: Penguin, 2000), 42.

13. Butterfield, *History of Human Relations,* 56.

14. Maritain, *On the Philosophy of History,* 160–61.

15. Ibid., 150–51.

16. Butterfield, *History of Human Relations,* 13–14.

17. Martin D'Arcy, *The Meaning and Matter of History* (New York: Noonday Press, 1967), 41–45.

18. Marc Bloch, *The Historian's Craft,* trans. Peter Putnam (New York: Vintage Books, 1954), 32.

19. Hans Ur Von Balthasar, *A Theology of History* (New York: Sheed & Ward, 1963). The entire work develops the theme of the Incarnation as the key to history.

20. Danielou, *The Lord of History,* 111–13.

21. Balthasar, *A Theology of History,* 57–58.

22. Maritain, *On the Philosophy of History,* 43–76.

23. Balthasar, *A Theology of History,* 6–7.

24. D'Arcy, *The Meaning and Manner of History,* 238–39.

25. Christopher Dawson, *The Dynamics of World History,* ed. John J. Mulloy (LaSalle, IL: Sherwood Sugden, 1978), 235.

26. Christopher Dawson, *Progress and Religion* (New York: Sheed & Ward, 1929), 193.

Chapter 9 ◆ *Edward King,* **Secularized Christendom and the Age of Revolution** (pages 135–168)

1. Christopher Dawson, *The Gods of Revolution* (New York: New York University Press, 1972), 14. It is from the introductory paragraph of the chapter "The Historic Origins of Liberalism," originally published in *The Review of Politics,* vol. 11 (1954, but written circa 1937).

2. The following are important: Christopher Dawson, "Introduction" to *The Making of Europe* (London: Sheed & Ward, 1932); "The Significance of the Western Development," introductory chapter to *Religion and the Rise of Western Culture* (London: Sheed & Ward, 1950); "The Study of Christian Culture As a Means of Education," *Lumen Vitae,* vol. 1 (January 1950): 178–79, 182–86. This article became chapter 1 "How to Understand Our Past." in *Understanding Europe* (London: Sheed & Ward, 1952); "The Study of Christian Culture," introductory chapter to *Medieval Essays* (London: Sheed & Ward, 1953), 4–6; Sheed & Ward pamphlet introducing "The Makers of Christendom" series (1954), 4 pages; "The Cultural Consequences of Christian Disunity," introductory chapter to *The Dividing of Christendom* (New York: Sheed & Ward, 1965), 5–8.

3. Christopher Dawson, "How to Understand Our Past," chapter 1, *Understanding Europe* (London: Sheed & Ward, 1952), 13.

4. Christopher Dawson, *Progress and Religion* (London: Sheed & Ward, 1929).

5. Most of it forms chapter 4, "The Missionary Expansion of Western Christendom," Roger Aubert, *The Movement of World Revolution* (London: Sheed & Ward, 1959).

6. Christopher Dawson, *The Church in Secularized Society* (London: Darton, Longman, & Todd, 1978).

7. W. S. F. Pickering, *New Blackfriars,* vol. 58, no. 690 (November, 1977): 538.

8. Dawson, *Progress and Religion* (London: Sheed & Ward, 1929).

9. Note the following: Christopher Dawson, "The Secularization of Western Culture and the Rise of the Religion of Progress," chapter 8 of Dawson, *Progress and Religion* (London: Sheed & Ward: 1929); "The Age of Science and Industrialism: the Decline of the Religion of Progress," chapter 9 of Dawson, *Progress and Religion* (London: Sheed & Ward, 1929); "Religion in an Age of Revolution," *The Tablet* (August 29, September 5 and 12, October 10, 17, and 24, 1936); *The Gods of Revolution* (New York: New York University Press, 1972); "The Revolt Against Europe," chapter 11 of *Understanding Europe* (London: Sheed & Ward, 1952); "Rationalism and Revolution," chapter 3 of *The Movement of World Revolution* (London: Sheed & Ward, 1959).

10. Christopher Dawson, "Europe and the Seven Stages of Western Culture," chapter 2 of *Understanding Europe* (London: Sheed & Ward, 1952), 44.

11. Note the following: Christopher Dawson, "Herr Spengler and the Life of Civilisations," *Sociological Review,* vol. 14, no. 3, (July 1922): 194–201; "History and the Idea of Progress," chapter 2 of *Progress and Religion* (London: Sheed & Ward, 1929); "The Catholic Interpretation of History," *Christendom,* vol. 4, no. 15 (Oxford: September 1934), 173–93. This became chapter 5, "Communism and the Christian Interpretation of History" of *Religion and the Modern State* (London: Sheed & Ward, 1935); "The Politics of Hegel," *The Dublin Review,* vol. 213, no. 427 (October 1943): 97–107. It became chapter 10, "Intellectual Antecedents: Hegel and the German Ideology" of *Understanding Europe* (London: Sheed & Ward, 1952); "Germany and Central Europe," chapter 4 of *Understanding Europe.*

12. Christopher Dawson, "The Politics of Hegel," *The Dublin Review,* vol. 213, no. 427 (October 1943): 97–107.

13. The following are important: "Preface to Oscar Halecki, *The Limits and Divisions of European History* (London: Sheed & Ward, 1950), vii–xi; "Christian Culture in Eastern Europe," *The Dublin Review,* vol. 224, no. 448, (Second Quarter, 1950): 17–35.

14. Christopher Dawson, Concluding paragraph to the Preface, in Oscar Halecki, *The Limits and Divisions of European History* (London: Sheed & Ward, 1950), x-xi.

15. Much of it became chapter 5 "Eastern Europe and Russia," Christopher Dawson, *Understanding Europe* (London: Sheed & Ward, 1952).

16. Note the following: Christopher Dawson, "The Significance of Bolshevism," *The English Review,* vol. 55, (September 1932): 239–50. It forms chapter 2 of *Enquiries into Religion and Culture* (London: Sheed & Ward, 1933); "What is Russia?" *The Changing World* (1941); "Russia and Asia," chapter 4 of *Understanding Europe* (London: Sheed & Ward, 1952).

17. Dawson, "The Significance of Bolshevism," *The English Review,* Vol. 55, (September 1932): 241, 242, 243.

18. *Bolshevism, Theory and Practice* (London: Sheed & Ward, 1932).

19. Note the following: "The Passing of Industrialism," *The Sociological Review,* vol. 12 (Spring 1920): 6–17. Fourth essay in *Enquires into Religion and Culture* (London: Sheed & Ward, 1932); "The Evolution of the Modern City," *Town Planning Review,* vol. 10 (1923): 6–17. Chapter 1 in part 1, section III, *The Dynamics of World History* (London: Sheed & Ward, 1957); "The World Crisis and the English Tradition," *The English Review,* vol. 56 (March 1933): 248–60. Third essay in *Enquires into Religion and Culture* (London: Sheed & Ward, 1932); *The Spirit of the Oxford Movement* (London: Sheed & Ward, 1933); *Beyond*

Politics (London: Sheed & Ward, 1939); "Introducing the Ideas and Beliefs of the Victorians" and "The Humanitarians," *The Ideas and the Beliefs of the Victorians* (London: Sylvan Press, 1949), 26–30, 247–53; "The Victorian Background: The Vanishing Protection of the Last Hundred Years," *The Tablet*, vol. 196, no. 5757 (September 23, 1950): 245–46.

20. Jean Cardinal Danielou, "The Victorian Background: The Vanishing Protection of the Last Hundred Years," *The Tablet*, vol. 196, no. 5757 (September 23, 1950): 245–46.

21. Christopher Dawson, *Religion and the Modern State* (London: Sheed & Ward, 1935).

22. Note the following: "The New Leviathan," *The Dublin Review*, vol. 185, no. 310 (July 1929): 88–102. First essay in *Enquiries into Religion and Culture* (London: Sheed & Ward, 1933); "The Birth of Democracy," written circa 1937 and first published in 1957 in the *Review Of Politics*, vol. 19 (1957): 48–61. It appeared as chapter 3 in *The Gods of Revolution* (New York: New York University Press, 1972); "Europe Overseas: The New World of America, chapter 9 of *Understanding Europe* (London: Sheed & Ward, 1952); *The Crisis of Western Education,* chapter 6, "The Development of the American Educational Tradition"; chapter 8, "Education and the State"; chapter 14, "American Culture and the Liberal Ideology" (London: Sheed & Ward, 1961); *America and The Secularization of Modern Culture* (Houston: University of St. Thomas, 1960). A small booklet giving the Smith History Lecture at the University of Saint Thomas which Dawson delivered in that same year.

23. Christopher Dawson, "Religious Liberty and the New Political Forces" *The Month,* vol. 183, no. 955 (London, January 1947): 44–45.

24. Taken from Herman Melville, *White Jacket* (1850), chapter 36 (174).

25. Herman Melville, *Claret,* vol. 2, 249–50, 175.

26. Christopher Dawson, "Education and the State" chapter 8 of *The Crisis of Western Education* (London: Sheed & Ward, 1961).

27. Christopher Dawson, "Europe Overseas: The New World of America," chapter 9 of *Understanding Europe* (Sheed & Ward, 1952).

28. Alexis de Tocqueville, *Democracy in America,* vol. 2, part 3, chap. 6.

29. Note the following: Christopher Dawson, "The New Leviathan," *The Dublin Review,* vol. 185, no 310 (July 1929): 88–102; "Western Man and the Technological Order," chapter 15 in *The Crisis of Western Education* (London: Sheed & Ward, 1961); "The Future of Christian Culture," *Commonweal,* (March 19, 1954): 595–98; "Total Secularization or a Return to Christian Culture," chapter 13 in *Understanding Europe* (London: Sheed & Ward, 1952); "Education and the State," *Commonweal,* (January 25, 1957): 423–27.

30. Christopher Dawson, *Religion and the Modern State* (London: Sheed & Ward, 1935), 143, 144.

31. Note the following: "The New Decline and Fall," *Commonweal* (January 20, 1932): 320–22; "The Yogi and the Commissar," *Blackfriars,* vol. 26, no. 307 (October 1945): 366–71; "The Humanitarians," in *The Ideas and the Beliefs of the Victorians* (London: Sylvan Press, 1949), 247–53.

32. Christopher Dawson, *The Revolt of Asia* (London: Sheed & Ward, 1957), 6. This small booklet was included in *The Movement of World Revolution* (London: Sheed & Ward, 1959).

33. The following are important: Christopher Dawson, "Religion and the Life of Civilisation," *The Quarterly Review,* vol. 244, (January, 1925): 98–115. Included in *Enquiries into Religion and Culture* (London: Sheed & Ward, 1933); "Religion," chapter 5 of *The Modern Dilemma* (London: Sheed & Ward, 1932); *Beyond Politics* (London: Sheed & Ward, 1939);

Religion and the Modern State (London: Sheed & Ward, 1935); *The Gods of Revolution* (New York: Sheed & Ward, 1972).

34. Dawson, *Religion and the Modern State,* 69.

35. Christopher Dawson, "The Totalitarian State and the Christian Community," chapter 3 of *Beyond Politics* (London: Sheed & Ward, 1939), 65.

36. Christopher Dawson, "The Catholic Attitude to War," *The Tablet,* vol. 169, no. 5053 (March 13, 1937), 368.

37. From the concluding paragraph of chapter 7, "The Religious Solution," in Dawson, *Religion and the Modern State.*

Chapter 10 ◆ *Carl B. Schmitt, Jr.,* Galahad Naif: The Experience of a Student Wrestling With the Enlightenment
(pages 171–190)

1. That persistently Trinitarian vision is centered on Christ as bridegroom, priest, and victim. The triad of family-society-person was based on this and was related to an aesthetic triad of lyric, epic, and dynamic (circle, square, and triangle). Art involves creating (analogically and symbolically) the combination of all three in imaginative form, with its beauty being based on the intuition of created being as analogical to the divine Being.

2. I recall wrestling with the extreme way my father made this comparison between the death of the Church and Christ's death. But he explained that this took nothing away from the divinity of the Church: When Christ died His divinity remained united to His dead body. Cf. *Catechism of the Catholic Church* (Citta del Vaticano: Libreria Editrice Vaticana, 1994), 626.

3. All were certainly impressed by whatever they might have caught of my father's wisdom, but the insightful comment of one friend has stayed with me: "The real saint here, of course, is your mother."

4. Thus the child in the family is treated as a person from the first and as growing into the responsible use of freedom. Socialization begins within the family, but the social stage comes more explicitly with "schooling" that starts at "the age of reason."

5. The transition from Romanesque to Gothic architecture may be seen as typifying this "crossing balance." Another is seen in the way the Church developed a new clerical caste and institutional character, such that "Church" increasingly designated its ecclesiastical establishment as distinct from the laity, giving it a new dualistic character.

6. Our own times are comparable in this extreme unbalance to what happened at the end of the first millennium—but in reverse, because of the difference between these two ages. "Aristocracy and the sense of hierarchy," my father would say, "are as absent from the twentieth century as a middle and the sense of equality were in the tenth."

7. This helped me understand why none of them could really be committed to Marxists, even as most acknowledged that Marx had added an economic and broader social dimension to the study of history; and why none of them could truly be called Freudians, even though many felt Freud helped them realize that human actions *(mirabile dictu!)* are not always rational.

8. Several years later I had a long conversation with Carleton J. H. Hayes on this. He spoke strongly of the "comparative health" of the history profession, contending that because of this inherent realism that study of the past imposes, the profession is preserved, on the whole, from ideological excess—"especially among the best and the brightest."

9. In this I began to distinguish the Enlightenment *Project* from the Enlightenment itself. The "Project" involved working from the base supplied by this latter in the eighteenth century. That meant being committed to an anti-faith rationalism that went deeper and therefore criticized even its own immediate past "triumphs" in what amounted to successive "revolutions" of thought. The true mark of the "liberal" is ever to be in what amounted to be "open to the left, no opening to the right." I began to wrestle with how a Catholic must recognize a *legitimate human progress* there, even as he sustained a "conservative" stance against its blind destructiveness. A Catholic, it seemed, had to be both liberal and conservative without fully embracing either—though for quite different reasons in each case and not merely "balancing" one against the other.

10. As I got to know Taylor better, I discovered how deep and personal was that wrestling, and with questions that very much involved the faith. In due time I found that the rest of my professors were in fact wrestling with the same thing. Crane Brinton, the most brilliant and consistently "rational" of these, labeled *any* ideologues "true believers" in the naïveté of their optimism—taking pot shots especially at Arthur Schlesinger, Jr. and often pointing out *mistakes* they commonly made regarding the Catholic faith.

11. There was no "millenarianism" in this, although I had some fear that this millennial schema could be perceived as carrying some esoteric numerological connotation that was alien to Christian thought and to a sensible approach to history.

12. Christopher Dawson gave a succinct summary of this in speaking of how in this epoch, "In every walk of life men leagued themselves together in voluntary associations for social objects under religious auspices" and of "the great movements of communal activity which transformed the social life of medieval Europe." He goes on to point out how this "vast complex of social organisms" stood in contrast to the earlier and dominant "feudal insubordination." Christopher Dawson, *Progress and Religion* (New York: Sheed & Ward, 1929), 168.

13. There was a millennial story to be traced out there—from the way the money economy first began to intrude upon the aristocratic ethos in the eleventh and twelfth centuries and gradually transform it on through Henry VIII's remaking of the aristocracy or Louis XIV's effective reduction of it.

14. Joseph R. Strayer, *On the Medieval Origins of the Modern State* (Princeton, NJ: Princeton University Press,1970) gives a brief survey of the earlier but telling developments in terms of the consequent millennial continuity—as the title itself suggests.

15. The Church in fact led the way in developing these new social forms, providing a model for kings and princes as well as an impetus in the new use of Roman law; likewise the "clerics" coming out of the schools provided the "new men" who staffed the new royal bureaucracies and courts.

16. Marshall W. Baldwin, *The Medieval Church* (Ithaca, NY: Cornell University Press, 1953) supplies the overview of this development of the Church's "ecclesiastical dimension" as a "social" institution. Even by the mid-twelfth century, as Baldwin says, "the church had been transformed from an institution struggling to preserve its authority against centrifugal forces of an imperfectly civilized feudal society into an organization of authority capable of exerting an influence of its own" (45).

17. The Reformation and Counter-Reformation combined to pitch this dualism into this new phase. The priesthood of all believers, disconnected from a sacred priesthood, left human works and human freedom divorced from any divine meaning and carried this dualism to a radical extreme. Trent's reaffirmation of priestly power and church authority meanwhile strengthened the image of the Church itself as a clerical reality vis-à-vis the non-clerical world.

18. The French Revolution not only marked a critical moment in this anti-clerical development, but thenceforth shaped its course. On the Church's side, Pius IX's *Syllabus of Errors* is often taken as epitomizing this divorce.

19. St. Augustine, *City of God,* trans. D.B. Zema, SJ and G.G. Walsh, SJ, vol. 8 of *The Fathers of the Church* (Washington, DC: Catholic University of America Press, 1962), book 5, chap. 9, 258.

20. To preserve man's freedom, Cicero could not see *logically* where there was room for divine foreknowledge, because his logic did not encompass in His very Being: The Judeo-Christian personal Creator-God was unknown to him. What was significant for me here is that Augustine was not simply stating that faith takes us beyond reason, for the issue is freedom and divine power to create *free beings.* Hence, the critical word here is "devout": St. Augustine saw that the answer to Cicero meant raising his "logic" to the order of *being*—where human freedom can be expressed only in man's recognizing his creatureliness—in an act of worship.

21. *Trinal* intelligence, of course. Rationality is bracketed by the first-plane embrace of the real and the third-plane awareness of man's total dependency. The rational is open to faith only because human intelligence encompasses all three levels—the use of which ends in "devout faith." I felt a new fraternity with St. Augustine: Fellow Catholic, his thought was trinal.

22. Not the least of the lights I found here was how St. Augustine stood so securely in his conviction—*devoutly* embracing the mystery of man's freedom in God's—that avoided *casting himself in a defensive role.* Far from indulging in any ringing condemnation of his adversary, he found it easy to be gracious to Cicero for his noble love of human freedom.

23. With his famous distinction between "the two cities"—those who love God even to hatred of self and those who love self even to the hatred of God—the entire sweep of history from creation to final judgment was set in terms of its origin and end in God's love.

24. It is not that Christians are always better or that virtue raised to the order of grace is better than pagan virtue in a temporal sense—though it often is. What is significant here is that grace has *temporal* effects, and St. Augustine was explicit about the many ways this is so.

25. This was mainly because his interest was in showing both Christians and pagans that temporal felicity—even when enhanced by the effects of grace—was *not the Christian true purpose*: To think that Christ died to save the Empire was a mistake, and in any case temporal felicity was in the hands of God's providence.

26. This was forcefully shown when one of the readers of my paper wrote a scathing objection to some "Catholic implications" I had drawn in my conclusion. He was particularly outraged by my quoting Hilaire Belloc (among four others) to show that these Augustinian principles were much alive among representative Catholic thinkers today. In spite of this—further irony—my paper was awarded the Washburn Prize for the best thesis in history that year.

27. Harvard granted me a fellowship for a year's study in France, with no particular requirements attached to it and with ample funds for travel. While there, I applied for and received a Fullbright scholarship to spend another year of study in Europe, this time in Florence—and with like opportunities.

28. I had seen why St. Augustine wanted to emphasize eternal felicity even though he allowed that Christianity would produce a measure of temporal felicity, but still I wrestled with a satisfactory explanation of why, as a part of his apologetic, he was not led into making use of the good temporal effects Christianity could have (which my senior paper dwelt on)

and especially in view of the fact that this aspect of his thought so obviously shaped the historical apologetic of the current Catholic writers I cited in the conclusion of my senior paper.

29. Thus Christians could be good citizens of the Empire even as it persecuted them—all authority is from God, not just spiritual authority.

30. Regarding the three examples just cited: In affirming the true transcendence of God in the first millennium (in confronting the paganism of both the ancient world and then in the barbarian world), no Christian would have even thought of singing of brother Sun; none could have given divine honors to Emperor or king; and even in adapting the basilica, Christians consciously avoided using the pagan temple as a model.

31. It might be noted here that in my father's scheme of things paganism is characteristic of "first-plane" perception of reality as instinctively and directly finding something transcendent in it; "divinizing" created reality is a mark of the first age (allowing the expression "the good pagan") in contrast to the analytical (logical, scientific) approach to reality of "second plane" thinking, which involves having de-divinized it.

32. Historians have marked the fifteenth and sixteenth centuries as "the Age of Discovery" because of the geographical explorations that began with Henry the Navigator. It took little, however, to see that these had their roots in much earlier *discoveries and developments*—in everything from trade and commerce to shipbuilding, map making, astronomy, and navigation that had begun in Genoa and Venice—since the eleventh century.

33. Etienne Gilson, "Intelligence in the Service of Christ the King," in *A Gilson Reader*, ed. Anton C. Pegis (Garden City, NY: Hanover House, 1957), 40. (emphasis mine).

34. My introduction to a closer examination of the Reform was provided by the excellent study of Gert Tellenbach, *Church, State and Christian Society at the Time of the Investiture Contest* (Oxford: Basil Blackwell, 1948). Getting into the manifold ways in which the Reform provoked the cultural revolution that led to what are called the High Middle Ages and the distinctive characteristics of the second millennium as a whole was more random work, and I pursued many angles.

35. His achievement marked the triumph in the way human reason (a created reality) related to faith, and it is often cited as a paradigm of the medieval synthesis. Moreover, his work stood as the culminating development in that process of "discovery and exploration" that had been going on in the schools since the new millennium began.

36. The "Committee" seemed to present the most suitable way to continue my project in an academic setting. Its association with Jacques Maritain and other great lights, together with its uniquely structured degree program that allowed the student to set his own goals, made it very attractive to me.

37. Etienne Gilson, *The Spirit of Medieval Philosophy,* Gifford Lectures, 1931–32 (New York: Charles Scribner's Sons, 1936), chap. 3.

38. In coming upon Frederick Wilhelmsen's *The Paradoxical Structure of Existence* (Dallas: University of Dallas Press, 1970) many years later I was happy to find a more studied explication of this point. His eighth chapter is titled "Existence and History." It was at this time, however, that I began to consider the difference between theological (and philosophical) language and the language of the historian. "God created man; God became man" are theological statements; "God created Adam; God became incarnate in the man Jesus" are historical statements.

39. In effect the Enlightenment, ignorant of its own origins, drew on a Christian inheritance. It was at this time that I began to think that "secularism" as an ideology had to be sharply distinguished from simply "secular" as referring to what God created and gave

into man's hand in the double command to increase and multiply and to work in service to Him and to all men for His glory. It began to dawn on me that the Enlightenment's rejection of Christianity deprived it of clearly understanding its own presuppositions, of its own *cultural* roots, and that secularism, then, is even a specifically Christian heresy. Only much later did I come upon the work of Fr. Stanley Jaki that elucidates in one particular area—that of scientific inquiry—how this "discovery, exploration, and development" was pursued from medieval times right into our own.

40. St. Augustine's apologetic purpose was to show that the sack of Rome said nothing with regard to the truth of Catholicism. Indeed, whether Rome rose or fell could be of no ultimate concern to the Christian. What had changed since St. Augustine's time, of course, was that society had become wholly Christian and temporal action was always appropriately Christian or not—the heart and soul of the medieval "synthesis" and the making (or unmaking) of Christian culture.

41. Pondering this, I concluded that Providence is not a univocal term, but *triune*. In the first and general way Providence is understood, God certainly works in all events with an absolute freedom through His power over all that He created (God the Father)—in terms of its varied and interrelated goodness and embracing all their actions and inter-reactions. from merely material up through the hierarchy of living beings to man and including therefore even human freedom. But God also and additionally works in a *distinct* way by His inspiration and grace in spiritual beings (God the Holy Spirit).

42. Or more exactly perhaps, He freed us from what was *sinful* in each sinful action, everything *else* there being lovable.

43. Man, having been created free and then suffering the consequences of its misuse, is caught in a desperate search for freedom—a search in which every man is involved every time he makes a free act. But he can find it only in Christ who purchased our freedom through its perfect use, and part of that perfection was that He suffered every sin, identifying Himself with every action of man for the redemption of all.

44. This connection was properly *historical* in that St. Thomas is seen as bringing this further theological insight that more fully clarifies a Christian view of history.

45. In effect I was tying together, through St. Thomas's *real* connection with St. Augustine, the unresolved dichotomy reflected in my senior paper on St. Augustine—Providence at work in salvation history *as distinct from* its workings in temporal history.

46. G. K. Chesterton, *Orthodoxy* (New York: John Lane Company, 1909), 153.

47. Christopher Dawson, *Christianity and the New Age* (Manchester, NH: Sofia Institute Press, 1985), 103.

48. It was as an undergraduate that I read in Edmund Wilson's *To the Finland Station* (Garden City, NY: Doubleday and Company, Anchor Books, 1972; first printed in 1940), 151, about Karl Marx's own background in response to realism after reading Feuerbach in 1848: "The Philosophers hitherto have only interpreted the world in various ways: the thing is, however, to change it." My reaction at the time was: *Indeed! And yet how pathetic a way he offers!* My own breakthrough—this breakthrough to "realism" with which I conclude this account—came with encountering the following: "You worry about building up your culture. But what you really need to build up is your soul. Then you will work as you should—for Christ. In order that He may reign in the world, it is necessary to have people of prestige who with their eyes fixed on heaven, dedicate themselves to all human activities, and through those activities exercise quietly—and effectively—an apostolate of professional character." Josemaria Escrivá, *The Way*, (Princeton, NJ: Scepter Publishers), 84, 3, no. 347, cf. nos. 11,

346. The quotation in the text is taken from St. Josemaria's homily, "Christ the King," in *Christ Is Passing By* (Princeton, NJ: Scepter Publishers, 1974), no. 183.

Chapter 11 ◆ *Patrick Foley,* **Recovering a Legacy through History: The Catholic American Southwest and West** (pages 191–209)

1. George Lockhart Rives, *The United States And Mexico, 1821–1848,* vol. 1 (New York: Charles Scribners Sons, 1918; New York: Kraus Reprint Co., 1969), 18–19.

2. For a discussion of the Roman Catholic spiritual, cultural, and intellectual transmigration from Spain to the New World, see Patrick Foley, "De España a las Américas: Una Síntesis del Legado Católico, Espiritual e Intelectual de España," *Aportes: Revista de Historia Contemporánea* 8, no. 21 (November 1992–February 1993): 91–97.

3. Félix D. Almaráz Jr., "Social Interaction between Civil, Military and Mission Communities in Spanish Colonial Texas during the Height of the Bourbon Reforms, 1763–1772," *Revista Complutense de Historia de América,* no. 21 (1995): 11–28.

4. For a discussion of the historic union between altar and throne in Spain for many centuries, see Stanley G. Payne, *Spanish Catholicism: An Historical Overview* (Madison: University of Wisconsin Press, 1984), 3–70; José María Iraburu, *Hechos de los Apóstoles de América* (Pamplona: Fundación Gratis, 1992), 16–117; Warren H. Carroll, *Isabel of Spain: The Catholic Queen* (Front Royal, VA: Christendom Press, 1991); Felipe Fernandez-Armesto, *Ferdinand and Isabella* (New York: Taplinger, 1975), 46–163; *The Roman Catholic Church in Colonial Latin America,* ed. and intro. Richard E. Greenleaf (New York: Alfred E. Knopf, 1971), 19–42, 87–120, 151–206; Rhea Marsh Smith, *Spain: A Modern History* (Ann Arbor: University of Michigan Press, 1965), 52–189; William H. Prescott, *A History of the Conquest of Mexico: With a Preliminary View of the Ancient Mexican Civilization and the Life of the Conqueror Hernando Cortés* (London: George Routledge and Sons, n.d.), 67–102.

5. Robert Ricard, *The Spiritual Conquest of Mexico: An Essay on the Apostolate and the Evangelizing Methods of the Mendicant Orders in New Spain, 1523–1572* (Berkeley: University of California Press, 1966; original title *Conquete Spirituelle de Mexique,* vol. 20 of *Travaux et Memoires de L'Institut d'"Ethnologie* [Paris: University of Paris, 1933]), 15.

6. Gilbert R. Cruz, *Let There Be Towns: Spanish Municipal Origins in the American Southwest, 1610–1810* (College Station: Texas A&M University Press, 1988), 165.

7. Thomas J. Noel, *Colorado Catholicism and the Archdiocese of Denver, 1857–1989* intro. J. Francis Stafford, Archbishop of Denver (Denver: University Press of Colorado, 1989), 2.

8. On the archival resources dedicated to studying the Catholic Spanish heritage of New Spain as well as the labors of the Franciscans and their missions from Texas to California, just a few of the numerous outstanding sources would be Lino Gómez Canedo, "Archivos eclesiásticos en México," *Anuario de Bibliotecología y Archivología e Informática* 2, no. 3 (1971): 151–74; W. Michael Mathes, "Humanism in Sixteenth and Seventeenth-Century Libraries of New Spain," *Catholic Historical Review* 82, no. 3 (July 1996): 412–35; *Letters and Memorials of Fray Mariano de los Dolores y Viana, 1737–1762: Documents on the Missions of Texas from the Archives of the College of Queretaro,* trans. Fr. Benedict Leutenegger, OFM, intro. Fr. Marion Habig, OFM (San Antonio, TX: Old Missions

Historical Research Library, Our Lady of the Lake University, 1985); *Guide to the Spanish and Mexican Manuscript Collection at the Catholic Archives of Texas,* comp. Dedra S. McDonald, ed. Kinga Perzynska (Austin: Catholic Archives of Texas, 1994). It would be remiss not to mention that in recent years the Franciscan missionaries and their missions have come under attack by a few historians writing from mainly biased sociological purviews rather than historical ones. The most noted of these writers is Robert H. Jackson. If his works are read at all they should be studied with great caution, because he not only reflects anti-missions attitudes, but reveals that he knows little of the substance of Catholic Spanish history.

9. On the maturation of a Roman Catholic culture and society in the municipalities of northern New Spain, especially along the Rio Grande, see Gilberto Rafael Cruz, *Let There Be Towns*; Donald E. Chipman, *Spanish Texas, 1519–1821* (Austin: University of Texas Press, 1992); Carlos Eduardo Castañeda, *Our Catholic Heritage in Texas, 1519–1936,* vol. 5: *The Missions Era: The End of the Spanish Regime, 1780–1836* (Austin, TX: Von Boeckmann-Jones, 1942); Paul Horgan, *Great River: The Rio Grande in North American History,* vol. 1: *Indians and Spain,* (Austin: Texas Monthly Press Reprint; originally published in New York: Rinehart, 1954) 328–86. On Catholic life in the *jacales,* see Henry Granjon, Bishop of Tucson, *Along the Rio Grande: A Pastoral Visit to Southwest New Mexico in 1902,* ed. and annotation, Michael Romero Taylor, trans. Mary W. de Lopez (Albuquerque: University of New Mexico Press, published in cooperation with the Historical Society of New Mexico, 1986).

10. John J. Mulloy, "Herbert Eugene Bolton: Trailblazer to the Spanish Borderlands," *Dawson Newsletter* 10 (Winter 1992): 5.

11. On the Catholic Irish immigrants in nineteenth-century Texas, see Rachel Bluntzer Hébert, *The Forgotten Colony, San Patricio de Hibernia: The History, The People, and the Legends of the Irish Colony of McMullen-McGloin* (Burnet, TX: Eakin Press, 1981); John Brendan Flannery, *The Irish Texans* (San Antonio: University of Texas Institute of Texan Cultures at San Antonio, 1980); and Patrick Foley, "The Shamrock and the Altar in Early Nineteenth-Century Texas: Irish Catholics and Their Faith," in *The Irish in the West,* ed. Timothy J. Sarbaugh and James P. Walsh (Manhattan, KS: Sunflower University Press, 1993), 87–92.

12. Bluntzer Hébert, *The Forgotten Colony,* 3.

13. On Catholic devotions in the United States during the nineteenth century, see Ann Taves, *The Household of the Faith: Roman Catholic Devotion in Mid-Nineteenth-Century America* (Notre Dame, IN: University of Notre Dame Press, 1986), 128–33.

14. Patrick Foley, "Jean-Marie Odin, C.M., Missionary Bishop Extraordinaire of Texas," *Journal of Texas Catholic History and Culture* 1, no. 1 (March 1990): 42–60.

15. Paul Horgan, *Lamy of Santa Fe: His Life and Times* (New York: Farrar, Straus, and Giroux, 1975).

16. Gerald McKevitt, SJ, *The University of Santa Clara: A History, 1851–1977* (Stanford, CA: Stanford University Press, 1979).

17. Robert E. Wright, OMI, "Pioneer Religious Congregations of Men in Texas before 1900," *Journal of Texas Catholic History and Culture* 5 (1994): 65–90.

18. Christine Morkovsky, CDP, "The Challenge of Catholic Evangelization in Texas: Women Religious and Their Response," *Journal of Texas Catholic History and Culture* 4 (1993): 65–96.

19. Félix D. Almaráz Jr., *Knight without Armor: Carlos Eduardo Castañeda, 1896–1958* (College Station: Texas A&M University Press, 1999).

20. Chipman, *Spanish Texas, 1519–1821*; Rupert N. Richardson, et al., *Texas: The Lone Star State* (Englewood Cliffs, NJ: Prentice-Hall, 1993; originally published in 1943).

21. Robert A. Calvert and Arnoldo De Leon, *The History of Texas* (Arlington Heights, IL: Harlan Davidson, 1990), 24.

22. Ibid., 349.

23. Robert Divine, et al., *America Past and Present,* 3rd ed. (New York: Harper Collins, 1991), 20.

24. Ibid.

25. Ibid., 21.

26. Among the more prominent of the "revisionists" are Gilberto Miguel Hinojosa; Moises Sandoval; Ana Maria Diaz-Stevens; David Badillo; and Marina Herrera. Though not an apologist for liberation theology, Jeannette Rodriguez could be considered an iconoclastic feminist with her recent publication of *Our Lady of Guadalupe: Faith and Empowerment among Mexican American Women* (Austin: University of Texas Press, 1994).

27. John Gilmary Shea's insistence upon laying a foundation of archival research as the basis for the writing of Catholic history—so clearly mirrored in his late-nineteenth-century book, *New History of the Catholic Church in the United States* (New York: P. J. Kenedy, Excelsior Catholic Publishing House, passim)—seemed revolutionary in the latter nineteenth century. He was the innovator, because today such a dependence on primary sources is commonplace among truly scholarly historians.

28. In addition to those archives mentioned in the text of this essay, the Archives of the University of Notre Dame; the de Andreis–Rosati Memorial Archives (Vincentians) originally located at St. Mary's of the Barrens Seminary in Perryville, Missouri; the Archives of the Archdiocese of St. Louis; the Antoine Blanc Memorial Archives of the Archdiocese of New Orleans; the Archives of the Catholic University of America; and the Archives of the new Archdiocese of Galveston-Houston all are repositories of excellent primary source materials on the Roman Catholic history of the American Southwest and West.

 Index